I0634430

John Dun

British banking statistics

With remarks on the bullion reserve and non-legal-tender note circulation of the

United Kingdom

John Dun

British banking statistics
With remarks on the bullion reserve and non-legal-tender note circulation of the United Kingdom

ISBN/EAN: 9783337146849

Printed in Europe, USA, Canada, Australia, Japan

Cover: Foto ©Suzi / pixelio.de

More available books at **www.hansebooks.com**

BRITISH
BANKING STATISTICS;

WITH

REMARKS ON THE BULLION RESERVE

AND

NON-LEGAL-TENDER NOTE CIRCULATION

OF THE

UNITED KINGDOM.

BY JOHN DUN,

GENERAL MANAGER OF PARR'S BANKING COMPANY, LIMITED.

LONDON:
EDWARD STANFORD, 55, CHARING CROSS, S.W.

1876.

PREFACE.

THE following paper is reprinted from the *Journal of the Statistical Society.*

In Sections I to VI the author has in a great measure trodden in the track traced by Mr. Newmarch in 1851, and Mr. Palgrave in 1872. That he has carried the investigation of the banking liabilities and assets of the United Kingdom to a point not previously attained, is due to the circumstance that in 1875 much more copious data were available for the purpose than in 1851 or even in 1872.

In the course of the paper many important practical points in connection with the constitution and management of banking institutions are dealt with. Attention is specially directed to the utter inadequacy of the present ultimate bullion reserve.

Section VII is devoted to the discussion of non-legal-tender note issues.

The Chancellor of the Exchequer has intimated to a deputation of English bankers, that the Government have it in contemplation to legislate on the subject of banking and note issues " in a broad and comprehensive way, with a view to giving " proper effect to the principles of Sir Robert Peel's measures" of 1844-45, and he has explained these principles to be "that " you should separate your dealing with issue and with banking ; " and that with regard to banking you should endeavour to " make it as free as possible, while with regard to issue the " State should provide proper regulations to prevent excess or " regulate issues."

In common with many of the mature statesmen of the present day, Sir Stafford Northcote has imbibed his currency ideas from Sir Robert Peel, and it may be feared that he both overrates the advantages and underrates the disadvantages to the public of an exclusive State or State-bank issue; whilst at the same time he underrates the advantage to the public of a well regulated system of non-legal-tender issues supplementary to the legal-tender issues of the State or a State bank.

Be this as it may, the author trusts that the collation of facts in this paper may be found of some service in the controversy which must ensue when the subjects of banking and currency are again brought before Parliament with a view to legislation.

The author is under great obligations to Mr. Newmarch for valuable information and advice upon many of the most important points embraced in the paper.

He thankfully records his acknowledgments for the ready response which his inquiries almost invariably elicited from the officials of banks whom he had occasion to trouble for information.

He would also gratefully acknowledge the invaluable assistance received from Mr. W. D. Hughes and other officers of Parr's Banking Company, Limited, in compiling and checking the tables and in making and verifying the innumerable calculations which the investigation involved. Although no effort was spared to secure perfect accuracy, it cannot but be, where such masses of figures had to be dealt with, that some errors have crept in, and any reader who detects an inaccuracy, will confer an obligation on the author by pointing it out by letter addressed to him at Warrington.

WARRINGTON,
June, 1876.

CONTENTS.

B

2

3

8

THE BANKING INSTITUTIONS

OF THE

UNITED KINGDOM.

I.—Enumeration and General Review of Joint Stock Banks.

The "Banking Almanac" for 1875, published in December, 1874, gives the joint stock banks in England and Wales as 121. Omitting the Bank of England, two Isle of Man banks, the Cheque Bank (Limited), and the Shropshire Banking Company, since absorbed by Lloyd's Banking Company (Limited), the City and County Bank (suspended), and adding the Ludlow and Tenbury Bank, which, though a bank of issue, does not appear in the "Almanac," the total number stands at 116.

These are—

	Number.
Purely London	12
London and Provincial	7
Purely Provincial	97
Total England and Wales	116

Add—

Isle of Man	2
Scotland	12
Ireland	9
Total joint stock banks, United Kingdom	139

The following tables, compiled from the "Investors' Monthly "Manual" for August, 1875, the "Banking Almanac" of 1875, and the balance sheets or statements of the banks where these were available, show the date of establishment, number of offices, number of shareholders, paid-up capital, reserve-fund, shares, dividend, market price, and yield to the investor :—

Table I of the Purely London Banks.
  ,, II of the London and Provincial Banks.
  ,, III of the Purely Provincial Banks, roughly classified in districts.
  ,, IV of the Scotch Banks.
  ,, V of the Irish Banks.

TABLE I.—*Purely London*

Number.	Names.	1 Date of Establishment.	2 Number of Offices.	3 Paid-up Capital.	4 Reserve and Balance after last Dividend.
		Year.	No.	£	£
1	LONDON AND WESTMINSTER BANK...........	1834	8	2,000,000	667,501
2	LONDON JOINT STOCK BANK	'36	6	1,200,000	522,713
3	UNION BANK OF LONDON........................	'39	5	1,395,000	411,123
4	CITY BANK	'55	6	600,000	137,554
5	IMPERIAL BANK, *Limited*	'62	3	675,000	97,132
6	ALLIANCE BANK, *Limited*	{ '62 '71	1	800,000	170,000
7	CENTRAL BANK OF LONDON, *Limited*	'63	5	100,000	25,260
8	METROPOLITAN BANK, *Limited*	'67	1	190,583	2,500
9	St. James' Bank, *Limited*	'71	1	6,620	100
10	W. LONDON COMML. BANK, *Limited*	'66	2	22,269	981
11	London Banking Association, *Limited*†	'72	1	—	—
12	MERCHANT BANKG. CO. OF LONDON, *Limd.*	'63	1	375,000	103,980
	Totals	—	40	7,364,472 11 banks,	2,138,844 11 banks,
	Averages...............................	—	3½	669,497	194,440

* 90,160l. of capital consisting of deferred shares received no dividend.
† The business of this Association is not that of ordinary London bankers, and their Exchange.

TABLE II.—*London and Provincial*

Number.	Name.	1 Establishment Date of lishment.	2 Number of Offices.	3 Paid-up Capital.	4 Reserve and Balance after last Dividend.
		Year.	No.	£	£
1 {	NATIONAL PROVINCIAL BANK OF ENGLAND ⎤ " " ⎥ " " New, 1874 ⎦	1833	138	1,462,500	742,444
2	LONDON AND COUNTY BANK	'36	149	1,425,000	719,657
3 {	LONDON AND SOUTH-WESTERN BANK, ⎤ *Limited* ⎦	'62	27	166,180	14,012
4	CONSOLIDATED BANK, *Limited*.................	'63	4	800,000	125,876
5	MIDLAND BANKING COMPANY, *Limited*....	'63	28	300,000	45,000
6	LONDON AND PROVINCIAL BANK, *Limited*	'64	55	150,000	34,818
7	LONDON AND YORKSHIRE BANK, *Limited*	'72	11	121,284	2,331
	Totals	—	412	4,424,964	1,684,138
	Averages...............................	—	59	632,138	240,591

Joint Stock Banks, 1875.

5 Number of Proprietors.	6 Number of Shares.	7 Amount per Share.	8 Paid per Share.	9 Dividend and Bonus per Cent. for 12 Months.	10 Price per Share, August, 1875.	11 Premium per Cent.	12 Yield per Cent. at Price.	Number.
No.	No.	£	£	Per cnt.	£	Per cnt.	£ s. d.	
4,800	100,000	100	20	16	64½	222½	4 19 3	1
2,560	80,000	50	15	18½	47	213⅓	5 17 11	2
2,800	90,000	50	15½	15	44	183⅞	5 5 9	3
830	60,000	20	10	9	13	30	6 18 6	4
530	45,000	50	15	8	17½	16⅔	6 17 2	5
1,240	80,000	25	10	7	12½	25	5 12 –	6
350	20,000	10	5	8	8	60	5 – –	7
500 {	18,031	10	10	} 8*	9⅞	Discount	—	8
	6,849	10	1½					
28	—	20	10	5½	—	—	—	9
109	4,005	10	3 to 6	5	—	—	—	10
—	—	—	—	—	—	—	—	11
260	15,000	100	25	10	36	44	6 18 11	12
14,007	—	—	—	—	—	—	—	
				11 banks,			8 banks,	
1,167	—	—	—	11	—	—	5 18 8	

shares were privately subscribed for and no quotation applied for on the Stock

Joint Stock Banks, 1875.

5 Number of Proprietors.	6 Number of Shares.	7 Amount per Share.	8 Paid per Share.	9 Dividend and Bonus per Cent. for 12 Months.	10 Price per Share, August, 1875.	11 Premium per Cent.	12 Yield per Cent. at Price.	Number.
No.	No.	£	£	Per cnt.	£	Per cnt.	£ s. d.	
3,312 {	20,000	50	21	23	85	304⅘	5 13 7½	} 1
	77,500	20	12	23	49	308⅓	—	
	28,125	20	4	23	36	—	—	
3,250	60,000	50	20	18	62	210	5 16 2	2
580	8,309	100	20	8	24	20	6 13 4	3
1,650	200,000	10	4	10	7½	87½	5 6 9	4
887	15,000	100	20	9	27⅜	38⅛	6 10 4	5
625	30,000	10	5	10	9½	90	5 5 3	6
539	13,476	50	9	4	5½	Discount	6 10 11	7
10,843	—	—	—	—	—	—	—	
1,549	—	—	—	11 4/7	—	—	5 19 5¾	

TABLE III.—*Purely Provincial English*

Number.	Name. [*Italics*—Small or Large—denote Banks of Issue, CAPITALS—Italic or Plain—Banks which publish Balance Sheets.]	1 When Estab- lished.	2 Number of Offices.	3 Paid-up Capital.
	I. Cumberland, Northumberland, and Westmoreland.	Year.	No.	£
1	*CARLISLE CITY AND DISTRICT BANK*	1837	6	80,162
2	*CARLISLE AND CUMBERLAND BKG. CO.*	'36	6	75,000
3	*CUMBERLAND UNION BANK, Limited*	'29	18	225,000
4	*BANK OF WHITEHAVEN, Limited*	'37	4	98,530
5	*Whitehaven Joint Stock Bank*	'29	6	45,000
6	*Bank of Westmoreland*	'33	2	25,680
7	NORTH EASTERN BANKING COMPANY, *Limited*	'72	17	260,000*
8	INDUSTRIAL BANK, *Limited*, NEWCASTLE	'72	1	20,323
9	NORTHN. COUNTIES' BANKING CO., *Limd.*, NEWCASTLE	'71	2	21,690
	II. Liverpool.			
10	Bank of Liverpool	1831	1	625,000
11	LIVERPOOL UNION BANK	'35	1	600,000
12	,, COMMERCIAL BANK, *Limited*	'32	1	350,000
13	NORTH WESTERN BANK, *Limited*, LIVERPOOL	'64	1	405,000
14	NATIONAL BANK OF LIVERPOOL, *Limited*	'63	3	450,000
15	ADELPHI BANK, *Limited*	'61	2	130,110
16	*NORTH AND SOUTH WALES BANK*	1836	37	420,000
	III. Manchester District.			
17	MANCHESTER AND LIVERPOOL DISTRICT BANK	1829	52	905,000
18	,, COUNTY BANK, *Limited*	'62	27	660,000
19	,, Salford Bank	'36	9	600,000
20	UNION BANK OF MANCHESTER, *Limited*	'36	21	440,000
21	MANCHESTER JOINT STOCK BANK, *Limited*	'73	2	90,000
22	LANCASHIRE AND YORKSHIRE BANK, *Limited*	'72	9	250,000
23	*Lancaster Banking Company*	'26	14	275,000
24 {	PRESTON BANKING COMPANY	'44	7	191,484
	,, New A Shares	—		50,000
25	PARR'S BANKING COMPANY, *Limited*, WARRINGTON	1865	17	290,000
26	Bank of Bolton	'36	3	225,000
27	Bury Banking Company	'36	1	109,080
28	ROCHDALE JOINT STOCK BANK, *Limited*	'72	1	22,656
29	Ashton, Stalybridge, &c., Bank	'36	1	50,000
	IV. Yorkshire.			
30	*Darlington District Bank*	1831	8	68,000
31	*SWALEDALE, &c., BANKING COMPANY*	'36	4	63,000
32	*Knaresborough and Claro Banking Company*	'31	6	unknown
33	*YORKSHIRE BANKING COMPANY*	'43	22	250,000
34	*York City and County Bank*	'30	15	125,000

* Viz., 40,000 ordinary shares—6l. paid and 1,000 20l. shares deferred; no dividend as yet on the latter.

Joint Stock Banks, 1875.

4 Reserve and Balance after Last Dividend.	5 Number of Proprietors.	6 Number of Shares.	7 Amount per Share.	8 Paid-up per Share.	9 Dividend per Cent. per Annum for 12 Months, including Bonus.	10 Price per Share, August, 1875.	11 Premium per Cent.	12 Yield per Cent. at Price.			Number.
£	No.	No.	£	£	Per cnt.	£	Per cnt.	£	s.	d.	
93,025	413	6,415	25	12½	20	44¼	254	5	13	–	1
103,836	325	15,000	20	5	21	22½	350	4	13	4	2
85,724	780	18,000	30	12½	18	44	252	5	2	3	3
96,797	304	9,853	30	10	20	37¼	272½	5	7	4	4
28,195	209	3,000	100	15	25	64	326⅔	5	17	2	5
15,000	106	2,140	100	12	10	19	58⅓	6	6	4	6
80,412	1,028	40,000	20	6	3¾	5¾	Dis.	3	18	3	7
1,500	211	6,873	5	3	10	3¼	8⅓	9	4	8	8
1,777	36	723	50	30	7¾	34	13⅓	6	16	9	9
317,778	527	50,000	100	12½	16	25⅛	101	7	19	2	10
164,365	156	30,000	20	20	10	29	45	6	18	–	11
205,729	280	35,000	20	10	12½	18	80	6	18	10½	12
101,179	367	54,000	20	7½	7	10	33⅓	5	5	–	13
106,400	752	30,000	25	15	6⅝	17⅜	15⅝	5	18	–	14
7,194	357	13,011	20	10	5	10	Par	5	–	–	15
235,328	852	42,000	10	10	18¾	32¾	227½	5	14	6	16
571,774	1,250	90,500	20	10	20	36½	265	5	9	7	17
354,885	730	44,000	100	15	15	40½	170	5	11	1	18
250,000	230	75,000	20	8	11⅛	14	75	6	7	7	19
150,097	384	40,000	25	11	12	23½	$113\frac{7}{11}$	5	12	4	20
31,630	263	15,000	20	6	10	12¼	104⅙	4	17	11	21
34,145	450	25,000	20	10	6	13⅞	38¾	4	6	5¾	22
276,216	324	11,000	25	25	30	155	520	4	16	9¼	23
49,900	110	2,000	100	100	Nil	23	—	Nil			24
		2,000	25	25	10	33	32	7	11	6½	
85,768	265	14,500	100	20	15	60	200	5	–	–	25
—	247	15,000	20	15	6	21½	43⅓	4	3	9	26
120,000	151	18,180	10	6	23	24	300	5	15	–	27
4,446	148	5,664	20	4	7¼	5	25	5	16	–	28
16,005	148	12,500	10	4	10⅝	8	100	5	6	3	29
29,416	78	4,000	100	17	10†	23	35⅓	7	7	10	30
33,000	121	8,400	100	7½	20	‡	—		—		31
24,000	104	—	—	20	15	—	—		—		32
163,000	425	20,000	25	12½	24	57	356	5	5	3	33
100,000	167	5,000	100	25	18	70	180	6	8	7	34

† And also 1*l*. per share added to capital. ‡ Shares very rarely dealt in.

TABLE III.—*Purely Provincial English*

Number	Name. [*Italics*—Small or Large—denote Banks of Issue, CAPITALS—Italic or Plain—Banks which publish Balance Sheets.]	1 When Estab-lished.	2 Number of Offices.	3 Paid-up Capital.
	IV. Yorkshire—*Contd.*	*Year.*	*No.*	*£*
35	*York Union Banking Company*	1833	10	132,000
36	*Hull Banking Company*	'33	4	90,990
37	BANK OF LEEDS, *Limited*	'64	1	151,300
38	LEEDS AND COUNTY BANK, *Limited*	'62	6	230,000
39	EXCHANGE AND DISCOUNT BANK, *Limited*, LEEDS	'66	2	89,250
40	*BRADFORD COMMERCIAL BANKING CO.*	'33	1	193,500
41	„ *BANKING COMPANY*	'27	1	408,000
42	BRADFORD DISTRICT BANK, *Limited*	'62	2	227,500
43	„ OLD BANK, *Limited*	'64	3	423,160
44	*Halifax Joint Stock Bank*	'29	3	150,000
45	*HALIFAX COMML. BANKING CO., Limited*	'36	2	120,000
46	*Halifax and Huddersfield Union Bank*	'36	2	250,000
47	*Huddersfield Banking Company*	'27	4	382,500
48	*West Riding Union Bank*	'32	3	200,000
49	*Wakefield and Barnsley Union Bank*	'32	3	100,000
50	*Barnsley Banking Company*	'32	2	40,575
51	SHEFFIELD UNION BANKING COMPANY	'43	6	180,000
52	*SHEFFIELD AND ROTHERHAM BKG. CO.*	'36	5	160,704
53	*SHEFFIELD BANKING COMPANY*	'31	4	293,160
54	„ *AND HALLAMSHIRE BANK*	'36	1	183,200
	V. Midland Counties—Agricultural.			
55	*Chesterfield and North Derby Bank*	1834	1	35,000
56	*Derby and Derbyshire Bank*	'33	3	62,500
57	DERBY COMMERCIAL BANK, *Limited*	'68	1	30,000
58	*BURTON, UTTOXETER, &c., BANK*	'39	3	130,000
59	*Nottingham and Notts Banking Company*	'34	8	203,500
60	*Moore and Robinson's Notts Banking Company, Limited*	'36	2	203,000
61	NOTTINGHAM JOINT STOCK BANK, *Limited*	'65	6	95,500
62	*Lincoln and Lindsey Banking Company*	'33	12	87,500
63	*STAMFORD, SPALDING, &c., BANKING CO.*	'32	19	200,000
64	*Pares's Leicestershire Banking Company*	'36	6	310,000
65	*LEICESTERSHIRE BANKING COMPANY*	'29	11	275,000
66	*Coventry Union Banking Company*	'36	2	56,000
67	„ *and Warwickshire Bank*	'35	1	78,080
68	*Leamington Priors and Warwickshire Bank*	'35	4	32,000
69	*Northamptonshire Banking Company*	'36	4	78,000
70	„ *Union Bank*	'36	4	132,500
	VI. Black Country.			
71	LLOYD'S BANKING COMPANY, *Limited*	1865	32	400,000
72	BIRMINGHAM, DUDLEY, AND DISTRICT BANK	'36	8	228,160

Joint Stock Banks, 1875—*Contd.*

4 Reserve and Balance after Last Dividend.	5 Number of Proprietors.	6 Number of Shares.	7 Amount per Share.	8 Paid-up per Share.	9 Dividend per Cent. per Annum for 12 Months, including Bonus.	10 Price per Share, August, 1875.	11 Premium per Cent.	12 Yield per Cent. at Price.			Number.
£	No.	No.	£	£	Per cnt.	£	Per cnt.	£	s.	d.	
76,234	179	6,600	100	20	20	60	200	6	13	4	35
80,892	207	6,066	100	15	20	54½	263⅓	5	10	1	36
42,327	144	6,052	100	25	7	31¾	27	5	10	3	37
65,385	374	9,200	100	25	9½	40¼	61	5	18	–	38
39,000	314	20,000	10	5	12½	10¼	105	6	1	11¼	39
163,558	250	10,000	100	20	18	61	205	5	18	–	40
264,574	211	6,800	100	60	25	183	205	8	3	11	41
115,554	216	6,500	100	35	11¾	90	157 1/7	4	11	4	42
108,904	362	21,158	50	20	14⅜	60	200	4	15	10	43
106,445	410	15,000	25	10	18	28	180	6	8	7	44
70,000	297	12,000	20	10	14	24	140	5	16	8	45
183,080	458	25,000	20	10	17½	29¼	192½	5	19	8	46
124,269	330	17,000	100	22½	10	42½	88⅝	5	5	10½	47
32,346	320	20,000	100	10	15	26	160	5	15	4½	48
85,014	193	8,000	50	12½	17½	38½	208	5	13	7½	49
37,273	77	2,705	100	15	20	52	246⅔	5	15	4½	50
50,000	252	15,000	20	12	11¼	25	108⅓	5	8	–	51
86,169	289	5,022	100	32	18¾	86	168¾	6	19	6¼	52
106,404	232	1,500 3,000	200 50	140 35	17	308 75	120 114 2/7	7 	14 —	6½ 	53
55,581	326	7,328	100	25	15	57	128	6	11	7	54
13,049	90	2,500	100	14	10	21	50	6	13	4	55
20,000	184	5,000	50	12½	8	20	60	5	–	–	56
3,000	160	6,000	20	5	5	8	60	3	2	6	57
67,469	213	13,000	20	10	20	27	170	7	8	1¾	58
35,000	230	8,140	50	25	8	38	52	5	5	4	59
100,000	320	50,575	10	4	15	10½	162½	5	14	3½	60
34,477	208	10,000	50	10	8½	15¾	57½	5	7	11¼	61
71,400	225	1,250	200	70	25	280	300	6	5	–	62
102,577	307	10,000	20	20	16½	70	250	4	14	3¼	63
148,201	440	20,000 12,000	12½ 12½	12½ 5	14	33 14¾	164 195	5 	6 —	–¾ 	64
87,000	296	5,000 10,000	100 25	40 7½	14	95 20	137½ 166⅔	5 	17 —	10¾ 	65
17,000	144	8,960	20	6¼	12	13	108	5	15	4½	66
21,000	130	9,760	50	8	10	14¼	78⅛	5	12	3¼	67
14,555	60	3,200	20	10	12½	21½	115	5	16	3¼	68
18,612	324	15,600	20	5	9	8	60	5	12	6	69
146,056	726	26,500	25	5	16	18¼	265	4	7	8	70
200,000	1,130	50,000	50	8	20	26¾	228⅛	6	1	10¾	71
87,934	384	25,000 7,040	20 10	8 4	12½	16⅞ 8¼	111 —	5 	18 —	5 	72

TABLE III.—*Purely Provincial English*

Number.	Name. [*Italics*—Small or Large—denote Banks of Issue, CAPITALS—Italic or Plain—Banks which publish Balance Sheets.]	1 When Estab-lished.	2 Number of Offices.	3 Paid-up Capital.
	VI. Black Country—*Contd.*	Year.	No.	£
73	BIRMINGHAM BANKING COMPANY, *Limited*	1866	2	158,070
74	„ JOINT STOCK BANK, *Limited*	'61	3	203,900
75	Birmingham and Midland Bank	'36	3	300,000
76	*COUNTY OF STAFFORD BANK*	'36	1	60,000
77	*WOLVERHMPTN. AND STAFFDSH. BKG. CO.*	'32	1	100,000
78	STAFFORDSHIRE JOINT STOCK BANK, *Limited*	'64	9	174,500
79	*STOURBRIDGE AND KIDDERMINSTER BK.*	'34	14	100,000
	VII. Western and Southern Counties.			
80	Bala Banking Company, *Limited*	1864	3	8,155
81	Glamorganshire Banking Company	'36	6	250,000
82	Swansea Bank, *Limited*	'73	4	170,784
83	*Whitchurch and Ellesmere Banking Company*	'40	2	—
84	*Ludlow and Tenbury Bank* *	'40	1	—
85	*WORCESTER CITY & COUNTY BANK, Limited*	'40	14	250,000
86	*W. OF ENGLAND AND S. WALES DIST. BK.*	'34	43	750,000
87	DEVON AND CORNWALL BANK	'32	15	128,000
88	*Helston Banking Company*	'36	2	—
89	THREE TOWNS' BANKING COMPANY, *Limited*	'63	2	50,000
90	*Stuckey's Banking Company*	'26	34	301,900
91	*County of Gloucester Bank*	'36	12	181,000
92	*Gloucestershire Banking Company*	'31	27	450,000
93	*North Wilts Banking*	'35	16	85,000
94	*WILTS AND DORSET " BANKING COMPANY*	'35	50	250,000
95	BUCKS AND OXON UNION BANK, *Limited*	'66	9	80,000
96	HAMPSHIRE BANKING COMPANY	'34	29	150,000
97	NORTH KENT BANK, *Limited*	'64	2	22,390
	Totals	—	823	19,361,993
	Averages	—	97 banks. 8½	93 banks. 208,193

* The general business of the Ludlow and Tenbury Bank is merged in the Worcester City and

Joint Stock Banks, 1875—*Contd.*

4 Reserve and Balance after Last Dividend.	5 Number of Proprietors.	6 Number of Shares.	7 Amount per Share.	8 Paid-up per Share.	9 Dividend per Cent. per Annum for 12 Months, including Bonus.	10 Price per Share, August, 1875.	11 Premium per Cent.	12 Yield per Cent. at Price.	Number.
£	No.	No.	£	£	Per cent.	£	Per cent.	£ s. d.	
132,866	569	31,614	50	5	15	14⅜	187½	5 4 4	73
221,219	581	20,390	100	10	20	33⅞	233¾	5 19 10	74
266,229	249	6,000	50	50	20	170	240	5 17 7¾	75
34,982	100	12,000	10	5	18	16⅛	222½	5 11 7½	76
41,526	162	10,000	50	10	10	18⅞	88¾	5 5 11½	77
64,542	273	10,000	100	20	8¾	29	45	6 – 8¼	78
96,582	191	10,000	25	10	20	28¼	182½	7 1 7	79
5,462	145	{ 5,000 1,137	1 10	½ 5	} 10	—	—	—	80
184,874	226	{ 2,000 10,000	100 10	100 5	} 15	{ 200 15½	100 200	7 10 – 5 – –	} 81
31,453	716	28,464	20	6	7½	9	58⅓	4 14 8¾	82
—	82	—	20	3½	12½	6	71½	7 5 9¼	83
—	11	—	—	—	—	—	—	—	84
101,044	447	20,000	50	12½	12⅔	25½	100	6 3 9	85
150,356	1,808	50,000	20	15	14	28	90	7 7 4	86
83,000	320	4,000	100	32	16¼	80	150	6 10 –	87
—	9	—	—	—	—	—	—	—	88
900	163	2,000	50	25	5	18	Dis.	6 18 10¾	89
150,864	111	—	—	50	—	—	—	—	90
69,068	383	7,240	100	25	10	48	92	5 4 2	91
194,792	650	20,000	50	22½	13⅓	52⅞	135	5 13 5½	92
86,484	192	17,000	25	5	20	20	300	5 – –	93
155,213	796	25,000	15	10	22	41½	315	5 6 –¼	94
18,100	350	16,000	25	5	20	17½	250	5 14 3½	95
40,220	281	15,000	50	10	16	30	200	5 6 8	96
1,600	30	2,239	50	10	8	12	20	6 13 4	97
9,150,236	32,105	—	—	—	—	—	—	—	
93 banks. 98,390	331	—	—	—	94 banks. 14¼	—	—	91 banks. 5 17 3	

County Bank, but it has retained its note circulation, and in that respect has a separate existence.

TABLE IV.—*Scotch*

Number.	Name. [All are Banks of Issue, and all publish Balance Sheets.]	1 Date when Established.	2 Number of Offices.	3 Paid-up Capital.	4 Reserve and Balance after last Dividend.
		Year.	No.	£	£
1	BANK OF SCOTLAND	1695	77	1,000,000	401,493
2	ROYAL BANK OF SCOTLAND	1727	107	2,000,000	527,301
3	BRITISH LINEN COMPANY BANK	'46	68	1,000,000	430,311
4	COMMERCIAL BANK OF SCOTLAND	1810	101	1,000,000	407,294
5	NATIONAL BANK	'25	92	1,000,000	418,300
6	ABERDEEN TOWN & COUNTY BK.	'25	41	252,000	117,608
7	UNION BANK OF SCOTLAND	'30	117	1,000,000	403,195
8	N. OF SCOTLAND BANKING CO.	'36	47	320,000	100,295
9	CLYDESDALE BANKING COMPANY	'38	80	1,000,000	519,133
10	CALEDONIAN BANKING COMPANY	'38	22	150,000	78,362
11	CITY OF GLASGOW BANK	'39	123	1,000,000	461,519
	Totals	—	875	9,722,000	3,864,811
	Averages	—	79½	883,820	351,346

* Bonus of 2½ per cent., chiefly from a special fund. Ordinary

TABLE V.—*Irish Joint*

Number.	Name. [*Italics*—Small or Large—denote Banks of Issue, CAPITALS—Italic or Plain—Banks which publish Balance Sheets.]	1 Date of Establishment.	2 Number of Offices.	3 Paid-up Capital.	4 Reserve and Balance after last Dividend.
		Year.	No.	£	£
1	Bank of Ireland	1783	50	2,769,230	1,072,000
2	Northern Banking Company	1825	44	300,000	170,000
3	HIBERNIAN BANK	'25	32	500,000	239,216
4	Provincial Bank of Ireland	'25	44	540,000	213,255
5	Belfast Banking Company	'27	36	250,000	196,080
6	NATIONAL BANK	'35	106*	1,500,000	150,000
7	ULSTER BANKING COMPANY	'36	44	250,000	291,568
8	ROYAL BANK OF IRELAND	'36	5	300,000	200,670
9	MUNSTER BANK, Limited	'64	40	350,000	167,251
	Totals	—	401	6,759,230	2,700,040
	Averages	—	44½	751,025	300,004

* In

Banks, 1875.

5 Number of Proprietors.	6 Number of Shares.	7 Amount per Share.	8 Paid-up per Share.	9 Dividend and Bonus per Cent. per Annum for 12 Months.	10 Price per Share, August, 1875.	11 Premium per Cent.	12 Yield per Cent. at Price.	Number.
No.	No.	£	£	Per cnt.	£	Per cnt.	£ s. d.	
1,409	Stock	—	100	14	305	205	4 11 10	1
1,468	,,	—	100	9½	220	120	4 6 4	2
1,208	,,	—	100	13	276	176	4 14 2	3
1,170	,,	—	100	15	304	204	4 18 8	4
1,623	,,	—	100	16	309½	209½	5 3 4	5
844	36,000	20	7	12½	18⅛	157½	4 16 4	6
1,250	Stock	—	100	15	272	172	5 10 4	7
1,420	80,000	20	4	12½	11⅞	196⅞	4 4 2	8
1,383	Stock	—	100	16½*	268	168	6 3 2	9
801	60,000	10	2½	14	7½	200	4 13 4	10
1,212	Stock	—	100	11	227½	127½	4 16 8	11
13,788	—	—	—	—	—	—	—	
1,253	—	—	—	13½	—	176	4 18 –	

dividend 14 per cent., at which yield per cent. *5l. 4s. 6d.*

Stock Banks, 1875.

5 Number of Proprietors.	6 Number of Shares.	7 Amount per Share.	8 Paid-up per Share.	9 Dividend and Bonus per Cent. per Annum for 12 Months.	10 Price per Share, August, 1875.	11 Premium per Cent.	12 Yield per Cent. at Price.	Number.
No.	No.	£	£	Per cnt.	£	Per cnt.	£ s. d.	
—	Stock	—	100	13	306	206	4 5 –	1
718	5,000	92	30	15	91½	205	4 18 4	2
	5,000	100	30	7½	46	53⅓	4 17 8	
1,380	20,000	100	25	12	57½	130	5 4 4	3
2,000	20,000	100	25	18	88¼	253	5 2 –	4
	4,000	10	10		34¼	242½	5 5 1	
648	5,000	100	25	20	103¼	313	4 16 10	5
	5,000	100	25	8	41¼	65	4 16 11	
4,000	50,000	50	30	11	69½	131⅔	4 15 –	6
1,020	100,000	10	2½	20	10½	320	4 15 3	7
1,350	30,000	50	10	14½	29¾	197½	4 17 6	8
1,163	100,000	10	3½	12	8¾	150	4 16 –	9
12,279	—	—	—	—	—	—	—	
8 banks, 1,535	—	—	—	15	—	212	4 16 8	

Ireland.

Date of Establishment.

The first column in these five tables gives the date of establishment, and from it is compiled Table VI, showing the number of the existing banks founded previously to 1826, between 1826 and 1830, thence in successive periods of five years down to 1870, and in the four years 1871 to 1874.

TABLE VI.—*United Kingdom. Number of Existing Joint Stock Banks, December, 1874, exclusive of Bank of England, Classified according to Date of Establishment.*

Period of Establishment.	English Banks.				Scotch Banks.	Irish Banks.	Total, United Kingdom.
	Purely London.	London and Provincial.	Purely Provincial.	Total.			
Before 1826	—	—	—	—	6	4	10
1826–30	—	—	10	10	1	1	12
'31–35	1	1	26	28	—	1	29
'36–40	2	1	31	34	4	2	40
'41–45	—	—	3	3	1	—	4
'46–50	—	—	—	—	—	—	—
'51–55	1	—	—	1	—	—	1
'56–60	—	—	—	—	—	—	—
'61–65	4	4	18	26	—	1	27
'66–70	2	—	3	5	—	—	5
'71–74	2	1	8	11	—	—	11
	12	7	99	118	12	9	139
Before 1841	3	2	67	72	11	8	91
1841–60	1	—	3	4	1	—	5
Since 1860	8	5	29	42	—	1	43
	12	7	99	118	12	9	139

The following are the noteworthy features of this table. None of the English banks date from before 1826, as that was the year in which the establishment of joint stock banks in England was first made legal. Of the existing English banks seventy-two were founded during the period 1826 to 1840, three during the period 1841 to 1845, only one, the City Bank, London, from 1846 to 1860, and forty-two since 1860.

In Scotland six, and in Ireland four of the present banks were already in existence before 1826.

In Scotland eleven banks, being all the present banks of issue, were established before 1841. The North British Bank, established in 1845, does not carry on banking business, and is, I am informed, to all intents and purposes, in liquidation. No bank has been successfully established since that date. The monopoly of banking in Scotland, given to the eleven banks of issue by the legislation of 1845, is thus complete.

In Ireland eight of the nine banks were established before 1841, none from 1841 to 1860, and one since 1860, viz., the Munster Bank, Limited, in 1864. That only one bank in Ireland is of more recent foundation than 1845 is probably due in a great measure to the legislation of that year.

The lull in the establishment of joint stock banks in England between 1840 and 1862 is very remarkable. The gross abuse of joint stock banking prior to 1840 doubtless created an ignorant prejudice against its use. This prejudice was both evidenced and fostered by the course of the parliamentary inquiry of 1840 and by the speeches of Sir Robert Peel and others in the debates on the banking legislation of 1844. That legislation prevented the establishment of any new bank of issue, and the public were slow to learn that provincial banking could be profitably carried on without the privilege of issue. But by far the most powerful bar to progress lay in the liability of any shareholder to have judgment decrees and orders against the company enforced against him individually, whether he were a member at the time the cause of action arose, or had been a member within three years. This liability was abolished by an Act of 1857. The banking failures of 1847 and 1857 no doubt contributed likewise to retard the development of joint stock banking, and it was reserved for the much abused principle of limited liability under the sanction of the Companies Act of 1862 to inaugurate a fresh point of departure in the extension of joint stock bank enterprise. The forty-two banks of England and Wales, which date their foundation since 1860, are all limited companies, as also is the sole Irish bank established since that year.

Number of Banks.

Table VII has been compiled from the Banking Almanacs, to show the variations in number of joint stock and private banks in England and Wales since 1860.

TABLE VII.—*Number of Banks (Joint Stock and Private), excluding the Bank of England, existing in England and Wales, including the Isle of Man, but excluding the Channel Islands, at Dates as under.*

	1860.	1865.	1870.	1875.
Joint Stock—				
Purely London..........................	7	11	12	12
London and provincial	2	9	8	7
Provincial...............................	85	93	92	99
Total joint stock	94	113	112	118
Private—				
Purely London..........................	53	46	47	55
Provincial...............................	239	211	207	196
Total private	292	257	254	251
Total joint stock and private	386	370	366	369

It will be seen from Table VII that during the last fifteen years there has been a decided diminution in the number of private banks in the provinces of England and Wales. Against 239 provincial private banks in 1860, there are now only 196, showing a diminution of 43. Of these 28 disappeared between 1860 and 1865, 4 between 1865 and 1870, and 11 between 1870 and 1875.

The revival of joint stock banking after 1862 induced a good many private bankers to transfer their business to joint stock companies. This tendency received a rude but, as it appears, only a temporary check, from the events of 1866, which revealing a fearful amount of reckless and dishonest management on the part of new banks and financial companies, threw discredit for the time on the joint stock system. The public is now, however, convinced that it was neither the joint stock system nor its modern phase of limited liability which was at fault, but solely the vices of management. It must not be forgotten that two of the most scandalous smashes of 1866, those of Overend, Gurney, and Co., Limited, and Barned's Banking Company, Limited, were in reality failures of private banks, both concerns having been insolvent when within a year of their suspension they were converted into joint stock companies.

The joint stock banks in England and Wales have increased in number thus since 1860:—

Purely London 5
London and Provincial 5
Provincial, including Isle of Man 14

Total 24

It will probably be found that three or four have been added in the provinces during 1875.

Number of Bank Offices.

In the following table the number of bank offices and the average number of offices per bank are shown for the whole United Kingdom:—

TABLE VIII.—*Number of Banks and Bank Offices in the United Kingdom, December, 1874.*

Banks.	Number of Banks.	Number of Bank Offices.	Average Number of Offices per Bank.
England and Wales—			
JOINT STOCK—			
Bank of England	1	11	11
Purely London	12	40	3⅓
London and provincial	7	412	59
Purely provincial	97	823	8½
	117	1,286	11
Isle of Man	2	9	4½
Total joint stock	119	1,295	11
PRIVATE—			
Purely London	55	61	1
Provincial	196	523	2¾
Channel Isles	6	6	1
Total private	257	590	2¼
Total joint stock and private	376	1,885	5
Scotch—			
Joint stock	11	875*	79½
Private	—	—	—
Irish—			
Joint stock	9	409*	45
Private	3	3	1
Total Irish	12	412	34
Grand total	399	3,172	8

* Including London offices.

The joint stock bank with the largest number of offices is the London and County, with 149; next comes the National Provincial Bank of England, with 138; then the City of Glasgow Bank, with 123 (now 126). The Union Bank of Scotland has 117, and the National Bank (Ireland), 114. In the English provinces the banks having the largest number of offices are:—

Manchester and Liverpool District Bank 52
Wilts and Dorset Banking Company 50
West of England and South Wales District Bank 43

Twenty of the purely provincial English joint stock banks have no branches at all. These banks are chiefly in Liverpool and the manufacturing towns of Lancashire and Yorkshire.

TABLE IX.—*Proportion of Banks and Bank Offices to Inhabitants, December*, 1874.

Locality.	Number of Banks.	Number of Inhabitants to One Bank.	Number of Bank Offices.	Number of Inhabitants to One Bank Office.
England and Wales (including Bank of England)	376	63,700	1,885	12,600
Scotland	11	317,750	873	4,000
Ireland	12	441,477	404	13,100
United Kingdom	399	82,000	3,162	10,300

These figures bring out in salient relief one great distinguishing characteristic of English as compared with Scotch and Irish banking. In England there are many small local banks and few banking offices. In Scotland and Ireland there are few or no small banks and many banking offices. The comparatively local character of English banking is in a great measure the result of the maintenance, till 1826, of the monopoly of the Bank of England, by the restriction of banking to private firms with not more than six partners.

In England a comparison with previous investigations gives the following results :—

England.	Number of Bank Offices.	Number of Inhabitants to One Bank Office.
1851. Mr. Newmarch	962	18,700
'54. Mr. Gilbart	—	16,500
'70. Present Inquiry	1,651	13,500
'75. ,,	1,885	12,600

In Scotland the progress in the number of bank offices, according to Table LXXVII, p. 188, which brings the figures down six months later than I have done, has been

Scotland.	Number of Bank Offices.	Number of Inhabitants to One Bank Office.
1845	382	7,178
'55	480	6,200
'65	654	4,870
'75	884	3,954

In Ireland a comparison with previous investigations gives these results :—

Ireland.	Number of Bank Offices.	Number of Inhabitants to One Bank Office.
1851. Mr. Newmarch	170	38,300
'72. Mr. Palgrave	365	14,800
'75. Present Inquiry....	404	13,100

Paid-up Capital.

The total paid-up capital shown by Tables 1, II, III, IV, V, with the addition of that of four London discount companies and of the Bank of England, is as under :—

TABLE X.— *United Kingdom, Capital paid-up of Joint Stock Banks as under, August,* 1875. [000's omitted.]

Number of Banks.	Locality	Paid-up Capital.	Average per Bank.
	England and Wales—	£	£
11	Purely London banks	7,364,	669,
7	London and provincial	4,425,	632,
93	Purely provincial	19,362,	208,
4	„ not stated, say	250,	50,
2	Isle of Man	59,	30,
117	Total England and Wales	31,460,	268,
11	Scotch	9,722,	884,
9	Irish	6,759,	751,
137	Total United Kingdom...............	47,941,	350,
	To which add—		
4	London Discount Companies	2,717,	679,
141		50,658,	359,
	Add further—		
1	Bank of England	14,553,	14,553,
142	Grand total, United Kingdom....	65,211,	459,

Next to the Bank of England, the following are the banks with the largest paid-up capital :—

	£
Bank of Ireland	2,769,230
London and Westminster.................	2,000,000
Royal Bank of Scotland	2,000,000
National Bank (Ireland) ,..............	1,500,000
National Provincial Bank of England........	1,462,500
London and County	1,425,000
Union Bank of London.................	1,395,000
London Joint Stock	1,200,000
Seven Scotch banks, each	1,000,000
Manchester and Liverpool District	905,000
Alliance Bank, *Limited*.................	800,000
West of England and South Wales District...........	750,000

Note.—Banks of issue are distinguished by *italics.*

The proportion of paid-up capital to population is :—

		Per head.
		£ s.
England and Wales, including Bank of England	....	1 18
„ excluding „	....	1 6
Scotland	....	2 16
Ireland	....	1 6

The value of this comparison is much diminished by the circumstance that it cannot include private banks, of which there are 251 in England and Wales, none in Scotland, and 3 in Ireland.

Liability of Shareholders.

It will be seen from Table XI, that of the 139 joint stock banks of the United Kingdom, 84 are under unlimited and 55 under limited liability.

TABLE XI.— *Number of Limited and Unlimited Joint Stock Banks in the United Kingdom, December, 1874.*

Banks.	Unlimited.	Limited.
England and Wales—		
Bank of England	—	1
Purely London	4	8
London and provincial	2	5
Purely provincial	63	34
Isle of Man	—	2
Total England and Wales.......	69	50
Scotland	8	3
Ireland	7	2
Total number United Kingdom	84	55

All the joint stock banks established in England since 1860, 42 in number, are on the principle of limited liability, whilst the following seven old established banks have since 1862 transformed themselves into limited companies :—

		Established.
Cumberland Union Banking Company	....	1829
Liverpool Commercial Bank	....	'32
Halifax Commercial Banking Company	....	'36
Union Bank of Manchester	....	'36
Moore and Robinson's Nottinghamshire Bank	....	'36
Bank of Whitehaven	....	'37
Worcester City and County Bank	....	'40

The five banks printed in *italics* are banks of issue : but the Act of 1862 provides that the limitation of liability shall not apply to notes in circulation.

Adverse opinions have been expressed in various quarters, and even very recently, as to the soundness of applying the principle of limited liability to banking. The principle is, however, by no means an innovation. The liability of the proprietors in the Bank of England is absolutely limited to the capital paid up. The same is the case with the Bank of Ireland and with two Scotch banks, the Royal Bank of Scotland and the British Linen Company, both of which are incorporated by royal charter. In these four cases the proprietors are liable to no further calls in any event; the principle of limited liability is in fact pushed to its extreme. So far as I am aware, the only instance in which this extreme has been essayed by any bank established under the Companies' Act was that of the Metropolitan Bank, Limited. In that case the experiment did not succeed, and has been departed from. The Bank of Scotland is under limited liability, having been constituted by Act of Parliament. Its capital is 1,500,000*l.*, of which 500,000*l.* is uncalled. It should be explained that in the case of the three Scotch banks in which the liability is limited, there is no express limitation in the Act of Parliament or royal charter, as the case may be, but incorporation at the periods at which these banks were established may be held to infer limitation of liability, although some lawyers do not consider this point to be quite clear. Fortunately, the case has never had to be tried, and is never likely to be, considering the stability of the banks in question; but the report of the Committee of 1840 on Banks of Issue supports the view in favour of limited liability; Sir Robert Peel stated again and again, in the debates on the Bank Acts, that the liability of the three senior Scotch banks was limited, and these banks are specially exempted by the Act of 1845 from making any return of their partners, the reason being that the public could not look to the stockholders as individually responsible.

The obvious advantage of the system of limited liability is that each shareholder knows exactly the utmost amount he can possibly lose in the event of the failure of the bank. This unquestionably tends to attract as shareholders men of substance, who might decline to undertake an indefinite liability.

It cannot be denied, however, that from the creditor's point of view the limited bank exposes itself to unfavourable comparison with the unlimited bank, unless it maintains uncalled an adequate margin upon its shares. To ascertain what margin may fairly be deemed adequate, let us look at the calls made to liquidate banks which have failed in recent years. Through the kindness of the liquidators, or from other reliable sources, I am enabled to compile :--

TABLE XII.—*Calls made in Liquidation of Failed Banks.*

Failed Banks.	Date of Failure.	Amount per Share Paid-up at Date of Failure.	Total Calls per Share made during Liquidation.	Proportion of Calls to Paid-up Capital.	Amount per Share since Returned to Shareholders.
		£	£		£ *s.*
Liverpool Borough Bank	1857	10	. 5	0½	3 12
Royal Bank of Liverpool......	'67	10 original }	15	1½	5 16
		100 preference }	150	,,	58 _
Overend, Gurney & Co., L.....	'66	15	25	1¾	3 10
Birmingham Banking Co.	'66	10	10	1	1
Bank of London	'66	10	nil	nil	6 10*
Leeds Banking Company	'64	15	170	11½	10 −†
Northumberland and Durham Dist. Banking Co. }	'57	10	40	4	nil‡
Western Bank of Scotland....	'57	50 .	125	2½	68 −

* In addition to an apportionment of Atlantic and Great Western shares and bonds.

† A most exceptional case of mismanagement.

‡ Paid creditors 19s. 8d. per pound.

Barned's Banking Company, Limited, is not included in this table, because its business proved to have been hopelessly insolvent at the time it was taken over from Messrs. Barned and Co., a year before the failure of the Company. The case of the Leeds Banking Company is so extremely exceptional that it may fairly be left out of view. The calls required in the other cases were :—

Northumberland and Durham .... 4 times the paid-up capital.
Western Bank of Scotland .... 2½   „
Overend, Gurney, and Co., Limited .... 1¾   „
Royal Bank of Liverpool .... 1½   „
Birmingham Banking Company .... equal to the paid-up capital.
Liverpool Borough Bank .... half of   „
Bank of London.. no calls.

From these data the conclusion seems to be justified that a limited bank with an uncalled margin of three times the amount paid up on its shares is, *cæteris paribus*, so far as regards security to its creditors, practically as safe as an unlimited bank.

The following table contains a list of the limited banks of the United Kingdom, with the amount per share, the amount called per share, and the ratio of the uncalled margin to the amount paid up :—

TABLE XIII.—*England and Wales, Limited Banks, Proportion of Uncalled to Paid-up Capital,* 1875.

Limited Banks. [Banks of Issue in *Italics.*]	Amount per Share.	Paid-up per Share.	Ratio of Uncalled Margin to Amount Paid-up.
	£	£	Per cut.
Purely London—			
1 Imperial	50	15	233
2 Alliance	25	10	150
3 Central	10	5	100
4 Metropolitan {	10	10	Nil
	10	1¼	566
5 St. James'	20	10	100
6 West London Commercial	10	6	66
7 Merchant Banking Company	100	25	300
London and Provincial—			
1 London and South Western	100	20	400
2 Consolidated	10	4	150
3 Midland	100	20	400
4 London and Provincial	10	5	100
5 „ Yorkshire	50	9	455
Purely Provincial—			
1 Cumberland Union	30	12¼	140
2 *Bank of Whitehaven*	30	10	200
3 North Eastern, Newcastle	20	6	233
4 Industrial Bank, Newcastle	5	3	66
5 Northern Counties	50	30	66
6 Liverpool Commercial	20	10	100
7 North Western, Liverpool	20	7¼	166
8 National of Liverpool	25	15	66
9 Adelphi, Liverpool	20	10	100
10 Manchester and County	100	15	566
11 Union of Manchester	25	11	127
12 Manchester Joint Stock	20	6	233
13 Lancashire and Yorkshire	20	10	100
14 Parr's Banking Company	100	20	400
15 Rochdale Joint Stock	20	4	400
16 Bank of Leeds	100	25	300
17 Leeds and County	100	25	300
18 Exchange and Discount, Leeds	10	5	100
19 Bradford District	100	35	186
20 „ Old	50	20	150
21 *Halifax Commercial*	20	10	100
22 Derby Commercial	20	5	300
23 *Moore and Robinson's, Notts*	10	4	150
24 Nottingham Joint Stock	50	10·	400
25 Lloyd's, Birmingham	50	8	525
26 Birmingham Banking Company	50	5	900
27 „ Joint Stock Bank	100	10	900
28 Staffordshire „	100	20	400
29 Bala Banking Company	10	5	100
30 Swansea	20	6	233
31 *Worcester City and County*	50	12¼	300
32 Three Towns'	50	25	100
33 Bucks and Oxon Union	25	5	400
34 North Kent	50	10	400

We find from Table XIII that out of forty-six limited banks of England and Wales, twenty-six have a smaller margin of capital uncalled than three times the amount paid up, whilst eighteen have an uncalled margin equal to or greater than three times the amount paid up. Whilst deeming it instructive to work out these figures, I must distinctly disclaim any insinuation whatever that any of the established banks which fall below the assumed standard of uncalled margin is not in a sound position as regards its capital. It is impossible to lay down any hard and fast line on the subject, but it may be suggested that in the future establishment of banks on the principle of limited liability, it would be well to keep in view that the maintenance of a large margin of uncalled capital is most desirable, if not essential, in order to secure the confidence of the public.

Even in the case of unlimited banks, it is very expedient to have some uncalled margin on the shares, so that the directors may be enabled, if necessary, to obtain an accession to the paid-up capital without creating and placing new shares,—a process which, under certain circumstances, might be undesirable, if not impracticable, and in any case would be a much less expeditious method of raising money than a call upon existing shares. In an unlimited bank, probably an uncalled margin equal in amount to the sum paid up, would be very ample.

From Table XIV, it will be found that amongst the unlimited banks no London or London and provincial bank has an uncalled margin of capital of less than the amount paid up, whilst amongst the purely provincial unlimited banks six have no margin uncalled, nine have less uncalled than the amount paid up, forty-four have more, and for three we have not the figures.

The details are as follows :—

TABLE XIV.—*England and Wales. Unlimited Banks. Proportion of Uncalled to Paid-up Capital*, 1875.

	Unlimited Banks. [Banks of Issue in *Italics*.]	Amount per Share.	Paid-up per Share.	Uncalled per Share.	Ratio per Cent. of Uncalled to Paid-up.
	Purely London.	£	£	£	Per cnt.
1	London and Westminster	100	20	80	400·0
2	„ Joint Stock	50	15	35	233·3
3	Union	50	15½	34½	222·5
4	City	20	10	10	100·0
	London and Provincial.				
1	National Provincial Bank	50	21	29	138·0
2	London and County	50	20	30	150·0

TABLE XIV.—*England and Wales.   Unlimited Banks—Contd.*

	Unlimited Banks. [Banks of Issue in *Italics*.]	Amount per Share. £	Paid-up per Share. £	Uncalled per Share. £	Ratio per Cent. of Uncalled to Paid-up.
	Purely Provincial.	£	£	£	Per cnt.
1	*Carlisle City and District Bank*	25	12½	12½	100·0
2	„ *and Cumb. Banking Compy.*	20	5	15	300·0
3	*Whitehaven Joint Stock Bank*	100	15	85	566·7
4	*Bank of Westmoreland*	100	12	88	733·3
5	Bank of Liverpool	100	12½	87½	700·0
6	Liverpool Union Bank	20	20	—	fully paid up
7	North and South Wales Bank	10	10	—	„
8	Manchester and Liverpool Dist. Bank.	20	10	10	100·0
9	„ Salford Bank	20	8	12	150·0
10	*Lancaster Banking Company*	25	25	—	fully paid up
11	Preston Banking Company {	100	100 }	—	„
		25	25		
12	Bank of Bolton	20	15	5	33·3
13	Bury Banking Company	10	6	4	66·6
14	Ashton, Stalybridge, &c., Bank	10	4	6	150·0
15	*Darlington District Bank*	100	17	83	488·2
16	*Swaledale, &c., Banking Company*	100	7½	92½	1233·3
17	*Knaresboro' and Claro Banking Co.*	?	20	?	?
18	*Yorkshire Banking Company*	25	12½	12½	100·0
19	*York City and County Bank*	100	25	75	300·0
20	„ *Union Banking Company*	100	20	80	400·0
21	*Hull Banking Company*	100	15	85	566·7
22	*Bradford Commercial Banking Co.*	100	20	80	400·0
23	„ *Banking Company*	100	60	40	66·7
24	*Halifax Joint Stock Bank*	25	10	15	150·0
25	„ *and Huddersfield Union*	20	10	10	100·0
26	*Huddersfield Banking Company*	100	22½	77½	344·4
27	*West Riding Union*	100	10	90	900·0
28	*Wakefield and Barnsley Union*	50	12½	37½	300·0
29	*Barnsley Banking Company*	100	15	85	566·7
30	Sheffield Union Banking Company	20	12	8	66·7
31	*Sheffield and Rotherham Bankg. Co.*	100	32	68	212·6
32	„ *Banking Company* {	200	140	60	42·9
		50	35	15	42·9
33	„ *and Hallamshire*	100	25	75	300·0
34	*Chesterfield and North Derby*	100	14	86	614·3
35	*Derby and Derbyshire*	50	12½	37½	300·0
36	*Burton, Uttoxeter, &c.*	20	10	10	100·0
37	*Nottingham and Notts Banking Co.*	50	25	25	100·0
38	*Lincoln and Lindsey* „	200	70	130	185·7
39	*Stamford, Spalding, &c.* „	20	20	—	fully paid up
40	*Pares's Leicestershire Banking Co.* {	12½	12½	—	„
		12½	5	7½	150·0
		100	40	60	150·0
41	*Leicestershire* „ {	25	7½	17½	233·3
42	*Coventry Union* „	20	6½	13¼	220·0
43	„ *and Warwickshire*	50	8	42	525·0
44	*Leamington Priors and Warwickshire*	20	10	-10	100·0
45	*Northamptonshire Banking Company*	20	5	15	300·0
46	„ *Union Bank*	25	5	20	400·0
47	Birmingham, Dudley, and District {	20	8	12	150·0
		10	4	6	150·0

TABLE XIV. —*England and Wales. Unlimited Banks—Contd.*

	Unlimited Banks. [Banks of Issue in *Italics*.]	Amount per Share.	Paid-up per Share.	Uncalled per Share.	Ratio per Cent. of Uncalled to Paid-up.
	Purely Provincial—*Contd.*	£	£	£	Per cnt.
48	Birmingham and Midland	50	50	—	fully paid up
49	*County of Stafford*	10	5	5	100·0
50	*Wolverhampton and Staff. Bkg. Co.*	50	10	40	400·0
51	*Stourbridge and Kidderminster*	25	10	15	150·0
52	Glamorganshire Banking Company {	100	100	—	fully paid up
		10	5	5	100·0
53	*Whitchurch and Ellesmere Bkg. Co.*	20	3½	16½	471·4
54	*West of England and S. Wales Dist.*	20	15	5	33·3
55	Devon and Cornwall	100	32	68	212·5
56	*Helston Banking Company*	?	?	?	?
57	*Stuckey's* ,, ...	?	50	?	?
58	*County of Gloucester*	100	25	75	300·0
59	*Gloucestershire Banking Company*	50	22½	27½	122·2
60	*North Wilts* ,, ...	21	5	20	400·0
61	*Wilts and Dorset* ,, ...	15	10	5	50·0
62	Hampshire Banking Company............	50	10	40	400·0

Reserve-Fund.

The totals of reserve-fund, shown by Tables I, II, III, IV, and V, adding those of the four chief London Discount Companies and that of the Bank of England, are as follows :—

TABLE XV.—*United Kingdom Joint Stock Banks. Reserve Fund,*
August, 1875.   [000's omitted.]

Number of Banks.	Locality.	Reserve Fund.	Average per Bank.	Ratio to Paid-up Capital.
	England and Wales—	£	£	Per cnt.
11	Purely London	2,139,	194,	29
7	London and provincial	1,684,	241,	38
93	Purely provincial	9,150,	98,	47
2	Isle of Man	20,	10,	33
113	England and Wales	12,993,	115,	42
11	Scotch	3,865,	351,	40
9	Irish	2,700,	300,	40
133 {	United Kingdom (4 purely provincial English not included)	19,558,	147,	41
4	To which add— London Discount Companies	668,	167,	24·
137		20,226,	150,	40
1	Add further— Bank of England	3,104,	3,104,	21
138	Grand total............................	23,330,	170,	36

It may not be superfluous to exhibit the paid-up capital and reserve fund together:—

TABLE XVI.— *United Kingdom Joint Stock Banks.   Paid-up Capital and Reserve Fund, August,* 1875.

[000's omitted.]

Number of Banks.	Locality.	Paid-up Capital.	Reserve Fund.	Together.
	England and Wales—	£	£	£
11	Purely London	7,364,	2,139,	9,503,
7	London and provincial	4,425,	1,684,	6,109,
97	Purely provincial	19,612,	9,150,	28,762,
2	Isle of Man	59,	20,	79,
117		31,460,	12,993,	44,453,
11	Scotch	9,722,	3,865,	13,587,
9	Irish	6,759,	2,700,	9,459,
137	United Kingdom	47,941,	19,558,	67,499,
	To which add—			
4	London Discount Companies	2,717,	668,	3,385,
141		50,658,	20,226,	70,884,
	Add further—			
1	Bank of England	14,553,	3,104,	17,657,
142	Grand total	65,211,	23,330,	88,541,

The purposes of a reserve-fund are—1, to enable a bank to meet large and exceptional losses without an infringement on its paid-up capital, or with as little reduction in dividend as possible; 2, thereby to give steadiness to the market value of the shares; 3, to increase the basis of proprietors' funds upon which the liabilities rest, and so to strengthen public confidence in the stability of the bank.

Generally speaking, the reserve-fund is formed by the gradual accumulation of undivided profits; but so essential a feature is it now deemed to be, that there have been several recent instances in which, on the establishment of a new bank, the shares have been issued at a small premium in order to create a reserve-fund at the very outset. This practice seems to be a sound one, and it can readily be carried into effect in most cases, and especially where the bank is formed to take over an existing business. When the shares of an established bank have attained a fair premium in the market, and an increase of capital is found desirable, a considerable accession to the reserve fund may be very advantageously secured by issuing new shares at a premium, and carrying the amount of the premium to reserve-fund. This has recently been done by many of the English provincial banks. The new shares are frequently

D

allotted amongst the shareholders at a price considerably below their actual market value, and thus the operation, besides its other advantages, yields a welcome bonus to the proprietors.

It is worthy of remark that in the case of the following purely provincial English banks, the reserve-fund, including undivided profit carried forward, exceeds or nearly equals the paid-up capital.

Banks. [Banks of Issue printed in *Italics*.]	Paid-up Capital.	Reserve and Balance Forward.	Dividend and Bonus per Cent.
	£	£	£
1. *Carlisle City and District Bank*	80,162	93,025	20
2. ,, *and Cumberland Bankg. Co.*	75,000	103,836	21
3. *Bank of Whitehaven, Limited*........	98,530	96,797	20
4. *Lancaster Banking Company*	275,000	276,216	30
5. Bury Banking Company	109,080	120,000	23
6. *York Union Banking Company*	90,990	80,892	20
7. *Barnsley Banking Company*............	40,575	37,273	20
8. *Northamptonshire Union*	132,500	146,056	16
9. Birmingham Joint Stock Bank........	203,900	221,219	20
10. ,, and Midland Bank	300,000	266,229	20
11. *Stourbridge and Kidderminster*........	100,000	96,562	20
12. *North Wilts*................................	85,000	86,484	20

Nine of these twelve banks are banks of issue. As might naturally be supposed, the banks which have reserve-funds so large in relation to their paid-up capital, are found to pay very high dividends. In the above list eight of the banks pay 20 per cent., one 21, one 23, and one 30 per cent.

In ordinary circumstances, a reserve fund equal to one-half the paid-up capital is quite ample. When it considerably exceeds that proportion, it may be good policy to capitalise a portion of it, and several instances might be adduced of English country banks which have treated part of their accumulated profits in that way.

Number of Proprietors.

TABLE **XVII.**—*United Kingdom Joint Stock Banks. Number of Proprietors, December,* 1874.

Locality.	Proprietors.	Average per Bank.	Proportion of Proprietors to Population.
England and Wales—	No.	No.	1 Proprietor in
Purely London	14,007	1,167	—
London and provincial	10,843	1,549	—
Purely provincial	32,105	337	—
Isle of Man	574	287	—
Total for England and Wales (ex-cluding Bank of England)	57,529	487	416
Scotland	13,788	1,253	253
Ireland (exclusive of Bank of Ireland not ascertained)	12,279	1,535	433
Total for United Kingdom	83,596	610	391

The figures in the last column indicate that banks are more popular as investments with the Scotch than with the English or Irish.

Dividend.

TABLE XVIII.—*United Kingdom Joint Stock Banks. Dividend per Cent. per Annum, including Bonus, Twelve Months ending June,* 1875.

Locality.	Lowest.	Highest.	Average.
England and Wales.			
Purely London—			
3 senior banks	15	18½	16½
8 others	5	10	7¾
Total 11 banks	5	18½	11
London and provincial—			
2 senior banks (unlimited)	18	23	20½
5 other banks (limited)	4	10	8½
Total 7 banks	4	23	11½
Purely provincial—			
51 issuing banks	8	30	16½
43 non-issuing banks	3¾	23	11⅝
Total 94 purely prov¹. banks.	3¾	30	14¼
Scotland, 11 banks	9½	16½	13½
Ireland, 9 banks	11	20	15

The absolutely highest dividends are :—

	Per Cent.
Lancaster Banking Company	30
Whitehaven Joint Stock	25
Bradford Banking Company	25
Lincoln and Lindsey Bank	25
Yorkshire Banking Company	24
National Provincial Bank of England	23
Bury Banking Company	23
Wilts and Dorset Banking Company	22
Carlisle and Cumberland Banking Company	21

Note.—Banks of issue printed in *italics.*

Market Price.

For the purpose of comparison the premium per cent. on the capital paid up is the readiest measure of the market price. The averages are as follows :—

TABLE XIX.— *United Kingdom Joint Stock Banks. Premium per Cent. on Paid-up Capital, August, 1875.*

Locality.	Highest Premium per Cent.	Average Premium per Cent.
England and Wales.		
Purely London—		
3 senior banks	222½	206¾
5 others	60	35
1 „ at a discount	—	—
2 „ no return	—	—
London and provincial—		
2 senior banks, unlimited	305	257½
4 others, limited	90	59
1 „ at a discount	—	—
Purely provincial—		
49 issuing banks	520	18½
5 „ no return	—	—
39 non-issuing banks............................	300	112
1 „ no return	—	—
2 „ at a discount...........	—	—
1 „ at par.....................	—	—
Scotland	209½	176
Ireland	320	212

It is worthy of remark that only four of the banks in our tables are at a discount. For eight there is no market price ascertained. The absolutely highest premium is that of the Lancaster Banking Company, 520 per cent.—their 25*l.* share selling at 155*l.*

Yield to Investor.

TABLE XX.— *United Kingdom Joint Stock Banks. Yield per Cent. to Purchaser at Market Price of August, 1875, and at the Rate of Dividend and Bonus per Cent. per Annum paid for previous Twelve Months.*

Banks.	Lowest Yield.			Highest Yield.			Average Yield.		
	£	s.	d.	£	s.	d.	£	s.	d.
England and Wales.									
Purely London—									
3 senior banks	4	19	3	5	17	11	5	7	7
5 others..............................	5	–	–	6	18	6	6	5	4
8 banks...............................	4	19	3	6	18	6	5	18	8
London and provincial—									
2 senior banks	5	13	7	5	16	2	5	14	10
5 others	5	5	3	6	13	4	6	1	4
7 banks......... ..	5	5	3	6	13	4	5	19	6
Purely provincial—									
49 issuing banks	4	7	8	8	3	11	5	18	6
42 non-issuing banks	3	2	6	9	4	8	5	15	10
91 banks.............................	3	2	6	9	4	8	5	17	3
Scotland, 11 banks............................	4	4	2	6	8	2	4	18	–
Ireland, 9 banks............................	4	5	–	5	4	4	4	16	8

Whilst the smallness of the yield to the investor at the market price, and dividend and bonus per cent., may be taken in the case of established banks to be the test of the estimation in which the bank stands in the eyes of the public, allowance must be made for the circumstance that in very recently established banks the market price generally represents, more or less, the expectation rather than the actual realisation of success.

The absolutely lowest yield to the investor amongst the English banks was, at the date of my figures, 3*l.* 2*s.* 6*d.* per cent., in the case of the Derby Commercial Bank, *Limited.*

The absolutely highest yield is 9*l.* 4*s.* 8*d.* per cent. in the case of the Industrial Bank, *Limited,* Newcastle-on-Tyne.

The appreciably lower yield shown by the Scotch and Irish banks evidences the greater popularity of bank shares as an investment in these parts of the United Kingdom.

I revert to the yield to the purchaser, and the circumstances which regulate it, in dealing with the tables of banks which publish balance sheets.

Circulation of Notes.

The following is the number of the joint stock banks of issue of the United Kingdom :—

Bank of England 1
Of the ninety-seven purely provincial English banks 54
All the Scotch banks 11
Of the nine Irish banks... 6
                                                                                     ——
Total joint stock banks of issue 72
                                                                                     ——

The circulation of these banks was as follows on the average of the year 1874. (See Mr. Palgrave's Tables) :—

Joint Stock Banks.	Fixed Authorised Issue.	Actual Average Circulation, 1874, as per Mr. Palgrave's Tables.
	£	£
1 Bank of England............................	15,000,000	26,264,000
54 English provincial	2,662,707	2,360,000
11 Scotch	2,749,271	5,900,000
6 Irish	6,354,494	6,769,000
Total joint stock banks	26,766,472	41,293,000

This branch of my subject is fully discussed in Section VII.

II. PUBLISHED BALANCE SHEETS OF JOINT STOCK BANKS.

Tables. •

All the purely London joint stock banks are understood to publish balance sheets, but I have been able to obtain those of only seven, which are tabularised and analysed in Tables XXI, XXII, and XXIII.

All the seven London and provincial banks publish balance sheets, and these are treated in Tables XXIV, XXV, and XXVI.

Of the ninety-seven purely provincial English banks in Table III, fifty-six publish their balance sheets, and forty-one, so far as I have been able to discover, do not. Of the fifty-four English banks of issue, twenty-two publish balance sheets and thirty-two

TABLE XXI.—*Purely London Joint Stock Bank Balance*

[000's omitted, thus

		1	2	3	4
					Liabilities.
Number.	Purely London Banks.	When Established.	Subscribed Capital.	Uncalled Capital.	Paid-up Capital.
1	London and Westminster Bank............	1834	10,000,	8,000,	2,000,
2	London Joint Stock Bank	'36	. 4,000,	2,800,	1,200,
3	Union Bank of London	'39	4,500,	3,105,	1,395,
4	City Bank...	'55	1,200,	600,	600,
5	Imperial Bank, *Limited*	1862	2,250,	1,575,	675,
6	Central Bank, *Limited*	'63	200,	100,	100,
7	Alliance Bank, *Limited* *	'71	2,000,	1,200,	800,
	Totals	—	24,150,	17,380,	6,770,
	Averages	—	7,450,	2,483,	967,

* 49,450*l.* appearing on both sides of balance sheet as outstanding.
† Estimated.

appear not to do so. Of the forty-three banks of non-issue, thirty-four publish balance sheets and nine seem not to do so. In Tables XXVII, XXVIII, and XXIX have been summarised and analysed the balance sheets of forty-nine purely provincial English banks, of which twenty-two are banks of issue and twenty-seven are banks of non-issue, twenty-four are unlimited banks, and twenty-five are limited banks. For facility of comparison the banks are classified in districts as in Table III.

The balance sheets of the Scotch banks, all of which publish their accounts, will be found in Table XXX and their analysis in Table XXXI.

Of the nine Irish banks, the balance sheets of only five are published. These are treated in Tables XXXII, XXXIII, and XXXIV.

Sheets for Twelve Months ending December, 1874.

30,235 = 30,235,000*l*.]

5	6	7	8	9	10	11	12	
Liabilities.				Assets.				
Reserve, including Balance of Profit Carried Forward.	Money Lodged, including Dividend Due.	Acceptances.	Total Resources.	Bills and Advances.	Government and other Securities.	Cash.	Property Account.	Number.
1,015,	30,235,	1,038,	34,288,	26,428,	3,999,	3,861,	—	1
515,	16,132,†	4,527,†	22,374,	18,871,	1,080,	2,297,	126,	2
482,	14,227,	4,957,‡	21,061,	12,698,	2,941,	5,130,	283,	3
174,	3,318,	3,261,	7,353,	6,181,	329,	788,	54,	4
94,	2,142,	1,068,	3,979,	3,309,	72,	577,	22,	5
23,	773,	—	896,	591,	82,	186,	37,	6
191,	1,922,	582,	3,445,	2,726,	81,	638,	—	7
2,494,	68,749,	15,383,	93,396,	70,804,	8,584,	13,486,	522,	
356	9,821,	2,198,	13,342,	10,115,	1,226,	1,927,	—	

accounts of old bank to be realised is omitted in these columns.

‡ Cover in hand, amounting to 7,590,154*l*.

TABLE XXII.—*Purely London Joint Stock Bank Balance Sheets*

[00's omitted in Columns 2 and 4.]

		1	2	3	4	5	6
				Analysis.			
Number.	Purely London Banks.	Ratio per Cent. of Reserve Fund to Paid-up Capital.	Net Profit, less Charges. [00's omitted.]	Ratio per Cent. per Annum of Net Profits to Total Resources.	Charges or Working Expenses. [00's omitted.]	Ratio per Cent. of Charges to Net Profits.	Ratio per Cent. per Annum of Charges to Liabilities to Public.
		Per cnt.	£	Per cnt.	£	Per cnt.	Per cnt.
1	London and Westminster Bank...	51	412,0	1·20	151,5	36·8	0·48
2	London Joint Stock Bank	43	269,2	1·20	88,8	33·0	0·43
3	Union Bank of London	34	255,5	1·21 }	Not stated }	—	—
4	City Bank	29	61,6	0·84	42,6	69·1	0·65
5	Imperial Bank, *Limited*	14	59,4	1·50	23,3	39·2	0·72
6	Central Bank, *Limited*	23	11,3	1·26	14,2	126·0	1·84
7	Alliance Bank, *Limited* *	24	66,3	1·92	27,6	41·6	1·12
	Totals	—	1,135,3	—	6 Banks 348,0	—	—
	Averages	37	162,2	1·22	—	6 Banks 39·6	6 Banks 0·54

* 49,450*l*. appearing on both sides of balance sheet as outstanding

TABLE XXIII.—*Purely London Joint Stock Banks. Profits, Dividends, and Prices,*
January, 1875.

		1	2	3	4	5	6
				Dividends and Prices.			
Number.	Purely London Banks.	Ratio per Cent. of Net Profits to Paid-up Capital.	Dividend per Cent. per Annum, including Bonus.	Amount per Share Paid.	Market Price, Jan., 1875, Ex. Div.	Premium per Cent.	Yield per Cent. at Market Price.
							£ s. d.
1	London and Westminster Bank....	20·6	21	20	75	275	5 12 –
2	London Joint Stock Bank	22·4	21	15	51	240	6 3 6
3	Union Bank of London	18·3	17½	15½	45	190½	6 – 6
4	City Bank	10·3	10	10	13½	32½	7 10 11
5	Imperial Bank, *Limited*	8·8	8	15	18	20	6 13 4
6	Central Bank, *Limited*	11·3	8	5	8	60	5 – –
7	Alliance Bank, *Limited*	8·3	8	10	13	30	6 3 1
	Totals	—	—	—	—	—	—
	Averages	16·8	13½	—	—	—	6 3 4

for Twelve Months ending December, 1874, *Analysis.*

[000's omitted in Columns 8, 9, 10, and 13.]

7	8	9	10	11	12	13	14	
				Analysis.				
Number of Establishments.	Average Liabilities to Public at each Office.	Liabilities to Public.	Proprietors' Funds.	Ratio per Cent. of Proprietors' Funds to Liabilities to Public.	Ratio per Cent. of Uncalled Capital to Liabilities to Public.	Government Securities, Cash, &c.	Ratio per Cent. of Government Securities, Cash, &c , to Liabilities to Public.	Number.
No.	£	£	£	Per cnt.	Per cnt.	£	Per cnt.	
8	3,909,	31,273,	3,015,	9·6	25·6	7,860,	25·1	1
6	3,443,	20,659,	1,715,	8·3	13·6	3,377,	16·3	2
5	3,837,	19,184,	1,877,	9·8	16·2	8,080,	42·1	3
6	1,096,	6,579,	774,	11·8	9·1	1,117,	17·0	4
3	1,070,	3,210,	769,	24·0	49·1	649,	20·2	5
5	155,	773,	123,	16·0	13·0	268,	34·8	6
1	2,454,	2,454,	990,	40·4	48·9	719,	29·3	7
34	—	84,133,	9,263,	—	—	22,070,	—	
5	2,474,	12,019,	1,323,	11·0	20·7	3,153,	26·2	

accounts of old bank to be realised, is omitted in these columns.

TABLE XXVI.—*London and Provincial Joint Stock Banks.* *Profits, Dividends, and Prices*

		1	2	3	4	5	6	
Number.	London and Provincial Banks.	Ratio per Cent. of Net Profit to Paid-up Capital.	Dividend per Cent. per Annum, including Bonus.	Amount per Share Paid.	Market Price, January, 1875.	Premium per Cent.	Yield per Cent. at Price.	
		Per cnt.	Per cnt.	£	£	Per cnt.	£ s. d.	
1	National Prov. Bank of England..	24·41	23	{ 21 / 12 / 3 }	84 / 48 / 29½	3cc } / 300 } / 88₃	5 15 —	
2	London and County Bank	18·58	20	20	65¾	128¾	0 1 8	
3	Consolidated Bank, *Limited*	11·18	10	4	6⅛	72	5 16 4	
4	Midland Banking Co., *Limited*	9·60	9	20	27½	37½	6 10 11	
5	London and South-Western, *Limd.*	9·81	7¼	20	22½	12½	6 13 4	
6	,, Provincial B., *Limd.*	14·66	10	5	8⅛	65	6 1 3	
7	,, Yorkshire B., *Limd.*	3·96	4	9	6	Dis.	6 — —	
	Totals	—	—	—	—	—		
	Averages	17·6	12	—	—	119½	6 2 8	

TABLE XXIV.—*London and Provincial Joint*

[000's omitted thus

Number.	London and Provincial Banks.	1 When Estab- lished.	2 Subscribed Capital.	3 Uncalled Capital.	4 Liabilities. Paid-up Capital.	5 Reserve, including Balance of Profit Carried Forward.
1	National Provincial Bank of England .... CAPITAL. 20,000 shares at 50l. = 1,000,000l. 77,500 „ 20l. = 1,550,000l. 28,125 „ 20l. = 562,500l.	1833	3,112,	1,734,	1,378,	792,
2	London and County Bank	'36	3,750,	2,402,	1,348,	697,
3	Consolidated Bank, *Limited*	1863	2,000,	1,260,	800,	118,
4	Midland Banking Co., *Limited*	'63	1,500,	1,200,	300,	45,
5	London and South-Westn., *Limd.*	'62	831,	665,	166,	14,
6	„ Provincial B., *Lim*....	'64	300,	150,	150,	31,
7	„ Yorkshire B., *Lim*.....	'72	632,	518,	114,	2,
	Totals	—	12,125	7,869,	4,256,	1,699,
	Averages..................	—	1,732,	1,124,	608,	243,

* Includes

TABLE XXV.—*London and Provincial Joint Stock*

[00's omitted in Columns 2 and 4, thus 336,5 = 336,500l.]

Number.	London and Provincial Banks.	1 Ratio per Cent. of Reserve Fund to Paid-up Capital.	2 Net Profit, less Charges, [000's omitted.]	3 Ratio per Cent. per Annum of Net Profits to Total Resources.	4 Charges or Work- ing Ex- penses. [00's omitted]	5 Ratio per Cent. of Charges to Net Profits.	6 Ratio per Cent. per Annum of Charges to Liabilities to Public.
		Per cnt.	£	Per cnt.	£	Per cnt.	Per cnt.
1	National Prov. Bank of England..	57	336,5	1·28	298,9	88·8	1·24
2	London and County Bank	52	250,5	1·00	245,6	98·0	1·08
3	Consolidated Bank, *Limited*	15	89,4	2·09	29,3	32·8	·87
4	Midland Banking Co., *Limited*	15	28,8*	1·62	25,9	90·0	1·81
5	London and South-Westn., *Limd.*	8	16,3	1·48	23,1	141·7	2·52
6	„ Provincial B., *Lim*....	20	22,0	1·46	30,5	138·7	2·30
7	„ Yorkshire B., *Lim*.....	2	4,5	0·88	10,3	228·9	2·62
	Totals	—	748,0	—	663,6	—	—
	Averages..................	40	106,9	1·24	—	88·7	1·22

* Without deduction of 5,000l. taken from reserve fund to cover exceptional loss.

Stock Banks. *Balance Sheets for year* 1874.

,113, = 8,113,000*l.*]

6	7	8	9	10	11	12	
Liabilities.			Assets.				
Money Lodged, including Dividend due.	Acceptances.	Total Resources.	Bills and Advances.	Government and other Securities.	Cash, &c.	Property Account.	Number.
23,063,	1,043,	26,276,	15,637,	6,056,	4,168,	415,	1
20,072,	2,780,	24,897,	16,893,	2,083,	5,512,	408,	2
3,113,	246,	4,277,	3,089,	209,	807,	181,	3
1,432,	—	1,778,	1,518,	—	229;	30,	4
916,	1,	1,097,	804,	—	261,	33,	5
1,329,	—	1,510,	926,	864,	198,	22,	6
393,*	—	508,	437,	—	55,	16,	7
50,318,	4,070,	60,344,	39,304	8,712,	11,230,	1,105,	
7,188,	—	8,621,	—	—	—	—	

cceptances.

Banks. *Analysis of Balance Sheets,* 1874.

[000's omitted in columns 9, 10, 11, and 14.]

7	8	9	10	11	12	13	14	15	
Number of Branches.	Number of Sub-Branches.	Average Liabilities to Public at each Office, ex-Subs.	Liabilities to Public.	Pro-prietors' Funds.	Ratio per Cent. of Proprietors' Funds to Liabilities to Public.	Ratio per Cent. of Uncalled Capital to Liabilities to Public.	Govern-ment Securities, Cash, &c.	Ratio per Cent. of Government Securities, Cash, &c., to Liabilities to Public.	Number.
No.	No.	£	£	£	Per cnt.	Per cnt.	£	Per cnt.	
134	3	178,	24,106,	2,171,	9·0	—	10,225,	42·4	1
148†		153,	22,852,	2,045,	8·9	—	7,596,	33·2	2
3	—	840,	3,319,	919,	27·7	—	1,016,	30·6	3
22	5	62,	1,432,	346,	24·1	83·8	229,	16·0	4
26	—	34,	917,	180,	19·6	72·5	261,	28·4	5
54	—	24,	1,329,	181	13·6	11·3	562,	42·3	6
10	—	36,	393,	116,	29·4	132·0	55;	14·0	7
397	8	—	54,348,	5,958,	—	—	19,944,	—	
57	—	1,346,	777,0,	851,	10·9	—	—	36·7	

† Includes sub-branches.　　　　　　　*Note.*—For Table XXVI, see p. 41.

mber.	Purely Provincial Banks. [Banks of Issue are in *Italics*.]	When Established.	Date of Balance, 1874.	Subscribed Capital.	Uncalled Capital.	Paid-up Capital.	Reserve, including Balance of Profit Carried Forward.
	I. Cumberland and Northumberland.						
1	Carlisle and Cumberland Bank	1836	Dec.	300,	225,	75,	104,
2	Cumberland Union B. Co., Limtd.	'29	,,	540,	315,	225,	83,
3	*Carlisle City and District Bank*....	'37	,,	160,	80,	80,	91,
4	*Bank of Whitehaven, Limited*	'37	,,	222,	123,	99,	91,
5	North Eastern B. Co., *Limited* ...	'72	,,	800,	540,	260,*	81,
	II. Liverpool.						
6	Adelphi Bank, *Limited*	1861	Dec.	260,	130,	130,	5,
7	Liverpool Commercial B. Co., *Lim.*	'32	,,	700,	350,	350,	204,
8	,, Union Bank	'35	,,	600,	None	600,	164,
9	National Bank of Liverpool, *Lim.*	'63	,,	750,	300,	450,	93,
10	North Western Bank, *Limited*	'64	,,	1,080,	675,	405,	101,
11	*North and South Wales Bank*	1836	Dec.	420,	36,	384,	212,
	III. Manchester District.						
12 {	Manchester and Liverpool District Banking Company .... }	'29	,,	1,810,	905,	905,	572,
13	Manchester and County B., *Limd.*	'62	,,	4,400,	3,740,	660,	350,
14	Union B. of Manchester, *Limited.*	'36	June	947,	531,	417,	123,
15	Lancashire and Yorkshire B., *Lim.*	'72	Dec.	500,	250,	250,	34,
16	Manchester Joint Stock B., *Limd.*	1873	Dec.	288,	202,	86,	18,
17	*Parr's Banking Company, Limited*	'65	,,	1,450,	1,160,	290,	86,
	IV. Yorkshire.						
18	*Swaledale and Wensleydale B. Co.*	'36	,,	840,	777,	63,	33,
19	*Bradford Banking Company*	'27	,,	1,020,	612,	408,	265,
20	,, *Commercial J. Stock B.*	'33	,,	968,	774,	194,	163,
21	,, *District Bank, Limited*	'62	,,	650,	422,	227,	112,
22	,, *Old Bank, Limited*	'64	,,	983,	590,	393,	137,
23	Bank of Leeds, *Limited*	'64	,,	605,	454,	151,	42,
24	*Halifax Commercial B. Co., Lim.*	'36	June	240,	120,	120,	70,
25	*Yorkshire Banking Company*........	'43	Dec.	500,	250,	250,	148,
26 {	Sheffield Banking Company .... CAPITAL. 1,500 shares at 200*l.* = 300,000*l.* 2,375 ,, 50*l.* = 118,800*l.* }	'31	,,	419,	126,	293,	106,

* Of the capital of this bank 20,000*l.* is in deferred shares given in payment of the preliminary sharey

† Bills rediscounted, 131,600*l.*; credits, drafts, &c., 97,900*l.*; total, 229,500*l.*

								£	
617,	22,	—	818,	—	808,	—	9,	25,610	1
1,826,	35,	—	2,168,	1,634,	75,	413,	47,	35,395	2
658,	20,	—	850,	—	845,	—	5,	19,972	3
597,	27,	—	813,	715,	41,	49,	8,	32,681	4
314,	—	5,	659,	557,	56,	32,	13,	—	5
189,	—	—	324,	268,	—	34,	22,	—	6
1,227,	—	—	1,781,	1,540,	—	91,	150,	—	7
2,571,	—	774,	4,109,	2,947,	—	1,126,	36,	—	8
621,	—	40,	1,204,	1,071,	—	108,	25,	—	9
1,125,	—	230,†	1,860,	1,686,	—	141,	33,	—	10
3,891,	62,	59,	4,607,	3,289,	1,233,		85,	63,951	11
12,445,	—	150,	14,071,	9,645,	1,415,	2,860,	151,	—	12
5,794,	—	—	6,804,	—	6,766,	—	38,	—	13
1,588,	—	67,	2,195,	1,930,	232,		33,	—	14
626,	—	—	909,	754,	—	152,	3,	—	15
241,	—	—	346,	—	344,	—	2,	—	16
2,904,	—	—	3,280,	1,848,	101,	1,300,	30,	—	17
747,	49,	—	892,	658,	234,		—	54,372	18
2,071,	49,	—	2,702,	—	2,787,	—	5,	49,292	19
570,	20,	—	947,	—	937,	—	9,	20,084	20
716,	—	—	1,055,	—	1,035,	—	20,	—	21
1,165,	—	—	1,695,	—	1,675,	—	20,	—	22
423,‡	—	—	616,	577,	—	32,	7,	—	23
388,	11,	—	590,	—	585,	—	4,	13,733	24
2,444,	112,	—	2,954,	—	2,886,	—	68,	122,532	25
1,456,	37,	—	1,893,	—	1,870,	—	23,	35,843	26

expenses, the amount of which appears among the assets included in the item "bills and advances."
‡ Including acceptances.

TABLE XXVII.—*Purely Provincial English Joint Stock*

[000's omitted, thus

		1	2	3	4	5	6
						Liabilities.	
Number.	Purely Provincial Banks. [Banks of Issue are in *Italics*.]	When-Established	Date of Balance, 1874.	Subscribed Capital.	Uncalled Capital.	Paid-up Capital.	Reserve including Balance of Profit Carried Forward.
27	*Sheffield and Hallamshire Bank*	1836	June	733,	550,	183,	55,
28	„ *Rotherham Bank*	'36	Dec.	502,	341,	161,	86,
29	Sheffield Union Banking Company	'43	June	287,	115,	172,	47,
	V. Derby, Notts, Lincoln, Leicester.						
30	*Burton, Uttoxeter, &c., Union B.*	1839	Dec.	260,	130,	130,	69,
31	*Nottingham Joint Stock B., Limd.*	'65	„	477,	382,	95,	32,
32 {	*Stamford, Spalding, and Boston Banking Company.................*	'32	.,	200,	None	200,	103,
33	*Leicestershire Banking Company*	'29	„	500,	250,	250,	90,
	VI. Black Country.						
34	*Staffordshire Joint Stock B., Lim.*	1864	Dec.	872,	698,	174,	60,
35	*County of Stafford Bank*	'36	„	120,	60,	60,	35,
36	Lloyd's Banking Company, *Limited*	'65	,,	2,181,	1,832,	349,	129,
37	Birmingham Joint Stock B., *Lim.*	'61	„	2,039,	1,835,	204,	219,
38	„ Banking Co., *Limited*	'66	June	1,549,	1,394,	155,	121,
39	„ Town and District B.	'36	„	400,	240,	160,	61,
40 {	*Wolverhampton and Staffordshire Banking Company ....*	'32	Dec.	500,	400,	100,	41,
	VII. W. and S. Counties.						
41 {	*Stourbridge and Kidderminster Banking Company...................*	1834	June	250,	150,	100,	86,
42 {	*Worcester City and County Banking Company, Limited ....*	'40	„	1,000,	750,	250,	102,
43	Bucks and Oxon Union Bank, *Lim.*	'66	Dec.	400,	320,	80,	18,
44 {	*West of England and South Wales District Bank ....*	'34	„	1,000,	250,	750,	150,
45	Devon and Cornwall Banking Co.	'32	„	400,	272,	128,	87,
46	Three Towns Banking Co., *Limited*	'63	,,	100,	50,	50,	1,
47	*Wilts and Dorset Banking Co. ....*	'35	„	375,	125,	250,	155,
48	Hampshire Banking Company	'34	,,	750,	600,	150,	41,
49	North Kent Bank, *Limited*............	'64	,,	65,	43,	22,	2,
	Totals	—	—	36,413,	23,873,	11,940,	5,282,
	Averages..............	—	—	743,	487,	244,	108,

* Cash and brokers' bills.

Banks. *Balance Sheets of Forty-Nine Banks—Contd.*

733 = 733,000l., except in Col. 15.]

7	8	9	10	11	12	13	14	15	Number
Liabilities.				Assets.					
Money Lodged, including Dividend due.	Circulation of Notes.	Acceptances.	Total Resources.	Bills and Advances.	Government and other Securities.	Cash, &c.	Property Account.	Authorised Issue. £	
549,	22,	—	809,	—	804,	—	5,	23,524	27
1,618,	53,	—	1,918,	—	1,904,	—	15,	52,496	28
438,	—	—	658,	—	653,	—	5,	—	29
1,206,	48,	—	1,453,	—	1,432,	—	21,	60,701	30
576,	—	—	704,	—	689,	—	15,	—	31
1,265,	46,	—	1,614,	965,	410,	210,*	23,	55,721	32
1,349,	63,	—	1,752,	1,237,	265,	233,	17,	86,060	33
685,	—	—	920,	796,	37,	80,	6,	—	34
412,	9,	—	516,	400,	40,	68,	8,	9,418	35
4,974,	—	—	5,452,	—	5,395,	—	56,	—	36
1,632,	—	—	2,054,	1,647,	224,	164,	18,	—	37
1,119,	—	—	1,395,	1,084,	55,	234,	22,	—	38
943,	—	—	1,164,	1,033,	48,	63,	19,	—	39
878,	16,	—	1,036,	1,001,		30,	4,	35,378	40
1,133,	49,	—	1,368,	1,036,	25,	279,	27,	56,830	41
1,023,	2,	—	1,377,	1,123,	54,	173,	27,	6,848	42
702,	—	—	800,	—	786,	—	13,	—	43
4,436,	70,	—	5,416,	4,406,	502,	418,	90,	83,535	44
1,699,	—	—	1,914,	—	1,014,		—	—	45
46,	—	—	97,	93,	—	4,	—	—	46
3,086,†	75,	—	3,567,	1,553,	1,572,	395,	46,	76,162	47
2,116,	—	—	2,306,	1,431,	311,	524,	40,	—	48
80,	—	—	104,	91,	—	11,	2,	—	49
79,175,	906,	1,325,	98,625,	—	—	—	—	—	
1,616,	—	—	2,013,	—	—	—	—	—	

† Includes acceptances.

TABLE XXVIII.—*Analysis of Balance Sheets of Forty-*

[00's omitted in Columns 2 and 4, thus 18,7 = 18,700*l.*;

		1	2	3	4	5	6
imber.	Purely Provincial Banks. [Banks of Issue are in *Italics.*]	Ratio per Cent. of Reserve Fund to Paid-up Capital.	Net Profit, less Charges.	Ratio per Cent. per Annum of Net Profits to Total Resources.	Charges.	Ratio per Cent. of Charges to Net Profits.	Ratio per Cent. per Annum of Charges to Liabilities to Public.
	I. Cumberland and Northumberland.	Per cnt.	£	Per cnt.	£	Per cnt.	Per cnt.
1	Carlisle and Cumberland Bank	138	18,7	2·28	—	—	—
2	Cumberland Union B. Co., Limtd.	37	45,6	2·10	15,9	34·9	0·85
3	Carlisle City and District Bank....	113	21,3	2·50	—	—	—
4	Bank of *Whitehaven, Limited*	93	18,0	2·21	4,0	22·2	0·64
5	North Eastern B. Co., Limited	31	11,9	1·80	9,4	79·0	2·96
	II. Liverpool.						
6	Adelphi Bank, *Limited*	4	9,8	3·02	5,2	53·1	2·76
7	Liverpool Commercial B. Co., Lim.	58	43,7	2·45	—	—	—
8	„ Union Bank	27	89,3	2·17	—	—	—
9	National Bank of Liverpool, *Lim.*	20	35,4	2·94	—	—	—
10	North Western Bank, *Limited*	25	37,9	2·04	—	—	—
11	*North and South Wales Bank*	55	66,4	1·44	37,5	56·5	0·93
	III. Manchester District.						
12 {	Manchester and Liverpool District Banking Company ....}	68	211,1	1·50	93,2	44·1	0·74
13	Manchester and County B., *Limd.*	53	129,4	1·90	37,1	28·7	0·64
14	Union B. of Manchester, *Limited*	30	63,8	2·90	22,3	34·9	1·35
15	Lancashire and Yorkshire B., *Lim.*	14	19,5	2·14	9,2	47·2	1·47
16	Manchester Joint Stock B., *Limd.*	21	10,1	2·92	5,2	51·5	2·15
17	Parr's Banking Company, *Limited*	29	68,6	2·09	22,5	32·8	0·77
	IV. Yorkshire.						
18	*Swaledale and Wensleydale B. Co.*	52	15,9	1·78	4,4	27·7	0·55
19	*Bradford Banking Company*	65	72,3	2·51	—	—	—
20	„ *Commercial J. Stock B.*	84	40,0	4·22	—	—	—
21	Bradford District Bank, *Limited*	50	32,5	3·08	7,3	22·5	1·02
22	„ Old Bank, *Limited*	35	55,1	3·25	—	—	—
23	Bank of Leeds, *Limited*	28	14,0	2·27	3,2	22·8	0·76
24	*Halifax Commercial B. Co., Lim.*	59	17,1	2·92	—	—	—
25	*Yorkshire Banking Company*	59	90,2	3·05	—	—	—
26 {	*Sheffield Banking Company* .... CAPITAL. 1,500 shares at 200l. = 300,000l. 2,375 „ 60l. = 118,000l. }	36	52,5	2·77	—	—	—
27	*Sheffield and Hallamshire Bank*	30	27,9	3·44	—	—	—
28	„ *Rotherham Bank*	53	31,4	1·63	—	—	—
29	Sheffield Union Banking Company	28	21,9	3·33	—	—	—

Nine Purely Provincial English Joint Stock Banks, 1874.

000's omitted in Cols. 9, 10, 11, and 14.]

7	8	9	10	11	12	13	14	15	
Number of Branches.	Number of Sub-Branches.	Average Liabilities to Public at each Office, ex Subs.	Liabilities to Public.	Pro-prietors' Funds.	Ratio per Cent. of Proprietors' Funds to Liabilities to Public.	Ratio per Cent. of Uncalled Capital to Liabilities to Public.	Govern-ment Securities, Cash, &c.	Ratio per Cent. of Government Securities, Cash, &c., to Liabilities to Public.	Numb
No.	No.	£	£	£	Per cnt.	Per cnt.	£	Per cnt.	
5	—	106,	639,	179,	28·0	—	—	—	1
13	4	133,	1,860,	308,	16·6	16·9	488,	26·2	2
4	—	136,	678,	171,	25·2	—	—	14·4	3
3	—	156,	623,	190,	30·5	19·8	89,	14·4	4
14	2	21,	318,	341,	107·3	17·0	89,	27·9	5
1	—	94,	189,	135,	71·7	68·9	33,	17·8	6
—	—	1,227,	1,227,	554,	45·1	28·5	91,	7·4	7
—	—	3,345,	3,345,	764,	22·8	—	1,126,	33·7	8
2	—	220,	661,	543,	82·0	45·4	108,	16·3	9
—	—	1,354,	1,354,	506,	37·4	49·9	141,	10·4	10
27	9	143,	4,011,	596,	14·8	—	1,233,	30·7	11
41	10	300,	12,594,	1,477,	11·7	—	4,275,	33·9	12
17	9	322,	5,794,	1,010,	17·4	64·6	—	—	13
14	6	110,	1,655,	540,	32·6	82·1	232,	14·0	14
6	2	89,	626,	284,	45·3	40·0	152,	24·4	15
1	—	121,	241,	104,	43·3	83·5	—	—	16
9	7	290,	2,904,	376,	12·9	39·9	1,401,	48·2	17
3	—	199,	796,	96,	12·1	—	234,	29·4	18
—	—	2,120,	2,120,	673,	31·7	—	—	—	19
—	—	590,	590,	357,	60·5	—	—	—	20
1	—	358,	716,	339,	47·4	59·0	—	—	21
2	—	388,	1,165,	530,	45·5	50·6	—	—	22
—	—	423,	423,	194,	45·8	107·4	32,	7·7	23
1	—	200,	399,	190,	47·7	30·1	—	—	24
14	7	170,	2,556,	398,	15·5	—	—	—	25
3	—	378,	1,493,	400,	26·8	—	—	—	26
—	—	571,	571,	238,	41·8	—	—	—	27
4	—	334,	1,671,	247,	14·8	—	—	—	28
2	1	146,	438,	220,	50·2	—	—	—	29

TABLE **XXVIII.**—*Analysis of Balance Sheets of Forty-Nine*

[00's omitted in cols. 2 and 4, thus 27,5 = 27,500.

Number.	Purely Provincial Banks. [Banks of Issue are in *Italics*.]	1 Ratio per Cent. of Reserve Fund to Paid-up Capital.	2 Net Profit, less Charges.	3 Ratio per Cent. per Annum of Net Profits to Total Resources.	4 Charges or Working Expenses.	5 Ratio per Cent. of Charges to Net Profits.	6 Ratio per Cent. per Annum of Charges to Liabilities to Public.
			£		£		
	V. Derby, Notts, &c.						
30	Burton, Uttoxeter, &c., Union B.	53	27,5	1·89	—	—	—
31	Nottingham Joint Stock B., Limd.	34	10,7	1·52	5,2	48·6	0·90
32 {	*Stamford, Spalding, and Boston Banking Company*	51	32,4	2·01	—	—	—
33	*Leicestershire Banking Company*	36	37,3	2·13	—	—	—
	VI. Black Country.						
34	Staffordshire Joint Stock B., *Lim.*	35	21,1	2·29	—	—	—
35	*County of Stafford Bank*	58	12,3	2·38	—	—	—
36	Lloyd's Banking Company, *Limited*	37	88,1	1·61	—	—	—
37	Birmingham Joint Stock B., *Lim.*	107	48,7	2·37	—	—	—
38	,, Banking Co., *Limited*	78	30,8	2·21	—	—	—
39	,, Town and District B.	38	30,5	2·62	—	—	—
40 {	*Wolverhampton and Staffordshire Banking Company*	41	15,5	1·49	—	—	—
	VII. W. and S. Counties.						
41 {	*Stourbridge and Kidderminster Banking Company*	86	29,5	2·16	—	—	—
42 {	*Worcester City and County Banking Company, Limited*	41	33,3	2·42	18,5	55·5	1·80
43	Bucks and Oxon Union B., *Lim.*	23	18,1	2·26	—	—	—
44 {	*West of England and South Wales District Bank*	20	126,2	2·33	56,7	44·9	1·25
45	Devon and Cornwall Banking Co.	68	27,8	1·45	—	—	—
46	Three Towns Banking Co., *Limited*	2	2,6	2·67	1,6	61·5	3·45
47	*Wilts and Dorset Banking Co.*	62	55,3	1·55	33,4	60·4	1·06
48	Hampshire Banking Company	27	33,3	1·44	26,5	79·6	1·25
49	*North Kent Bank, Limited*	7	1,9	1·82	—	—	—
	Totals	—	2,046,2,	—	418,3	— 20 banks	— 20 banks
	Averages	44	42,1,	2·07	8,5	42·7	0·95

Purely Provincial English Joint Stock Banks—Contd.

000's omitted in Cols. 9, 10, 11, and 14.]

7	8	9	10	11	12	13	14	15
Number of Branches.	Number of Sub-Branches.	Average Liabilities to Public at each Office, ex-Súbs.	Liabilities to Public.	Proprietors' Funds.	Ratio per Cent. of Proprietors' Funds to Liabilities to Public.	Ratio per Cent. of Uncalled Capital to Liabilities to Public.	Government Securities, Cash, &c.	Ratio per Cent. of Government Securities, Cash, &c., to Liabilities to Public.
		£	£	£			£	
2	—	418,	1,254,	199,	15·9	—	—	—
5	—	96,	576,	128,	22·2	66·3	—	—
9	9	131,	1,311,	303,	23·1	—	621,	47·3
8	2	157,	1,412,	340,	24·1	—	498,	35·3
7	—	86,	685,	235,	34·3	101·9	117,	17·1
—	—	421,	421,	95,	22·5	—	108,	25·8
23	12	207,	4,974,	478,	9·6	36·8	—	—
2	—	544,	1,632,	423,	25·9	112·5	381,	23·8
1	—	559,	1,119,	276,	24·7	124·6	289,	25·8
7	—	118,	943,	221,	23·4	—	111,	11·7
—	—	894,	894,	141,	15·8	—	—	—
12	1	98,	1,182,	186,	15·8	—	304,	25·7
9	4	102,	1,025,	352,	34·3	73·2	227,	22·1
8	—	78,	702,	·98,	14·0	45·6	—	—
38	4	116,	4,515,	900,	19·9	—	919,	20·4
14	—	113,	1,699,	215,	12·6	—	—	—
—	—	46,	46,	51,	109·9	108·0	4,	9·3
41	8	75,	3,161,	405,	12·8	—	1,967,	62·2
29	—	70,	2,116,	191,	9·0	—	835,	39·5
1	—	40,	80,	24,	29·9	53·7	11,	13·7
403	97	—	81,404,	17,221,	—	— 25 banks	16,126, 29 banks	— 29 banks
8	—	180,	1,661,	351,	21·15	55·5	—	30·9

Table XXIX.—*Profits, Dividends, and Prices of Forty-Nine Purely Provincial English Joint Stock Banks*, 1874.

Number.	Purely Provincial Banks. [Banks of Issue are in *Italics*.]	1 Ratio per Cent. of Net Profit to Paid-up Capital.	2 Dividend per Cent. per Annum, including Bonus.	3 Amount per Share Paid.	4 Market Price, January, 1875.	5 Premium per Cent.	6 Yield per Cent. at Price.
	I. Cumberland and Northumberland.						£ *s.* *d.*
1	*Carlisle and Cumberland Bank*	25·0	22	5	19⅞	297½	5 10 8
2	*Cumberland Union B. Co., Limtd.*	20·3	18	12½	40	220	5 12 6
3	*Carlisle City and District Bank*....	26·6	20	12½	44	252	5 13 7
4	*Bank of Whitehaven, Limited*	18·3	20	10	38½	285	5 3 10
5	North Eastern Banking Co., *Lim.*	4·6	5⅕	6	6¾	12½	4 12 5
	II. Liverpool.						
6	Adelphi Bank, *Limited*	7·5	5	10	9	Dis.	5 11 1
7	Liverpool Commercial B. Co., *Lim.*	12·5	12½	10	18	80	6 18 10
8	" Union Bank..................	14·9	10*	20	29	45	6 17 11
9	National Bank of Liverpool, *Lim.*	7·9	6⅔	15	16¼	8⅓	6 3 1
10	North Western Bank, *Limited*	9·4	7	7½	9¾	30	5 7 8
11	*North and South Wales Bank*	17·3	20	10	31	210	6 9 –
	III. Manchester District.						
12	Manchester and Liverpool District Banking Company	23·3	20	10	35½	255	5 12 8
13	Manchester and County B., *Lim.*	18·2	15	15	42	180	5 7 1
14	Union Bank of Manchester, *Lim.*	15·3	11⅓	11	21⅜	94⅓	5 16 7
15	Lancashire and Yorkshire B., *Lim.*	7·8	6	10	13½	35	4 8 10
16	Manchester Joint Stock B., *Limd.*	6·0	10	6	11¼	87½	5 6 8
17	Parr's Banking Company, *Limited*	23·7	15	20	52½	162½	5 14 3
	IV. Yorkshire.						
18	*Swaledale and Wensleydale B. Co.*	25·2	20	7½	—	—	—
19	*Bradford Banking Company*........	17·7	25	40	154	285	6 9 10
20	" *Commercial J. Stock B.*	20·7	18	20	58½	192½	6 3 1
21	" District Bank, *Limited*	14·3	10½	35	71½	$104\frac{2}{7}$	5 2 10
22	" Old Bank, *Limited*........	14·0	13¾	20	50	150	5 10 –
23	Bank of Leeds, *Limited*	9·3	7	25	31¾	27	5 10 3
24	*Halifax Commercial B. Co., Lim.*	14·3	14	10	23⅞	138⅞	5 17 3
25	*Yorkshire Banking Company*......	36·1	24	12½	50	300	6 – –
26	*Sheffield Banking Company*	18·0	17	140	274	$95\frac{5}{7}$	8 13 8
27	" *and Hallamshire Bank*	15·2	15	25	49¾	99	7 10 9
28	" *Rotherham Bank*	19·5	18¾	32	83½	161	7 3 8
29	Sheffield Union Banking Company	12·7	12½	12	21	75	7 2 10

* 2*l.* 10*s.* per share = 75,000*l.* capitalised from surplus funds and profits.

Table XXIX.—*Profits, Dividends, and Prices of Forty-Nine Purely Provincial English Joint Stock Banks—Contd.*

Number.	Purely Provincial Banks. [Banks of Issue are in *Italics*.]	1 Ratio per Cent. of Net Profit to Paid-up Capital.	2 Dividend per Cent. per Annum including Bonus.	3 Amount per Share Paid.	4 Market Price, January, 1875.	5 Premium per Cent.	6 Yield per Cent. at Price.
	V. Derby, Notts, &c.						£ s. d.
30	*Burton, Uttoxeter, &c., Union B.*	21·1	20	10	27	170	7 8 2
31	Nottingham Joint Stock B., *Lim.*	11·2	8½	10	15	50	5 13 4
32	*Stamford, Spalding, and Boston Banking Company*	16·2	17	20	67¼	236¼	5 1 1
33	*Leicestershire Banking Company*	15·0	13¾	40 5	90 15½	125 210	6 2 2 4 8 8
	VI. Black Country.						
34	Staffordshire Joint Stock B., *Lim.*	12·1	8¾	20	28¼	41¼	6 3 11
35	*County of Stafford Bank*	20·5	18	5	16	220	5 12 6
36	Lloyd's Banking Company, *Limited*	25·3	20*	8	29	262½	5 10 4
37	Birmingham Joint Stock B., *Lim.*	23·9	20	10	34	240	5 17 7
38	„ Banking Co., *Limited*	[illegible]	13¾	[illegible]	15	[illegible]	4 11 8
39	„ Town and District B.	19·1	11¼	8	16¼	103⅛	5 10 8
40	*Wolverhptn. and Staffdsh. B. Co.*	15·5	10	10	18	80	5 11 1
	VII. W. and S. Counties.						
41	*Stourbridge and Kidderminster*	29·5	20	10	25	150	8 – –
42	*Worcester City and County Banking Company, Limited*	13·3	12⅜	12½	25¼	102	6 2 9
43	Bucks and Oxon Union B., *Lim.*	22·6	20	5	17½	250	5 14 3
44	*W. of Engl. and S. Wales Dist. B.*	16·8	14	15	33½	123⅓	6 5 4
45	Devon and Cornwall Banking Co.	21·7	16½	32	75	134⅜	7 – 9
46	Three Towns Banking Co., *Limited*	5·2	5	25	18	Dis.	—
47	*Wilts and Dorset Banking Co.*	22·1	22	10	40	300	5 10 –
48	Hampshire Banking Company	22·2	13	10	23	130	5 13 –
49	North Kent Bank, *Limited*	8·5	8	10	par	—	—
	Totals	—		—	—	45 banks	46 banks
	Averages	17·1	14⅛	—	—	151	5 19 6

* Profits equal to 6⅔ per cent. on old capital capitalised.

TABLE XXX.—*Scotch Joint Stock Bank Balance*

[000's omitted,

Number.	Banks. [All are Banks of Issue.]	When Established.	Date.	Subscribed Capital.	Uncalled Capital.	Liabilities.	
		1	2	3	4	5	6
						Paid-up Capital.	Reserve, including Balance of Profit Carried Forward.
1	Bank of Scotland	1695 {	Feb. 1874 „ '75	Stock „	500, ,,	1,000, ,,	371, 401,
2	Royal Bank of Scotland	1727 {	Sept. 1873 „ '74	„ „	Nil „	2,000, „	509, 521,
3	British Linen Company Bank	1746 {	Apr. 1873 „ '74	„ „	Nil ,,	1,000, „	361, 390,
4	Commercial Bank of Scotland	1810 {	Oct. 1873 „ '74	„ „	Nil „	1,000, „	394, 407,
5	National Bank of Scotland	1825 {	Nov. 1873 Oct. '74	„ „	Nil „	1,000, „	394, 418,
6	Union Bank of Scotland	1830 {	Apr. 1873 „ '74	„ „	Nil „	1,000, ,,	389, 403,
7	Clydesdale Banking Company	1838 {	Dec. 1873 „ '74	„ „	Nil „	900, 1,000,	353, 519,
8	City of Glasgow Bank	1839 {	June 1873 „ '74	„ „	Nil „	870, 1,000,	313, 451,
9	{ Aberdeen Town and County Banking Company }	1825 {	Jan. 1874 „ '75	720, „	468, „	252, „	116, 118,
10	{ North of Scotland Banking Company }	1836 {	Sept. 1873 „ '74	1,600, „	1,280, „	320, „	85, 100,
11	Caledonian Banking Company	1838 {	June 1873 „ '74	500, „	450, „	125, „	63, 63,
	Totals {	—	—	—	—	9,467, 9,697,	3,349; 3,792,
	Averages {	—	—	—	—	861, 882,	304, 345;

1 (1873-74) including balances due by other banks,
2 ('73) viz., on open accounts, 1,373,300*l.*, bills
3 ('73-74) including property account.
4 ('73-74) including cash in hands of London agents
5 ('73) heritable property yielding rent 61,400*l.*, bank
6 ('73-74) drafts and acceptances.
7 ('73) viz., on open accounts 2,305,100*l.*, bills
8 ('73-74) also Bank of Mona has 40,000*l.* under.

Sheets for the Years 1873 *and* 1874.
thus 252 = 252,000*l*.]

7	8	9	10	11	12	13	14	15	Numb
	Liabilities.				Assets.				
Money Lodged.	Notes in Circulation.	Accept-ances.	Total Resources.	Bills and Advances.	Government and other Securities.	Cash, &c.	Property Account.	Authorised Issue.	Numb
10,486,	628,	2,060,	14,545,	10,175,	3,830,⁴	846,	194,	343,	} 1
10,881,	627,	1,443,	14,352,	10,208,	3,522,	426,	196,	,,	
10,597,	842,	378,	14,326,	9,987,	3,248,¹	940,	151,	216,	} 2
10,546,	865,	428,	14,355,	10,431,	2,800,	951,	172,	,,	
8,118,	610,	332,	10,421,	7,086,⁷	2,706,⁴	502,	126,	438,	} 3
7,957,	676,	329,	10,352,	7,493,	2,222,	513,	124,	,,	
9,358,	1,024,	473,⁶	12,250,	8,383,	2,796,⁴	937,	133,	375,	} 4
9,588,	785,	433,	12,213,	8,585,	2,878,	606,	143,	,,	
10,480,	588,	1,856,⁶	13,918,	9,901,	3,417,¹	476,	123,	297,	} 5
11,084,	588,	1,224,	14,265,	10,515,	3,150,	475,	124,	,,	
9,874,	947,	305,	12,515,	9,030,	2,694,	638,	152,	454,	} 6
9,965,	776,	219,	12,364,	8,645,	2,977,⁹	586,	155,	,,	
6,776,	732,	275,	9,035,	6,319,²	1,597,⁹	952,¹	168,⁵	274,	} 7
6,859,	717,	256,	9,351,	6,472,	1,705,	1,006,	168,	,,	
7,998,	896,	929,	11,007,	7,955,⁸	2,059,¹	998,{	See Bills and Advances. }	73,⁸	} 8
8,489,	898,	793,	11,631,	8,798,	1,877,	957,	—	,,	
1,640,	172,	—	2,180,	1,460,	418,	270,¹	33,	70,	} 9
1,848,	193,	—	2,410,	1,880,	251,	240,	39,	,,	
2,204,	340,	—	2,949,	2,109,	516,	291,¹	33,	154,	}10
2,479,	397,	—	3,296,	2,834,	564,	357,	40,	,,	
942,	97,	—	1,227,	813,	266,	125,¹	23,	53,	}11
1,058,	113,	—	1,354,	897,	248,	184,	26,	,,	
78,572,	6,877,	6,109,	104,374,	78,217,	23,548,	6,470,	1,137,	2,749,	
80,699,	6,635,	5,120,	105,943,	76,258,	22,195,	6,301,	1,187,	2,749,	
		8 Banks.							
7,143,	625,	764,	9,489,	6,656,	2,141,	588,	—	250,	
7,386,	603,	640,	9,631,	6,938,	2,018,	573,	—	250,	

and cash in London.
4,945,500*l*. ; (1874) on open accounts, 1,904,200*l*., bills 4,567,400*l*.

and short loans.
buildings 106,400*l*.; (1874) heritable property yielding rent 62,400*l*., bank buildings 106,200*l*.

4,781,100*l*.; (1874) on open accounts, 2,784,100*l*., bills 4,708,700*l*.
Manx Acts.　　　　　　　　(1873-74) including short loans in London.

TABLE XXXI.—*Analysis of Scotch Joint Stock Bank*

[000's omitted in

		1	2	3	4	5	6	7
Number.	Banks.	Ratio per Cent. of Reserve Fund to Paid-up Capital.	Net Profits, (Less Charges). [00's omitted.]	Rate per Cent. per Annum of Net Profits to Total Resources.	Number of Branches.	Average Liabilities to Public at each Office.	Liabilities to Public.	Proprietors' Funds.
		Per cnt.	£	Per cnt.	No.	£	£	£
1	Bank of Scotland............{	37·1	165,2	1·14	76	171,	13,174,	1,371,
		40·1	175,6	1·22	,,	168,	12,951,	1,401,
2	Royal Bank of Scotland ....{	25·4	199,3	1·39	100	117,	11,818,	2,509,
		26·0	202,2	1·41	106	111,	11,834,	2,521,
3	{ British Linen Company } Bank .... }	36·1	134,2	1·29	61	146,	9,060,	1,361,
		39·0	163,4	1·58	67	132,	8,962,	1,390,
4	{ Commercial Bank of Scot- } land .... }	39·4	165,8	1·35	96	112,	10,855,	1,394,
		40·7	168,2	1·39	100	107,	10,805,	1,407,
5	National Bank of Scotland{	39·4	199,0	1·43	87	142,	12,524,	1,394,
		41·8	184,6	1·29	91	140,	12,847,	1,418,
6	Union Bank of Scotland....{	38·9	160,1	1·28	116	95,	11,126,	1,389,
		40·3	161,5	1·30	,,	94,	10,960,	1,403,
7	{ Clydesdale Banking Com- } pany .... }	39·2	153,7	1·70	76	101,	7,783,	1,253,
		51·9	146,1	1·56	79	98,	7,832,	1,519,
8	City of Glasgow Bank........{	36·0	114,7	1·04	122	80,	9,824,	1,188,
		45·1	129,8	1·12	,,	83,	10,181,	1,450,
9	{ Aberdeen Town and } County Banking Co. ..... }	46·0	32,9*	1·51	38	46,	1,812,	368,
		46·8	34,3	1·42	,,	52,	2,041,	370,
10	{ North of Scotland Bank- } ing Company .... }	26·6	40,2	1·36	44	56,	2,544,	405,
		31·2	45,2	1·37	46	61,	2,875,	420,
11	{ Caledonian Banking } Company........................ }	50·4	18,7	1·52	19	52,	1,039,	188,
		50·4	18,7	1·38	21	53,	1,166,	189,
	Totals { 1873............	—	1,383,8	—	835	—	91,558,	12,816,
	'74............	—	1,429,6	—	862	—	92,453,	13,489,
	Averages { 1873............	34·4	125,8	1·33	76	108,	8,323,	1,165,
	'74............	39·1	129,9	1·35	78	106,	8,405,	1,226,

* (1873) including 3,100l. "extra or casual profits
† ('74) also 25,000l., or 2¼ per cent. distributed

Balance Sheets for the Years 1873 *and* 1874.

Cols. 5, 6, 7, and 10.]

8	9	10	11	12	13	14	15	16	17	
					Profits, Dividends, and Prices.					
Ratio per Cent. of Proprietors' Funds to Liabilities to the Public.	Ratio per Cent. of Uncalled Capital to Liabilities to Public.	Government Securities, Cash, &c.	Ratio per Cent. of Government Securities, Cash, &c., to Liabilities to Public.	Ratio per Cent. of Net Profit to Paid-up Capital.	Dividend per Cent. per Annum including Bonus.	Amount per Share Paid.	Market Price, Jan., 1874 and 1875.	Premium per Cent.	Yield per Cent. at Market Price.	Number.
Per cnt.	Per cnt.	£	Per cnt.	Per cnt.	Per cnt.			Per cnt.	£ s. d.	
10·4	3·86	4,176,	31·7	16·52	13½	Stock	292	192	4 12 6	1
10·8	"	3,948,	30·5	17·56	14	"	315	215	4 8 11	
21·2	Nil	4,188,	35·4	9·96	9	Stock	198½	98½	4 10 8	2
21·3	"	3,752,	31·7	10·11	9½	"	230½	130½	4 2 5	
15·0	Nil	3,209,	35·4	13·42	13	Stock	275	175	4 14 6	3
15·5	"	2,735,	30·5	16·34	"	"	286½	186½	4 10 9	
12·8	Nil	3,733,	34·4	16·58	15	Stock	303	203	4 19 –	4
13·0	"	3,484,	32·2	16·82	"	"	311	211	4 16 5	
11·1	Nil	3,894,	31·1	19·90	16	Stock	306	206	5 4 7	5
11·0	"	3,626,	28·2	18·46	"	"	313	213	5 2 2	
12·5	Nil	3,332,	29·9	16·01	15	Stock	295	195	5 1 8	6
12·8	"	3,563,	32·5	16·15	"	"	"	"	5 1 8	
16·1	Nil	2,549,	32·7	17·08	14	Stock	279	179	5 – 4	7
19·4	"	2,711,	34·6	14·61	14†	"	284	184	4 18 7	
12·1	Nil	3,052,	31·1	13·18	10	Stock	224	124	4 9 3	8
14·2	"	2,833,	27·8	12·98	11	"	236	136	4 13 3	
20·3	—	687,	37·9	13·06	12½	7	15⅜	119 9/14	5 13 10	9
18·1	22·9	491,	24·0	13·61	"	"	17¾	153½	4 18 7	
15·9	—	807,	31·7	12·56	10	4	9¾	143¾	4 2 –	10
14·6	44·5	922,	32·1	14·12	11¼	"	10⅞	171⅛	4 2 9	
18·1	—	391,	37·6	14·96	14	2½	7½	200	4 13 4	11
16·2	38·6	431,	37·0	14·96	"	"	8	220	4 7 6	
—	—	30,019,	—	—	—	—	—	—	—	
—	—	28,497,	—	—	—	—	—	—	—	
14·0	—	—	32·8	14·62	12·91	—	—	167	4 16 6	
14·6	—	—	30·8	14·74	13·20	—	—	183	4 13 –	

during the year."
among the shareholders, being exceptional profit realised in sale of old bank premises.

58

TABLE XXXII.—*Irish Joint Stock Balance*
[000's omitted in Columns

Number.	Banks. [Issuing Banks in *Italics*.]	1 When Established.	2 Date of Balance.	3 Subscribed Capital.	4 Uncalled Capital.	Liabilities.	
						5 Paid-up Capital.	6 Reserve, including Balance of Profit Carried Forward.
				£	£	£	£
1	Hibernian Bank	1825	Oct., 1873	2,000,	1,500,	500,	241,
		"	" '74	"	"	"	239,
2	Munster Bank, *Limited*	1864	Dec., 1873	1,000,	650,	350,	169,
		"	" '74	"	"	"	167,
3	*National Bank*	1825	Dec., 1873	2,500,	1,000,	1,500,	134,
		"	" '74	"	"	"	156,
4	Royal Bank of Ireland	1836	Aug.,1873	1,500,	1,200,	300,	200,
		"	" '74	"	"	"	201,
5	*Ulster Banking Company*	1836	Aug.,1873	1,000,	750,	250,	288,
		"	" '74	"	"	"	292,
	Totals	—	1873	8,000,	5,100,	2,900,	1,032,
	"	—	'74	8,000,	—	2,900,	1,055,

* (1873) bills 1,151,000*l.*, advances 809,400*l.*; (1874) bills 1,265,200*l.*, advances 891,700*l.*

‡ (1873) bills 1,350,500*l.*, advances 555,300*l.*;

TABLE XXXIII.—*Analysis of Balance Sheets of Irish*
[00's omitted in Cols. 2 and 4, thus 61,3 = 61,300.]

Number	Banks. [Issuing Banks in *Italics*.]	1 Ratio per Cent. of Reserve Fund to Paid-up Capital.	2 Net Profit, less Charges. [00's omitted.]	3 Ratio per Cent. per Annum of Net Profit to Total Resources.	4 Charges or Working Expenses. [00's omitted.]	5 Ratio per Cent. of Charges to Net Profits.	6 Ratio per Cent. per Annum of Charges to Liabilities to Public.
		Per cent.	£	Per cnt.	£	Per cnt.	Per cnt.
1	Hibernian Bank	48	61,3	2·78	—	—	—
		48	58,3	2·42	30,9*	53·0	1·85
2	Munster Bank, *Limited*	48	44,5†	1·64	36,1	81·1	1·64
		48	43,8	1·47	40,4	92·2	1·64
3	*National Bank*	9	179,3	1·60	130,8	73·0	1·37
		10	187,1	1·62	134,8	72·0	1·36
4	Royal Bank of Ireland	67	53,0	2·29	20,5	38·7	1·13
		67	47,0	2·02	22,1	47·0	1·21
5	*Ulster Banking Company*	115	58,4	1·40	—	—	—
		117	53,6	1·26	—	—	—
	1873	—	396,5	—	—	—	—
	'74	—	389,8	—	—	—	—
						4 banks.	4 banks.
	Averages, 1873	36	—	1·75	—	—	—
	" '74	36	—	1·66	—	67·9	1·44

* Taken from returns to Committee on Banks of Issue.

59

Sheets for the Years 1873 *and* 1874.
headed £, thus 240, = 240,000*l.*

7	8	9	10	11	12	13	14	15	
	Liabilities.				Assets.				
Money Lodged, including Dividend Due.	Notes in Circulation.	Accept-ances.	Total Resources.	Bills and Advances.	Government and other Securities.	Cash, &c.	Property Account.	Authorised Issue.	Number.
£	£	£	£	£	£	£	£	£	
1,462,	—	—	2,203,	1,960,*	195,	—	48,	None	} 1
1,669,	—	—	2,408,	2,157,	190,	—	62,	,,	
2,194,	—	—	2,713,	2,217,	200,	259,	37,	None	} 2
2,458,	—	—	2,975,	2,493,	175,	240,	66,	,,	
8,200,	1,312,	36,	11,181,	7,069,†	2,448,	1,419,	244,	852,	} 3
8,571,	1,344,	—	11,571,	7,095,	2,679,	1,549,	248,*	,,	
1,813,	—	—	2,313,	1,906,‡	380,		27,	None	} 4
1,824,	—	—	2,325,	1,827,	468,		29,	,,	
3,025,	605,	—	4,168,	3,320,	311,	537,	—	311,	} 5
3,121,	589,	—	4,251,	3,292,	311,	648,	—	,,	
16,694,	1,917,	36,	22,578,	16,472,	5,749,		356,	1,163,	
17,643,	1,933,	—	23,530,	16,864,	6,261,		405,	1,163,	

† (1873) bills 4,697,100*l.*, advances 2,372,300*l.* ; (1874) bills 4,683,100*l.*, advances 2,411,900*l.*
(1874) bills 1,419,700*l.*, advances 407,100*l.*

Joint Stock Banks for the Years 1873 *and* 1874.
[000's omitted in Cols. 9, 10, 11, and 14, thus 64, = 64,000*l.*]

7	8	9	10	11	12	13	14	15	
Number of Branches.	Number of Sub-Branches.	Average Liabilities to Public at each Office, ex Subs.	Liabilities to Public.	Proprietors' Funds.	Ratio per Cent. of Proprietors' Funds to Liabilities to Public.	Ratio per Cent. of Uncalled Capital to Liabilities to Public.	Govern-ment Securities, Cash, &c.	Ratio per Cent. of Government Securities, Cash, &c., to Liabilities to Public.	Num-ber.
No.	No.	£	£	£	Per ent.	Per cnt.	£	Per cnt.	
22	3	64,	1,462,	741,	50·7	102·7	195,	13·3	} 1
27	4	60,	1,669,	739,	44·3	89·9	190,	11·4	
34	5	63,	2,194,	519,	23·6	29·6	459,	20·9	} 2
34	5	70,	2,458,	517,	21·1	26·4	416,	16·9	
83	29	114,	9,548,	1,634,	17·1	10·5	3,867,	40·5	} 3
83	29	118,	9,915,	1,656,	16·7	10·1	4,228,	42·6	
4	—	363,	1,813,	500,	27·6	66·2	380,	20·9	} 4
4	—	365,	1,824,	501,	27·4	66·3	468,	25·7	
40	—	88,	3,630,	538,	14·8	20·7	848,	23·4	} 5
43	—	84,	3,710,	542,	14·6	20·2	959,	25·8	
183	37	—	18,647,	3,932,	—	—	5,749,	—	
191	38	—	19,576,	3,955,	—	—	6,261,	—	
—	—	102,	3,729,	786,	21·1	27·2	—	30·8	
—	—	102,	3,915,	791,	20·2	26·0	—	32·0	

† (1873) also 75,000*l.*, being premium on new issue.

TABLE XXXIV.—*Profits, Dividends, and Prices of Irish Joint Stock Banks for the Years* 1873 *and* 1874.

Number.	Banks. [Issuing Banks in *Italics*.]	1 Ratio per Cent. of Net Profits to Paid-up Capital.	2 Dividends and Prices. Dividend per Cent. per Annum, including Bonus.	3 Amount per Share Paid.	4 Market Price, January, 1874, and January, 1875.	5 Premium per Cent.	6 Yield per Cent. at Market Price.
		Per cnt.	Per cnt.	£	£	Per cnt.	£ s. d.
1	Hibernian Bank	12·0	12	25	57⅞	131½	5 3 8
		11·7	12	,,	60	140	5 – –
2	Munster Bank, *Limited*	12·7	12	3½	8⅞	153 4/7	4 14 7
		12·5	13	,,	9	157 1/7	5 1 1
3	*National Bank*	12·0	10	30	57⅜	91¼	5 4 7
		12·5	11	,,	67½	125	4 17 9
4	Royal Bank of Ireland	17·7	15	10	28¾	187½	5 4 4
		15·7	15	,,	30½	205	4 18 4
5	*Ulster Banking Company*	23·4	20	2½	10⅜	315	4 16 5
		21·4	20	,,	,,	,,	4 16 5
		—	—	—	—	—	—
		—	—	—	—	—	—
	Averages, 1873	13·7	13·8			176	5 – 8
	'74	13·4	14·2			188	4 18 9

Publication of Balance Sheets.

If a bank be sound in position and ably managed, I venture to think it has much to gain and nothing to lose by the regular publication of a clear statement of its assets and liabilities. The public surely have a right to know something of the position, and the extent and character of the business, of the banks to which they entrust their money. The opinion that a balance sheet gives confidence to the public, and thus tends to enhance the value of a bank's shares in the market, seems to be corroborated by a comparison of the yield per cent. to the investor of publishing and non-publishing banks as shown in Table III. The Whitehaven Joint Stock Bank, which does not, I believe, publish a balance sheet, yields the investor $5l.$ $17s.$ $2d.$ per cent., as against $5l.$ $4s.$ yielded on the average by the four other Cumberland banks of issue, which do publish balance sheets. The shares of the Bank of Liverpool with, it is understood, the largest business in Liverpool, but not publishing, stand to yield $7l.$ $19s.$ $2d.$ per cent., against $6l.$ $18s.$ and $6l.$ $18s.$ $10d.$ yielded respectively by the Liverpool Union Bank and the Liverpool Commercial Bank, which do publish; whilst still less is yielded by the other Liverpool banks which publish. The Manchester and Salford Bank, not publishing, yields to the investor $6l.$ $7s.$ $7d.$ per cent., against $5l.$ $11s.$ per cent. yielded on the average by the three other leading banks of Manchester. The Darlington District Bank, as compared with the banks of its district, which publish, seems also to be a case in point. Ten Yorkshire banks, which do not publish, yield on the average $6l.$ $10s.$ $6d.$ per cent.; thirteen, which do publish, yield on the average $6l.$ $1s.$ $1d.$ per cent. In Group V, midland counties, agricultural, eight non-publishing banks yield on the average $5l.$ $12s.$, against $5l.$ $6s.$ $2d.$ per cent. yielded by five publishing banks. In addition to its other advantages the publication of a balance sheet is calculated to exercise an appreciable effect in preventing the management from straying far from the recognised lines of sound banking. The knowledge that the balance sheet must run the gauntlet of adverse criticism, may, without discredit, be admitted by directors and managers as an incentive to keeping advances within due limits, and maintaining ample reserves readily available for any emergency. I have never heard any valid argument against the publication of balance sheets. It is sometimes said that it holds out a temptation to competition; but how little there is in this objection becomes evident when it is considered that the success of banking can, irrespective of any balance sheet, be tested by the amount of the profits, the rate of dividend, and the market price of the shares, all of which are matters of publicity. It has been urged that the figures of a balance sheet afford little reliable information as to the real position of a bank; because although the assets may amount on paper to the totals stated under the various heads, half the bills may be rotten and half the loans irrecoverable. I must dissent strongly from this view. Balance sheets differ in the amount of information which they give, but they are issued with the imprimatur of the directors and of the auditor, who is generally a public accountant of standing, and the character of these gentlemen for business capacity, and even for veracity, is staked upon the correctness of the published accounts. This is no small safeguard to the public.

It is satisfactory to note that the practice of publishing balance sheets seems to gain ground. Table XXVII contains the balance sheets of forty-nine purely provincial English banks. For a similar table, which was prepared for 1870, and is printed at p. 94, the balances of not more than thirty-five purely provincial banks could be obtained. The Manchester and Liverpool District Banking Company, by far the largest joint stock bank out of London, published its balance sheet for the first time in the beginning of 1875; and we may hope that year by year the banks which practice concealment will rapidly become fewer in number.

A bank's liabilities consist of two chief sections. (1) Those to the proprietors, comprising the paid-up capital, the reserve-fund, and the balance of undivided profit; (2) Those to the public, comprising money lodged, drafts current, note circulation, and acceptances. These liabilities constitute the total resources. The mode of their employment is shown by the items of assets, which consist of :—(1) Bills and advances to customers; (2) Government and other securities and investments; (3) Cash on hand and at call; and, (4) Property account.

Although averse on general grounds to legislative interference with private enterprise, yet I would, in the interests of the public and in those of sound banking, advocate that all joint stock banks should be constrained by law to publish their balance sheets once a-year in a prescribed form, the chief features of which should be that (1) acceptances, (2) note circulation and (3) bills rediscounted, should be distinguished from one another and from (4) money lodged, and that on the other side of the account (1) bills, (2) advances on open accounts, (3) cash, (4) Government securities, and (5) other investments, should each be shown separately. The current expenses should also be stated.

I submit a form of balance sheet and relative account of profit and loss, which will serve as a key to the manner in which the various balance sheets have been summarised in the tables. As may be supposed, numerous difficulties have arisen in making these summaries, from diversities of practice on the part of the various banks in the classification of items, especially on the creditor side of the account.

TABLE XXXV.—*Pro forma General Balance Sheet*, 31*st December*, 1875.

Note.—The bracketed number opposite each principal item refers to the column in the tabularised summary in which it is included in Table XXVII.

LIABILITIES. Dr.	£	£	ASSETS. Cr.	£	£
TO THE PUBLIC.			LENT TO CUSTOMERS.		
Due on current and deposit accounts (7)	6,000,000		Bills 3,500,000		
Drafts current (7)	200,000		Advances on open account 2,210,000		
Note circulation (8)	500,000		Acceptances as per contra 700,000		
Acceptances (9)	700,000				
Bills rediscounted or other endorsements current (7 or 9)	100,000		Total lent to customers (11)	—	6,410,000
Total to the public		7,500,000	Bills rediscounted or other endorsements current as per contra (11)	—	100,000
TO THE SHAREHOLDERS.					
Capital paid up, 50,000 shares at 20*l.* per share (5)	—	1,000,000	CASH AND SURPLUS FUNDS.		
Reserve fund at last balance	480,000		English Government Securities (12)	1,000,000	
Now added (6)	20,000	500,000	Other first-class available investments (12)	750,000	
		1,500,000	Cash on hand (13)	375,000	
Balance of Profit—			Do. at call and short notice with Company's bankers, brokers' bills, &c. (13)	375,000	
Dividend to be now paid at 10 per cent. per annum (7)	50,000		Total cash and surplus funds	—	2,500,000
Bonus of 5 per cent. (7)	50,000				
Balance carried forward (6)	10,000		PROPERTY ACCOUNT.		
		110,000	Bank premises and furniture (14)	—	100,000
		9,110,000			9,110,000

Pro forma Profit and Loss Account for the Year 1875.

	£	£		£
To current expenses, including directors' and auditors' fees, stationery, rent, taxes, and all other charges	—	75,000	By balance brought forward 30th December, 1874	7,500
To rebate of discount carried forward	—	20,000	By gross profits for twelve months, including rebate from previous year, and after providing amply for bad and doubtful debts	267,500
To balance of profit for 12 months—				
Dividend paid for half year, to 30th June.	50,000			
Reserve fund as above	20,000			
Balance of profit carried to general balance sheet	110,000			
		180,000		
		275,000		275,000

Some banks publish twice a-year, some only once. It is, I think, scarcely prudent for any but very large banks to publish their accounts more frequently than once a-year. Six months seems too short a time to bring the results of a moderately-sized business regularly within the law of average.

III. ANALYSIS OF LIABILITIES.

Beginning with the debtor side of the balance sheet, I shall discuss *seriatim* the various items of the liabilities.

Ratio of Uncalled Capital to Liabilities to Public.

The ratio per cent. of the uncalled capital to the liabilities to the public is found to be as under :—

	Per Cent.
Purely London—	
4 senior banks, unlimited, average	18·7
Lowest—City Bank	9·1
Highest—London and Westminster	25·6
3 other banks, limited, average	44·7
Lowest—Central	13·0
Highest—Imperial	49·0
London and provincial—	
2 senior banks, unlimited, average	8·8
Lowest—National Provincial Bank	7·2
Highest—London and County	10·5
5 other banks, limited, average	50·3
Lowest—The London and Provincial Bank	11·3
Highest—London and Yorkshire	132·0
Purely provincial—	
24 unlimited (I have not thought it worth while to work them out)	—
25 limited, average	55·5
Lowest—Cumberland Union	16·9
Highest—Birmingham Banking Company	124·6

Proprietors' Funds and their Ratio to Liabilities to Public.

The proprietors' funds, consisting of (1) the paid-up capital, (2) the reserve fund, (3) the balance of undivided profit carried forward, form together the working capital of the bank, the basis upon which its business rests, and it is of much importance to ascertain the proportion which this basis bears to the superstructure of credit which is reared upon it. This is found to be as follows.

Ratio of proprietors' funds to liabilities to public :—

Purely London—   Per Cent.
  4 senior banks .... 9'5
  3 other   ,, ... 29'3
                  Average .... —— 11'0

London and provincial—
  2 senior banks .... 9'0
  5 other   ,, ... 23'4
                  Average .... —— 10'9

49 Purely Provincial, average .... 21'0
  22 banks of issue... 21'0
  21 banks of non-issue.. 20'0
   5   ,,   exceptional omitted ....
11 Scotch .... 14'6
  4 Irish .... 20'2

Various considerations combine to determine the amount of proprietors' funds which should form the basis of the business of a bank.

Banks of recent establishment, not having had time to acquire business in relation to their paid-up capital, will naturally show a large proportion of proprietors' funds to liabilities to the public. Such are :—

Limited Banks.	Established.	Ratio of Proprietors' Funds to Liabilities to Public.
		Per cent.
North-Eastern Bank................	1872	107'3
Lancashire and Yorkshire	'72	45'4
Manchester Joint Stock	'73	43'3
London and Yorkshire	'72	29'4

Small banks may be said to require a larger proportion of proprietors' funds than large banks.

TABLE XXXVI.—*England and Wales. London and Provincial and Purely Provincial Joint Stock Banks. Ratio of Proprietors' Funds to Liabilities to Public. Small Banks, Medium-sized Banks, and Large Banks.*

[000's omitted in Columns headed £.]

Locality.	Small Banks. Liabilities to Public under 1,000,000l.				Medium-sized Banks. Liabilities to Public 1,000,000l. to 2,000,000l.			
	Number of Banks.	Liabilities to Public.	Proprietors' Funds.	Ratio per Cent.	Number of Banks.	Liabilities to Public.	Proprietors' Funds.	Ratio per Cent.
Limited Banks—	No.	£	£	Per ent.	No.	£	£	Per cnt.
Purely provincial	9	4,865,	1,941,	39·9	8	11,037,	3,490,	31·6
London and provincial	2	1,310,	296,	22·6	2	2,761,	526,	19·1
Total limited	11	6,175,	2,237,	36·2	10	13,798,	4,016,	29·1
Unlimited Banks—								
Purely provincial	9	5.970,	1,719,	28·8	7	10,022,	1,890,	18·8
London and provincial	—	—	—	—	—	—	—	—
Total unlimited	9	5,970,	1,719,	28·8	7	10,022,	1,890,	18·8
Total limited and unlimited	20	12,145,	3,955,	32·6	17	23,820,	5,906,	24·8
Total purely provincial	18	10,835,	3,659,	33·8	15	21,059,	5,379,	25·5
Total London and provincial	2	1,310,	296,	22·6	2	2,761,	526,	19·1
	20	12,145,	3,955,	32·6	17	23,820,	5,905,	24·8

Locality.	Large Banks. Liabilities to Public over 2,000,000l.				Total.			
	Number of Banks.	Liabilities to Public.	Proprietors' Funds.	Ratio per Cent.	Number of Banks.	Liabilities to Public.	Proprietors' Funds.	Ratio per Cent.
Limited Banks—	No.	£	£	Per cnt.	No.	£	£	Per cut.
Purely provincial	3	13,671,	1,864,	13·6	20	29,573,	7,294,	24·7
London and provincial	—	—	—	—	4	4,071,	822,	20·2
Total limited	3	13,671,	1,864,	13·6	24	33,644,	8,116,	24·1
Unlimited Banks—								
Purely provincial	8	34,419,	5,403,	15·7	21	50,410,	9,012,	17·9
London and provincial	2	46,958,	4,216,	9·0	2	46,959,	4,216,	9·0
Total unlimited	10	81,377,	9,619,	11·8	26	97,369,	13,228,	13·6
Total limited and unlimited	13	95,048,	11,483,	12·1	50	131,013,	21,344,	16·3
Total purely provincial	11	48,089,	7,267,	15·1	44	79,984,	16,306,	20·4
Total London and provincial	2	46,959,	4,216,	9·0	6	51,029,	5,038,	9·9
	13	95,048,	11,483,	12·1	50	131,013,	21,344,	16·3

This table shows that the eighteen small purely provincial banks therein tabulated, whose respective liabilities to the public did not exceed 1,000,000*l.*, had proprietors' funds equal to 33·8 per cent. The fifteen middle-sized purely provincial banks whose respective liabilities to the public were between one and two millions, showed proprietors' funds equal to 25·5 per cent.; whilst the eleven large purely provincial banks, having respectively liabilities to the public of over 2,000,000*l.*, showed proprietors' funds equal to 15 per cent.

Banks confined to great mercantile centres, finding a ready outlet for their resources, and not collecting deposits by means of country branches, require a comparatively large basis of capital.

TABLE XXXVII.—*Ratio per Cent. of Proprietors' Funds to Liabilities to the Public of Forty-four Purely Provincial English Banks, classified according to the Number of their Branches.*

I. *Banks without Branches.*

[000's omitted.]

Banks.	Liabilities to Public.	Proprietors' Funds.	Ratio per Cent.
	£	£	
1. Liverpool Commercial Bkg. Co., *Limited*....	1,227,	554,	45·2
2. „ Union Bank	3,345,	764,	22·8
3. „ North-Western Bank, *Limited*..	1,354,	506,	37·4
4. Bradford Banking Company.....................	2,120,	673,	31·7
5. „ Commercial Joint Stock Bank ...	590,	357,	60·5
6. Bank of Leeds, *Limited*....................	423,	194,	45·8
7. Sheffield and Hallamshire Bank	571,	238,	41·8
8. County of Stafford Bank	421,	95,	22·5
9. Wolverhampton and Staffordsh. Bkg. Co.	894,	141,	15·8
	10,944,	3,523,	32·2

II. *Banks with One, Two, or Three Branches.*

[000's omitted.]

Banks.	Liabilities to Public.	Proprietors' Funds.	Ratio per Cent.
	£	£	Per cnt.
1. Bank of Whitehaven, *Limited*...................	623,	190,	30·5
2. National Bank of Liverpool, *Limited**	661,	543,	82·0
3. Swaledale and Wensleydale	796,	96,	12·1
4. Bradford District Bank, *Limited*	716,	339,	47·4
5. „ Old Bank, *Limited*	1,165,	530,	45·5
6. Halifax Comm. Banking Co., *Limited*........	399,	190,	47·7
7. Sheffield Banking Company	1,493,	400,	26·8
8. „ Union Banking Company	438,	220,	50·2
9. Burton, Uttoxeter, and Ashbourn Union....	1,254,	199,	15·9
10. Birmingham Joint Stock Bank, *Limited*....	1,632,	423,	25·9
11. „ Banking Company, „	1,119,	276,	24·7
12. North Kent Bank, *Limited*	80,	24,	29·9
	10,376,	3,430,	33·0

* Branches in Liverpool and Birkenhead only.

68

TABLE XXXVII.—*Ratio per Cent. of Proprietors' Fund—Contd.*

III. *Banks with Four to Ten Branches.*
[000's omitted.]

	Liabilities to Public.	Proprietors' Funds.	Ratio per Cent.
	£	£	
1. Carlisle and Cumberland Bank	639,	179,	28·0
2. „ City and District „	678,	171,	25·2
3. Sheffield and Rotherham „	1,671,	247,	14·8
4. Nottingham Joint Stock Bank, *Limited*	576,	128,	22·2
5. Leicestershire Banking Company	1,412,	340,	24·1
6. Staffordshire Joint Stock Bank, *Limited*	685,	235,	34·3
7. Birmingham Town and District Bank	943,	221,	23·4
8. Bucks and Oxon Union Bank, *Limited*	702,	98,	14·0
	7,306,	1,619,	22·2

IV. *Banks with more than Ten Branches.*
[000's omitted.]

	Liabilities to Public.	Proprietors' Funds.	Ratio per Cent.
	£	£	
1. Cumberland Union, *Limited*	1,860,	308,	16·6
2. North and South Wales Bank	4,011,	596,	14·8
3. Parr's Banking Company, *Limited*	2,904,	376,	12·9
4. Manchester and County Bank, *Limited*	5,794,	1,010,	17·4
5. Union Bank of Manchester, *Limited*	1,655,	540,	32·6
6. Manchester and Liverpool District Bank	12,594,	1,477,	11·7
7. Yorkshire Banking Company	2,556,	398,	15·5
8. Stamford, Spalding, and Boston Company	1,311,	303,	23·1
9. Lloyd's Banking Company, *Limited*	4,974,	478,	9·6
10. Stourbridge and Kidderminster	1,182,	186,	15·8
11. Worcester City and County, *Limited*	1,025,	352,	34·3
12. W. of England and S. Wales District Bank	4,515,	900,	19·9
13. Devon and Cornwall Banking Company	1,699,	215,	12·6
14. Wilts and Dorset „	3,161,	405,	12·8
15. Hampshire Banking Company	2,116,	191,	9·0
	51,357,	7,735,	15·1

Note.—The following banks are omitted, their figures being, from their recent establishment or other circumstances, quite exceptional, and calculated to disturb the representative ratios, viz., Adelphi Bank, *Limited;* Lancashire and Yorkshire Bank, *Limited;* North-Eastern Bank, *Limited;* Manchester Joint Stock Bank, *Limited;* Three Towns Banking Company, *Limited.*

This table shows ratio of proprietors' funds to liabilities to the public :—

			Per Cent.
9 purely provincial banks without branches			32
12	„	with 1, 2, or 3 branches	33
8	„	with 4 to 10 „	22
15	„	with more than 10 branches	15

TABLE XXXVIII.—*Ratio per Cent. of Proprietors' Funds to Liabilities to Public. English Purely Provincial, and London and Provincial Joint Stock Banks by Districts,* 1874.

Districts.	Number of Banks.	Average Number of Offices per Bank.	Liabilities to Public. [000's omitted.]	Proprietors' Funds. [000's omitted.]	Ratio per Cent.
	No.	No.	£	£	Per cnt.
1. Cumberland	4	8	3,800,	848,	22·3
2. Liverpool	4	1½	6,587,	2,367,	35·9
3. North and S. Wales Bank	1	37	4,011,	596,	14·8
4. Manchester	4	29	22,946,	3,403,	14·8
5. Yorkshire	12	4	12,938,	3,881,	30·0
6. Derby, Notts, Lincoln, &c.	4	4	4,553,	970,	21·3
7. Black country	7	8½	10,667,	1,869,	17·5
8. West. and South. Counties	8	16	14,480,	2,371,	16·4
	44		79,982,	16,305,	20·4
9. London and provincial	6	143½	53,995,	5,840,	10·8
	50		133,977,	22,145,	16·5

Note.—In this table the following banks, whose figures are exceptional, have been omitted, viz., the *North-Eastern Banking Company, Limited, Lancashire and Yorkshire Banking Company, Limited, Manchester Joint Stock Bank, Limited,* and the *London and Yorkshire Bank, Limited,* which are all of quite recent establishment ; and the *Adelphi Bank, Limited,* and *Three Towns Banking Company, Limited,* which are both on a small scale.

This table takes the banks by districts, and it will be remarked that the highest ratio is 36 per cent. in the case of the four chief purely Liverpool banks—the next being 30 per cent. in the case of the Yorkshire banks. If the figures of the Yorkshire Banking Company, the only bank of that district which has numerous branches be left out, the remaining eleven Yorkshire banks show a ratio of 33½ per cent. Amongst the purely provincial banks the district in which the ratio is lowest, is that of Manchester, showing nearly 15 per cent., and the four Manchester district banks comprised in the return have all numerous branches.

Distinguishing limited from unlimited banks, the ratios are—

	Per Cent.
Limited—Purely provincial	24½
„ London and provincial	20
Together	24
Unlimited—Purely provincial	18
„ London and provincial	9
Together	13½

The nature of the business done is of course an element of

prime importance in determining the proportion which proprietors' funds should bear to liabilities.

The character of the money lodged must be taken into special consideration. Creditor balances of parties engaged in commercial business are not held on nearly so certain a tenure as the sums generally known by the term of deposit money. Large sums are usually held on a more uncertain tenure than small sums. The basis of proprietors' funds should be larger in proportion to the uncertainty of the tenure of the money lodged.

If the loans or advances on current accounts, which cannot be said to be immediately or even proximately available, form a preponderant item in the assets, the proprietors' funds should be of solid proportions. If the advances are chiefly in the shape of bills, a smaller proportion of proprietors' funds will suffice.

If a bank has a much larger amount of deposits than it can employ in its ordinary business with its customers, it may with safety work with a comparatively small substratum of proprietors' funds. Hence it is necessary, before jumping to the conclusion that any bank has too small a basis of proprietors' funds, to see what proportion of its liabilities to the public are held immediately or proximately available outside of its business with its customers.

Generally speaking, banks in a rural district being subject to comparatively few fluctuations in the demand for money, may with propriety carry on business on a smaller basis of capital than banks placed in large commercial centres.

In the tables the absolutely lowest ratios of proprietors' funds to liabilities to public are that of the London Joint Stock Bank, 8·3, and amongst the purely provincial banks, 9 per cent. shown by the Hampshire Banking Company, and 9½ per cent., shown by Lloyd's Banking Company, Limited, of Birmingham.

The London and County Bank and the National Provincial Bank of England show each 9 per cent. Both these banks, as well as Lloyd's Banking Company, Limited, are increasing their capital by the issue of new shares.

The absolutely highest ratios are 110 per cent. in the case of the Three Towns Banking Company, Limited, and 107 per cent. in the case of the North-Eastern Banking Company, Limited, the former a very small concern, and the latter of recent establishment.

In Scotland the highest ratio is 21·3 in the case of the Royal Bank, and the lowest 10·8 in the case of the Bank of Scotland.

In Ireland the highest ratio is 44·3 for the Hibernian Bank, and the lowest 14·6 for the Ulster Banking Company.

So far as I am aware, the only authoritative dictum which we have on this branch of our subject is that of the late Mr. Gilbart, who makes the following remark in his "Practical Treatise on

" Banking :"—" Although the proportion which the capital of a bank " should bear to its liabilities may vary with different banks, perhaps " we should not go far astray in saying it should never be less " than one-third of its liabilities." It is well known that under Mr. Gilbart's own management this rule was widely departed from by the London and Westminster Bank, whose proprietors' funds at 31st December, 1874, bore the proportion of 9·6 per cent. to their liabilities.

I should be sorry to attempt to lay down any hard and fast rule upon the point, but should be disposed to think that for a well established bank, wh ch holds considerable deposits and systematically keeps readily available reserves to the extent of about one-third of its liabilities, the fair proportion of proprietors' funds to banking liabilities should be something between 15 and 20 per cent. The leading London joint stock banks have not only very large deposits of their own, but also hold the balances of a great many of the country banks, and these balances are specially liable to be drawn at a period of commercial distrust or financial pressure. The acceptance business of the great London joint stock banks is also naturally much more extensive than that of any of the provincial banks, and I hope I shall not be considered presumptuous if I venture to suggest that their proprietors' funds ought to bear a much more substantial proportion to their liabilities than they now do.

An incidental advantage of a large paid-up capital is that it keeps down the rate of the dividend. The bloated dividends of some of the principal banks have been remarked upon, and in many cases where the dividend reaches 20 per cent. or upwards, it will be found that the ratio of proprietors' funds to liabilities to the public is feeble.

It would seem to be sounder policy to pay a good dividend on a substantial capital than a very large dividend on a small capital; and one advantage of this policy is that it tends to prevent the shares from rising to a dangerously high premium on the Stock Exchange.

Money Lodged.

The various tables show this item as follows :—

[000's omitted.]

Joint Stock Banks.	Total.	Average.
	£	£
7 Purely London	68,749,	9,821,
7 London and provincial	50,318,	7,188,
49 Purely provincial	79,175,	1,616,
63	198,242,	3,147,
11 Scotch	80,699,	7,836,
5 Irish	17,643,	3,529,

The column of money lodged includes the amount of the dividend due. It comprises money held on current account and on deposit, and also such balances as are held from other banks. For the most part the money lodged is repayable at call; though in the country there is frequently an understanding, sometimes expressed, sometimes merely tacit, that a few days' notice will be given before any very large sum is withdrawn.

It has been frequently asserted that the Scotch banks, as compared with the English, hold a larger proportion of their deposits in small amounts, that in fact they act much more than the English banks do as savings banks for the people. In support of this view it is pointed out that the total savings banks deposits of England and Wales amount to 2l. 7s. per head of the population, whilst the Scotch savings banks deposits are only 1l. 10s. 10d. per head of the population in Scotland. The National Provincial Bank of England is the most eminently representative provincial bank of England. With its head office in London, it has one hundred and thirty-five branches in the provinces, and there is scarcely a county in England in which it has not an office. That bank and the Scotch banks submitted to the Committee on Banks of Issue in 1875 returns of their depositors and deposits classified according to the sums at credit of each depositor. These returns are embodied in :—

TABLE **XXXIX.**—*Number of Depositors, and Amount of Deposits in National Provincial Bank of England, and in the Eleven Banks of Scotland, classified according to the Amount at Credit of each Depositor.*

[000's omitted in Cols. 3 and 5.]

1	2	3	4	5	6	7	8	9
	National Provincial Bank of England.		The Eleven Scotch Banks.		Ratio Per Cent. to Totals.			
Classification of Sums at Credit, according to Amount.					National Provincial Bank of England.		Scotch Banks.	
	Number of Depositors.	Amount of Deposits.	Number of Depositors.	Amount of Deposits.	Number of Depositors.	Amount of Deposits.	Number of Depositors.	Amount of Deposits.
	No.	£	No.	£	Per cnt.	Per cnt.	Per cnt.	Per cnt.
Not exceeding 100*l.*	83,723	3,603	290,885	11,768	68·24	15·68	69·65	15·44
Above 100*l.* and not above 200*l.*	16,780	2,518	56,445	8,849	13·68	10·97	13·52	11·66
Above 200*l.* and not above 300*l.*	7,430	1,866	23,253	6,111	6·06	8·21	5·56	8·02
„ 300*l.* „ 400*l.*	4,027	1,432	12,395	4,562	3·28	6·23	2·97	5·83
„ 400*l.* „ 500*l.*	2,896	1,339	8,921	4,600	2·36	5·83	2·14	6·04
Above 500*l.* and not above 600*l.*	1,628	902	5,129	2,927	1·33	3·93	1·22	3·85
„ 600*l.* „ 700*l.*	1,045	687	3,277	2,148	0·85	2·99	0·78	2·96
„ 700*l.* „ 800*l.*	799	601	2,621	2,071	0·65	2·61	0·63	2·72
„ 800*l.* „ 900*l.*	549	470	1,773	1,537	0·45	2·04	0·42	2·02
„ 900*l.* „ 1,000*l.*	911	891	2,855	3,286	0·74	3·88	0·68	4·32
Above 1,000*l.* and not above 2,000*l.*	1,847	2,585	6,240	8,760	1·51	11·26	1·50	11·49
Above 2,000*l.* and not above 3,000*l.*	473	1,171	1,672	4,178	0·38	5·10	0·40	5·49
„ 3,000*l.* „ 4,000*l.*	202	721	736	2,497	0·16	3·14	0·18	3·29
„ 4,000*l.* „ 5,000*l.*	127	570	494	2,341	0·10	2·48	0·12	3·08
Above 5,000*l.* and not above 10,000*l.*	184	1,300	659	4,674	0·15	5·66	0·16	6·14
„ 10,000*l.* „ 15,000*l.*	28	352	146	1,593	0·02	1·52	0·04	2·09
„ 15,000*l.* „ 20,000*l.*	17	305	58	917	0·01	1·33	0·01	1·20
Above 20,000*l.*	34	1,640	98	3,324	0·03	7·14	0·02	4·36
	122,700	22,953	417,657	76,243	100	100	100	100

The very remarkable, and I may say unexpected, coincidence of the ratios to the totals, both of the number of depositors and the amount of deposits, in almost every line of the above table must, be held to prove conclusively that whatever may be the case in certain districts and with certain banks, yet over the length and breadth of England and Wales the money lodged of the banks is held on the average in similar amounts, and from the same classes of the people, as that of the banks in Scotland.

Progress of Money Lodged.

Some very interesting evidence was collected by the Committee on Banks of Issue in 1875 as to the progressive increase of deposits both in England and Scotland.

Table XL illustrates the remarkable progress made by the London joint stock banks since 1844, the figures for that date being taken from Mr. Palgrave's evidence before the Committee in 1875.

TABLE XL.—*Progress of London Joint Stock Banks*, 1844 *to* 1874.

[000's omitted.]

London Joint Stock Banks.	1844.		1874.	
	Capital.	Deposits.	Capital,	Deposits.
London and Westminster	800,	2,677,	2,000,	30,020,
,, Joint Stock	600,	2,245,	1,200,	16,000,
Union	423,	1,591,	1,395,	14,120,
Commercial	80,	240,	—	—
London and County	160,	1,231,	1,348,	20,072,
City	—	—	600,	3,290,
Imperial, *Limited*	—	—	675,	2,110,
Central, *Limited*	—	—	100,	770,
Alliance, *Limited*	—	—	800,	1,922,
Metropolitan, *Limited*..............	—	—	191,	300,
	2,063,	7,984,	8,309,	88,604,

The increase of money lodged here shown is no less than 1010 per cent.; an enormous augmentation, even if allowance be made for the absorption of several large private banks.

Mr. Palgrave obtained returns from thirty-six issuing banks in England in 1874 as compared with 1844, and these showed an average increase of 250 per cent, in other words the money lodged in 1874 was 3½ times as large as it was in 1844.

The evidence of Mr. Davidson, Treasurer to the Bank of Scotland, on the progress of Scotch banking at intervals of ten years from 1845, exhibits the following results as regards money lodged:—

Scotland.	Money Lodged.	Proportion to 1845.
	£	
1845......................	33,192,000	100
'55......................	43,271,000	130
'65......................	56,185,000	169
'75......................	78,405,000	239

Comparing Mr. Palgrave's figures for thirty-six English provincial banks of issue with the Scotch figures, it would appear that the increase of deposits has been more rapid in England than in

Scotland. But the progress in Ireland has been still more remarkable.

Dr. W. Neilson Hancock, in his Report to the Irish Government,
on "Savings Invested in Ireland" (Midsummer, 1875), gives the
money lodged in the Irish banks as follows :—

Ireland.	Money Lodged.	Proportion to 1840.
	£	
1840......................	6,125,000	100
'74......................	31,700,000	518

Dr. Hancock remarks, "the increase of deposits and cash
"balances in the Irish joint stock banks from 6,125,000l. in 1840,
"to 31,815,000l. in 1875, or of 25,690,000l., is the most important
"figure" of the growth of savings invested in Ireland during that
period. "Making every allowance," he adds, "for the extension of
"branches and the increased facilities of intercourse bringing to the
"banks money that was hoarded or kept in cash boxes and shop tills,
"this increase of 25,690,000l. must represent a very large and sub-
"stantial increase of wealth."

It may be interesting to note here the progress of the savings
bank deposits in England, Scotland, and Ireland, during the period
1844 to 1874.

TABLE XLI.—*United Kingdom Savings Banks Deposits, 1844 to 1874.*

[000's omitted.]

Year.	England and Wales.				Scotland.			
	Old Savings Banks.	Post Office.	Total.	Proportion to 1844.	Old Savings Banks.	Post Office.	Total.	Proportion to 1844.
	£	£	£	Per cent.	£	£	£	Per cnt.
1844........	25,713	—	25,713	100	1,043	—	1,043	100
'54........	30,197	—	30,197	117½	1,932	—	1,932	185
'64........	34,728	4,688	39,416	153	2,819	124	2,943	282
'74........	34,521	21,826	56,347	219	4,969	418	5,387	516½

Year.	Ireland.				Total United Kingdom.	Proportion to 1844.
	Old Savings Banks.	Post Office.	Total.	Proportion to 1844.		
	£	£	£	Per cent.	£	Per cnt.
1844........	2,749	—	2,749	100	29,505	100
'54........	1,608	—	1,608	58½	33,737	114½
'64........	1,973	182	2,155	79	44,514	151
'74........	2,016	914	2,930	107	64,664	219

From the " Commercial History and Review " of the years 1870 and 1874, published by the " Economist," and from the Table of balance sheets of thirty-four purely provincial English banks, prepared for 1870, and printed on pp. 92 to 95, and from Table XXVII, I am enabled to give the following view of the progress of deposits :—

1st of seven purely London banks.

2nd of five London and provincial banks.

3rd of thirty-four purely provincial banks.

TABLE XLII.—*Progress of Money Lodged in certain English Banks, Four Years*, 1870 *to* 1874.

[000's omitted in columns headed £.]

ENGLAND.	Money Lodged.		Increase or Decrease.	Increase or Decrease per Cent.
	1870.	1874.		
Purely London—	£	£	£	Per cnt.
London and Westminster..................	21,980,	30,020,	+ 8,040,	+ 37
,, Joint Stock (estimated)	14,000,	16,000,	+ 2,000,	+ 14
Union	11,210,	14,120,	+ 2,910,	+ 26
City	2,440,	3,290,	+ 850,	+ 35
	49,630,	63,430,	+ 13,800,	+ 28
Imperial	1,530,	2,110,	+ 580,	+ 38
Central	470,	770,	+ 300,	+ 64
Metropolitan	540,	300,	− 240,	− 44
	2,540,	3,180,	+ 640,	+ 25
London and Provincial—				
National Provincial	15,735,	22,953,	+ 7,218,	+ 46
London and County	13,390,	19,890,	+ 6,500,	+ 48
	29,125,	42,843,	+ 13,718,	+ 47
Consolidated	2,340,	3,070,	+ 730,	+ 31
Midland	1,035,	1,432,	+ 397,	+ 38
London and South-Western..............	540,	910,	+ 370,	+ 68
	3,915,	5,412,	+ 1,497,	+ 38
Purely Provincial—				
4 Cumberland banks	2,433,	3,739,	+ 1,306,	+ 54
4 purely Liverpool	3,186,	5,544,	+ 2,358,	+ 74
1 North and South Wales.................	2,157,	3,890,	+ 1,733,	+ 80
3 Manchester district banks	4,924,	10,285,	+ 5,361,	+ 109
10 Yorkshire banks	7,250,	11,581,	+ 4,331,	+ 60
3 Derby, Notts, and Lincoln............	2,400,	3,096,	+ 696,	+ 29
5 Black Country	5,481,	9,352,	+ 3,871,	+ 71
4 West and South Counties	5,362,	7,941,	+ 2,579,	+ 48
34 banks. Total	33,193,	55,428,	+ 22,235,	+ 67

TABLE XLIII.—*Progress of Money Lodged in Scotch and Irish Banks, Four Years, 1870 to 1874.*

[000's omitted in columns headed £.]

SCOTLAND.	Money Lodged.		Increase or Decrease.	Increase or Decrease per Cent.
	1870.	1874.		
Edinburgh Banks—	£	£	£	
Bank of Scotland	8,227,	10,881,	+ 2,654,	+ 32
Royal	8,686,	10,546,	+ 1,860,	+ 21
British Linen Company	7,283,	7,957,	+ 674,	+ 9
Commercial	7,533,	9,588,	+ 2,055,	+ 27
National	8,282,	11,034,	+ 2,752,	+ 33
Glasgow Banks—				
Union Bank	8,296,	9,965,	+ 1,669,	+ 20
Clydesdale	5,293,	6,859,	+ 1,566,	+ 29
City	6,107,	8,489,	+ 2,382,	+ 39
Country Banks—				
Aberdeen Town and County	1,448,	1,848,	+ 400,	+ 28
North of Scotland	1,862,	2,479,	+ 617,	+ 33
Caledonian	741,	1,053,	+ 312,	+ 42
	63,758,	80,699,	+16,941,	+ 26
IRELAND	24,366,	31,700,	+ 7,334,	+ 30

It will be observed that in these four years the increase of money lodged in the English provinces has been greater than that in London, Scotland, or Ireland.

Acceptances.

The tables show the acceptances to be as follows:—

[000's omitted.]

Joint Stock Banks—	£
7 London	15,383,
7 „ and provincial	4,070,
49 purely provincial	1,325,
11 Scotch	5,120,
1 Irish (the others not stated)	36,

The acceptances of a London bank may be classified as follows:

I. Acceptances of the drafts of its country correspondents drawn at seven, fourteen, or twenty-one days, for purposes of remittance.

II. Acceptances at various dates up to ninety days against credits established by banking correspondents in the country.

III. Acceptances on account of foreign and colonial banks having head offices in London.

IV. Acceptances to mercantile firms and companies abroad.

Acceptances of Class I are perfectly legitimate and unobjectionable. Those of Class II are likewise unobjectionable where the position of the country correspondent is undoubted. Acceptances of Class III should be kept within judicious bounds, and should be well covered by available securities. Those of Class IV are probably best avoided entirely. Being generally drawn against shipping documents surrendered to the bank on acceptance, they are much more within the province of the merchant than of the English bank or banker.

Acceptances differ from ordinary advances to customers simply in this, that instead of being made in cash, they are made by means of the bank's obligation to pay at a future fixed date. Their ultimate payment to the bank may, for argument's sake, be assumed to be as well secured as if the accommodation had been given in the shape of cash advanced. But the bank is committed to meet them as they become due. If the securities held are such as are certain of realisation before maturity of the acceptances granted against them, then the risk of the business is reduced to a minimum. If, however, the customer fails to provide for the acceptances, and the securities lodged cannot be realised in time to meet them, the bank must take them up. A bank largely under acceptance has need therefore to keep at all times a much larger reserve of cash and surplus funds in a readily available shape than a bank which confines its accepting business within strictly moderate limits.

The acceptances of the London Joint Stock Bank as included in the above amount are merely estimated. They were stated at December, 1873, to amount to 4,517,000l. I have assumed them at 4,527,300l. The reserves of this bank in cash and Government securities bear the ratio of 16·3 per cent. to its total liabilities to the public.

The absolutely highest amount of acceptances shown by any of the banks is 4,957,000l., in the case of the Union Bank of London, who mention having cover in hand amounting to 7,590,154l. Their acceptances are in the ratio of very nearly 35 per cent. to their money lodged. They have cash and Government securities amounting to 42·1 per cent. of their liabilities to the public.

The City Bank has acceptances equal to rather more than four times the amount of its proprietors' funds, and actually equal to the total of its money lodged, a very unusual feature. Its reserves in cash and Government securities are 17 per cent. of its liabilities to the public.

Nor is it at all clear that the City Bank derives a commensurate accession of profit from the extended use of its credit in accepting. The net profit earned by the three senior London banks is at the rate of 1·2 per cent. on their total resources, including acceptances, or at the rate of 1·4 per cent. on their total resources, excluding acceptances. The net profit earned by the City Bank is at the rate of 0·84 per cent. on its total resources, including acceptances, or at the rate of 1·5 per cent. on its total resources, excluding acceptances. Either, therefore, the general business of the City Bank must be very much less profitable than that of its neighbours, or the profits of its large acceptance business must be very inadequate. The latter seems to be the more probable inference of the two.

As a rule the acceptances of the purely country banks are *nil*. The Liverpool banks accept to a moderate extent, and the London and County Bank, in virtue of its metropolitan position, is led to do a considerable business in that way. When the capital and surplus funds of a bank and its *locale* warrant it, and when sufficient security is invariably held, such a use of its credit to a moderate extent may be legitimate. The Bank of England does not accept. The New German Bank Act provides that no bank of issue shall accept bills, and several witnesses before the Committee of the House of Commons on Banks of Issue, stated as a probable result of the Scotch banks establishing themselves in London, that they might be tempted to enter more largely on the business of accepting than might be prudent for banks entrusted with the responsible function of providing a sound note currency for their own country. In justification of this view it will be observed that the Bank of Scotland and the National Bank of Scotland, who have both been established in London for some years, accept more extensively than any of the other Scotch banks, the figures being for these two banks 2,667;000*l.*, against 2,453,000*l.*, for the other nine.

Estimated Distribution of Items of Liabilities.

The various items of the liabilities having thus been discussed systematically, it may now be instructive to calculate and collate the percentages of the individual items to their total in each of the territorial divisions of the investigation.

Adopting the figures of the tables in the case of the purely London, London and provincial, purely provincial English, and the Scotch banks, and basing on Dr. Hancock's figures for the Irish banks, we have the following results:—

TABLE XLIV.— *United Kingdom Liabilities of Joint Stock Banks.*
Estimated Percentage of Items to Total Resources, 1874.

Items of Liabilities.	England and Wales.			Scotland.	Ireland.
	Purely London.	London and Provincial.	Purely Provincial.		
	Per cnt.	Per cnt.	Per cnt.	Per cnt.	Per cnt.
Capital paid-up	7·3	7·1	12·1	9·2	14·0
Reserve fund	2·7	2·9	5·4	3·6	5·6
Proprietors' funds	10·0	10·0	17·5	12·8	19·6
Money lodged	73·5	83·2	80·3	76·1	65·5
Note circulation	—	—	0·9	6·2	14·9
Acceptances	16·5	6·8	1·3	4·9	—
Liabilities to public...........	90·0	90·0	82·5	87·2	80·4
Total	100·0	100·0	100·0	100·0	100·0

IV. ANALYSIS OF ASSETS.

Thus far we have considered only the debtor side of the balance sheets before us, the total resources of the banks, and the various heads under which they fall. We now turn to the creditor side of the balance sheets, showing the assets of the banks, and it should be premised here that as the diversity of practice in making up the balance sheets renders it impossible to attain perfect consistency in arranging the assets under their various heads of (1) Cash; (2) Government securities and other investments; (3) Bills and advances, the results attained must be understood to be by no means so accurate as could be desired.

Cash and Surplus Funds.

These are the cash balance and the Government and other securities and money placed in a readily available position outside of the business of the bank with its customers.

A bank's *first* line of defence against a possible demand for money on the part of its customers must be the actual legal tender in its coffers. This should always be sufficient for ordinary requirements, with an ample margin for sudden emergencies. The extent of that margin must be regulated according to the locality of the bank, and the rapidity with which it can replenish its actual cash balance from its *second* line of defence, which consists in its balances at call, especially with the Bank of England. Banks situated in London, or in close proximity to a branch of the Bank of England, may regard their balances with the Bank of England as practically

equivalent to cash in hand. Banks less favourably situated must
of course be more fully supplied with actual legal tender. Issuing
banks of undoubted credit, and in a position to add freely to their
circulation at any moment, may work with a comparatively smaller
balance of legal tender.

The Appendix to the evidence collected by the Committee of
1875 on Banks of Issue, contains amongst other interesting
particulars of the National Provincial Bank of England, the following return of their actual cash balance at 31st December, 1874.

	£
Gold	524,390
Silver	90,043
Bank of England notes.............................	467,045
	1,081,478
Notes of other banks...............................	113,875
	1,195,353

This is as nearly as possible 5 per cent. of their liabilities to the
public, and it may be assumed that a non-issuing country bank,
with branches, requires to maintain nearly that proportion of its
liabilities as till money in the shape of legal tender.

The *third* line of defence lies in readily available investments.
In the first rank of these come English Government securities,
which are generally available either for immediate sale or as security
for an advance. Amongst the other readily convertible investments
suitable for a bank are the Government securities of India and the
Colonies, first class English railway debenture stock, and, to a
moderate extent, well selected foreign government securities; the
last named having this great advantage, that being saleable on
foreign markets, they are less liable to depreciation than English
securities during any financial pressure affecting only the London
market. Metropolitan corporation bonds are held by many banks,
and good local corporation bonds may also be taken to a moderate
extent, but these are seldom realisable to any large amount on a
sudden emergency.

Every investment held by a bank should be written down to
such a price as it would be certain to realise under unfavourable
circumstances, otherwise the risk is run of a serious inroad upon
profits at the very time when these are specially apt to be diminished
by bad debts of exceptional amount. It is customary, therefore,
with the best banks to hold their English Government securities at
or under 90, and all other investments should be treated on a similar
principle.

All the principal London and London and provincial banks, all

the Scotch banks, and all the Irish banks, which publish balance
sheets hold English Government securities. So also do most of the
English provincial joint stock banks.

Twenty-three out of the fifty-six purely provincial English and
London and provincial banks in Tables XXVII and XXIV, do not
appear from their balance sheets to have any English Government
securities.

Several of the English country banks hold first-class home
railway debenture stocks. The Birmingham Joint Stock Bank
gives the following detail of its investments:—

	£
Consols	100,000
American Government securities....................	20,000
Indian ,, ...	10,000
English railway debenture stocks	70,000
	200,000

Under this line of defence may be included the bills discounted
for bill brokers, which are generally and legitimately available for
rediscount at any moment, and doubtless many of the banks which
hold no Government securities prefer to see their reserves in first-
class brokers' bills rather than in consols.

The *fourth* line of defence is money at short notice, generally
three, seven, or fourteen days, with the London discount houses, on
security of first-class bills, and with stock brokers of high standing
on first-class stocks, with a margin. The last named class. of
business should of course be kept within narrow limits.

When there are surplus funds on hand beyond what are
required to furnish amply these various lines of defence, the
remaining balance may be employed, without undue risk and with
a fair profit, in loans for one, two, or three months, on first class
home railway stocks, with a good margin.

The *fifth* line of defence of a bank lies in the best of its bills
discounted for customers. Nothing, as I have indicated, can be
more legitimate than for a bank to bring into the discount market,
as occasion requires, the bills it may have previously discounted for
the discount houses; but it is also by no means uncommon for
English provincial banks in mercantile centres, and without large
deposits, to rediscount their customers' bills frequently, if not
habitually. This, however, is a custom more honoured in the
breach than the observance, for it is evident that the bank
habitually dependent on rediscounting is exposed to the risk of
finding its usual channels of discount suddenly stopped during a
period of financial difficulty. The rediscounting of customers' bills
is a consequence of what may be styled the one-sided character of a

good many of the English provincial banks. There may be said, speaking broadly, to be three classes of English country banks:—

1st. Those which are chiefly deposit banks, and have not a sufficient outlet for the employment of their money lodged in customers' bills or advances. Such are many banks in the agricultural districts.

2nd. Deposit banks which from having offices in commercial centres have a sufficient banking outlet for the funds at their command.

3rd. Banks which being situated in large commercial centres, and not holding large deposits, have to draw from the London bankers and brokers, by rediscounting their own customers' bills, a considerable portion of the funds which they employ in the business of their district.

In consequence of the great increase of money lodged during the last twenty years, banks of the third class are now much fewer in number than they used to be; but habitual rediscounting being a practice to be deprecated, the interests of sound banking would be served by the extensive fusion of banks of Class 3 with those of Class 1.

A careful comparison of the balance sheets analysed has convinced me that it is impossible to deal with the three columns, "bills and advances," "Government and other securities," and "cash, &c.," as representing respectively the same items throughout, and that, therefore, any conclusions deduced from them cannot be accepted without some correction.

With the London banks, as a rule, money at notice and short loans on stocks seem to be included in "bills and advances," and only cash on hand and at call falls into the "cash" column.

With the London and provincial banks money at notice seems to fall generally under the column for "cash," whilst short loans on stocks are probably included in "bills and advances."

Of the English purely provincial banks some class notice-money with "cash," some with "Government and other securi-"ties;" some rank short loans on stocks with "Government and "other securities," and some with "bills and advances."

With all the Scotch banks notice-money and short loans in London seem to fall under the head of "Government and other "securities."

Of the Irish banks, some rank notice-money with "bills and "advances," and some with "Government and other securities."

With all the banks, except one or two of those in the English provinces, brokers' bills discounted seem to fall under "bills and "advances," instead of under "Government and other securities," to which head they seem more correctly to belong.

It has been stated that some of the London joint stock banks habitually call in advances from the Stock Exchange, at the close of each half-year, in order to parade in their published balance sheets a show of strength in cash reserves which they do not normally maintain. The practice is discreditable.

Ratio of Cash and Surplus Funds to Liabilities to Public.

Subject to these very needful explanations, I proceed to deal with the ratios of surplus funds, *i.e.*, " Government securities " and "cash " to liabilities to public.

These are :—

Average Ratio of Cash and Surplus Funds to Liabilities to Public.

ENGLISH : Purely London—		
4 senior banks, unlimited	26·3 per cent.	
5 other „ limited	25·4 „	
London and provincial—		
2 senior banks, unlimited	38·0 „	
5 other „ limited	28·6 „	
Purely provincial—29 banks	30·9 „	
SCOTCH—11 banks	30·8 „	
IRISH—5 banks	32·0 „	

Amongst the London banks the highest ratio is 42·1 per cent., shown by the Union Bank ; the lowest 16·3, shown by the London Joint Stock Bank.

Amongst the London and provincial banks the highest ratio is 42·4 per cent., that of the National Provincial Bank; the lowest 14·0 per cent., that of the London and Yorkshire Bank, *Limited.*

Amongst the purely provincial English banks the highest ratios are :—

	Per Cent.
Wilts and Dorset	62·2
Parr's Banking Company, *Limited*	48·2
Stamford, Spalding, and Boston	47·3

And the lowest :—

Liverpool Commercial, *Limited*	7·8
Bank of Leeds, *Limited*	7·7

With regard to the two latter and other banks, which show an apparently feeble ratio of cash and surplus funds to liabilities to the public, it must be explained that where first-class bills from the discount brokers are largely held, and are classed under " bills and " advances," the ratio of cash and surplus funds to liabilities to the public ceases to afford any indication of the strength of the banking reserves held outside of the business of the bank with its customers.

Amongst the Scotch banks the highest ratios are :—

	Per Cent.
Caledonian Bank	37·0
Clydesdale	34·6

And the lowest :—

City of Glasgow	27·8
Aberdeen Town and County	24·0

Amongst the five Irish banks whose balance sheets are published, the highest ratios are :—

	Per Cent.
National Bank	42·6
Ulster Banking Company	25·8

And the lowest :—

Munster Bank, *Limited*	16·9
Hibernian	11·4

The ratios shown by the London banks would probably be on the average higher than those shown by the Scotch banks, if like the latter the London banks included notice-money and short loans on stocks amongst their surplus funds.

Probably the fair proportion for a bank to hold in cash and convertible investments, and in other readily available forms, is, speaking generally, about 30 per cent. of its liabilities to the public. Anything materially below 25 per cent. would seem to be quite inadequate, but, as already indicated, allowance must be made, not only for the local circumstances of the bank, but likewise for the diversities in the mode of classing the assets in the published balance sheets.

Money Lent.

The proportion of money lent to customers in the discount of bills and as loans or overdrafts on current accounts, must depend in a great measure on local circumstances. In some localities, and especially in rural districts, the course of trade gives rise to comparatively few bills, and the bill case, if maintained at anything like an adequate point, must consist mainly of bills obtained from the London brokers.

Generally speaking, good customers' bills are to be preferred to advances, whether on open accounts or in the shape of fixed loans. They can readily be made use of to a considerable extent by rediscounting on an emergency, when it would injure a bank's business, and perhaps seriously affect its credit, to call in, or even to restrict, its cash advances.

Loans to customers or advances on current accounts are probably more remunerative than bills, but they have this characteristic, which should never be lost sight of by the prudent banker, that so far from being an asset from which he can derive available funds on an emergency, they have a decided tendency to increase during a period of financial or commercial pressure, and due allowance must be made for this tendency in regulating the amount of surplus funds which should be kept proximately available.

Country banks are in the practice of giving advances to their customers on current accounts, either unsecured or covered by collateral security.

Unsecured advances should of course be made only to parties whose means, character, and standing amply warrant the accommodation. Any customer seeking an advance, and not covering it by satisfactory security, should be required to satisfy the banker as to his capital and his ability to repay the advance within a reasonable time.

The securities upon which English country banks usually make advances are :—

1. Guarantees by third parties. This mode of advance is practically the same as the cash credit system of Scotland.

2. Mortgage, or deposit of deeds by way of equitable mortgage, of property of sufficient ascertained value. If advances are exceptionally made against the deeds of works or other manufacturing premises, these should not be relied upon beyond their undoubted value under the adverse circumstances of a forced sale, and denuded of trade fittings and machinery. There seems to be a considerable advantage both to the English banks and the public in the system of equitable mortgage by deposit of title deeds, a mode of security foreign to Scotch law.

3. Good railway and other stocks transferred to the bank.

4. Foreign, and Colonial Government, and other first-class bonds to bearer.

The London banks do not, I believe, grant over-drafts on current accounts. They give cash advances of a fixed amount, and for a fixed time. The securities they accept are pretty much the same as those admitted by the country banks, with the addition to the list of dock warrants and other vouchers for goods and produce, which are rarely seen by country banks, except at the principal seaports. The West End London bankers naturally advance more on deeds of property than the City bankers.

Proportion of Bills to other Advances.

It is the practice of very few of the banks to distinguish in their published balance sheets between money advanced on loans to their customers and money advanced in the discount of bills.

None of the London or of the London and provincial banks do so.

Only thirteen of the purely country banks make the distinction so clearly as to enable us to use the figures as the basis of any calculation. The details are as follows :—

Thirteen English Provincial Joint Stock Banks separating Bills from Advances on Current Accounts.

Banks. [000's omitted.]		Bills.	Advances on Current Accounts.
	£	£	£
Liverpool Commercial	—	902,	637,
„ Union	—	1,727,	1,219,*
Parr's Banking Company	—	695,	1,153,
Bradford Banking Company—			
Cash and bills	916,		
Off, 16 per cent. of total resources, for cash	447,		
Bills estimated		469,	1,712,
Bradford Old Bank—			
Cash and bills	709,		
Off, 16 per cent. of total resources, for cash	271,		
		438,	915,
Leicestershire Banking Company	—	267,	970,
Staffordshire Joint Stock Bank	—	386	410,
Lloyd's Banking Company	—	1,830,	—
Advances on current accounts, consols, freehold, Government, and other securities	2,697,		
Off, 11 per cent. of total resources, for Government securities and freehold	600,		
Estimated advances		—	2,097,
Birmingham Joint Stock	—	888,	759,
„ Banking Company	—	645,	489,
„ Town and District	—	590,	444,
Worcester City and County	—	510,	613,
Halifax Commercial	—	—	—
Current accounts and bankers	287,		
Say, off, for bankers	37,		
		283,	250,
		9,630,	11,618,

* Includes advances by acceptance, 773,000*l.*

In calculating from these data it must not be forgotten that they are not sufficiently representative or extensive to form a basis for any absolutely certain conclusion. The result of the figures is that bills represent 45 per cent. and advances 55 per cent. of the aggregate total of the two.

I have endeavoured to check this calculation by means of the amount of rebate.

The practice of banks varies somewhat in the matter of rebate. In strictness the proper rate of rebate for each bill would be the rate at which it was discounted, but this would involve such multiplicity of calculations that it is not generally adopted, though I am informed it is the practice with the Bank of England and the London and Westminster Bank. The ordinary practice is to rebate all the bills on hand at a general balance at one rate, which may be, (1) an approximate estimate of the average rate at which the bills were discounted, or (2) the Bank of England minimum rate of the day, or (3) the outside market rate of the day, or (4) a fixed rate of say 5 per cent. Probably the best practice is to adopt the Bank of England rate of the day, but never less than 5 per cent. Some few banks may set aside a lump sum sufficient amply to cover rebate without making any detailed calculation, but these must be quite the exception.

From inquiry and reflection, I am of opinion that the average unlapsed currency of the bills held by country banks may be taken as forty-nine days.

Eight purely provincial banks show in the aggregate bills and advances 20,458,000l. and rebate 85,000l. Assuming the rebate to be at 5 per cent., the market rate of 31st December, 1874, the bills at forty-nine days to run would amount to 12,660,000l., showing bills to be 62 per cent. of the conjoined total of bills and advances. But these eight banks are all in commercial districts, where customers' bills are more abundant than in rural areas, and I venture to think that for the whole of provincial England the bills and advances may be taken to stand to one another in the very equal ratio of 50 to 50.

Only two of the Scotch banks separate their bills from their other advances; these are—

Scotch Banks.	Bills.	Current Accounts.	
	£	£	
British Linen Company	4,709,000	2,784,000	
Clydesdale	4,567,000	1,904,000	-
	9,276,000	4,688,000	.

If these two banks might be considered fairly representative, it would appear that relatively to the total of bills and open accounts, bills stand in Scotland for 66 per cent. and open advances for 34 per cent. A few years ago the figures of a third leading Scotch bank showed the ratio of 70 to 30. As the bills include brokers' bills, and the amount of these held must fluctuate greatly, the normal ratio of bills to advances can at best be little more than a matter of conjecture. After inquiry and reflection, I think that in placing the average ratio for the whole of the Scotch banks at 60 to 40, I shall not be very wide of the mark. None of the Scotch banks publish the amount of their rebate, so this estimate cannot be checked by that means.

In Ireland, three out of five banks publishing balance sheets separate bills from advances. These are—

[000's omitted.]

Irish Banks.	Bills.	Advances on Current Accounts.
	£	£
Hibernian	1,265,	892,
National	4,683,	2,412,
Royal	1,420,	407,
	7,368,	3,711,

These banks show the following percentages to the total of bills and advances :—

Per Cent.

Bills 67

Advances on open accounts................................... 33

100

These ratios cannot be verified by means of the rebate. I will therefore set down the ratio as the same as for Scotland, viz., 60 to 40 on the average of all the banks.

With regard to the London and London and provincial banks, the only means of estimating the proportion of bills held is through the rebate.

We find that seven purely London banks with bills and advances amounting to 44,461,000*l.* show rebate amounting to 80,000*l.* At 5 per cent. and forty-nine days to run, this would show bills amounting to 12,000,000*l.*, or 28 per cent. of the conjoined total of bills and advances ; but as it is represented to me that the average unlapsed currency of the bills in the hands of the London banks is somewhat less than forty-nine days, I adopt the following percentages :—

Per Cent.

Bills discounted 30

Loans 70

100

No small portion of the loans of the London banks, be it remembered, is against bills lodged in security. The smallness of this proportion of bills is accounted for by the fact that not only short loans on stocks, but also notice-money, is by the London banks ranked under " bills and advances."

Five London and provincial banks, with aggregate bills and

advances of 23,222,000*l.*, show a total rebate of 75,000*l.* Assuming the average unlapsed currency in this case at forty-nine days, and taking the rebate at 5 per cent., the bills would amount to 11,180,000*l.*, or 48 per cent. of the aggregate total of bills and advances. From information kindly furnished to me, I am, however, satisfied that the following percentages rather understate the proportion of bills in this section of banks :—

	Per Cent.
Bills	50
Advances	50
	100

It will be remembered that with these banks "bills and advances" include short loans on stocks, but not notice-money.

To recapitulate, my estimates of the separate proportions of bills and advances in the column for "bills and advances" in the various tables are :—

Banks.	Bills discounted.	Advances.
Purely London	30	70
London and provincial	50	50
Purely provincial	50	50
Scotch	60	40
Irish	60	40

These figures do not show the proportional amounts of bills held by the different classes of banks. They simply show what proportion of the column "bills and advances" consists of bills.

Property Account.

The column for property account seems to call for little remark. It need scarcely be pointed out that all property should be held at or under its realisable value, and that where it is held on lease with less than twenty years to run, sufficient sums must from time to time be set aside to replace its cost before the expiry of the lease.

Estimated Distribution of Items of Assets.

An estimate of the distribution of the assets of the banks of the various divisions of the United Kingdom may now be attempted, although it will be evident that the endeavour is much more of a leap in the dark than that made with regard to the debtor side or liabilities.

The items of the purely London and of the London and provincial banks are contained in the tables, and bills may be reckoned as 30 per cent. in the former case, and as 50 per cent. in the latter case of the aggregate of "bills and advances."

With the purely provincial English banks it is not so easy to determine the proportional relations of the various columns of assets. I have, however, endeavoured to calculate them in the following manner :—

Number of Banks.	Total Resources. [000's omitted.]	Items as under, included in Total Resources. [000's omitted.]		Percentage to Total Resources.
No.	£		£	Per cut.
26	55,445,	Bills and advances	40,140,	72·5
26	55,445,	Government and other securities....	5,231,	9·5
27	56,481,	Cash at call and notice	9,226,	16·5
47	95,820,	Property account	1,332,	1·5
—	—		—	100·0

Assuming that the bills bear to the bills and advances the ratio of 50 per cent., as already estimated, the assets of the purely provincial banks would seem to be distributed in the following proportions :—

Bills discounted	36·2
Advances on open accounts	36·3
Government and other securities	9·5
Cash at call and notice	16·5
Property account.................................	1·5
	100·0

Pursuing the same method with the Irish banks, we have :—

Number of Banks.	Total Resources. [000's omitted.]	Items as under, included in Total Resources. [000's omitted.]		Percentage to Total Resources, nearly
No.	£		£	Per cut.
4	19,280,	Bills and advances...........................	13,572,	69
3	18,797,	Government securities	3,165,	16
3	18,797,	Cash.................................	2,437,	13
4	19,280,	Property	406,	2
				100

And dividing the percentage of bills and advances in the aggregate, between bills and advances in the proportion of 60 to 40 already arrived at, we have for the Irish proportion of assets :—

Bills discounted	41·5
Advances	27·5
Government securities, &c.	16·0
Cash.................................	13·0
Property	2·0
	100·0

For the Scotch banks we possess all the items, and have simply to separate bills from advances in the ratio of 60 to 40.

Placing the proportions side by side we have :—

TABLE XLV.—*United Kingdom Joint Stock Banks ; Estimated Percentage of Various Items of Assets to Total,* 1874.

Items of Assets.	Purely London.	London and Provincial.	Purely Provincial.	Scotch.	Irish.
	Per cnt.	Per cnt.	Per cnt.	Per cnt.	Per cnt.
Bills discounted	22·8	32·5	36·2	43·2	41·5
Advances	53·2	32·5	36·3	28·8	27·5
Together	76·0	65·0	72·5	72·0	69·0
Government securities, &c........	9·0	14·5	9·5	21·0	16·0
Cash	14·5	18·5	16·5	6·0	13·0
Together	23·5*	33·0	26·0	27·0	29·0
Property	0·5	2·0	1·5	1·0	2·0
	100·0	100·0	100·0	100·0	100·0

* Were short loans on stock and notice-money, or even notice-money alone, transferred from "bills and advances" to "cash and Government securities" in the case of the London banks, this ratio would of course be greatly strengthened.

TABLE XLVI.—*English Provincial Joint Stock Bank Balance*

[000's omitted in columns headed £,

		1	2	3	4	5	6	7	8
			Liabilities.				Assets.		
Number.	Bank.	Paid-up Capital.	Reserve and Undivided Profit.	Money Lodged and other Liabilities to Public.	Total Re-sources.	Bills and Advances.	Government and other Securities.	Cash, &c.	Property Account.
		£	£	£	£	£	£	£	£
1	Carlisle & Cumb. Bg. Co.	52,	44,	424,	520,	1,025,	510,	320,	10,
2	Cumbland. Union, *Lmtd.*	225,	67,	1,155,	1,446,		65,		35,
3	Carlisle City and Dist.....	80,	81,	409,	569,	359,	564,	74,	5,
4	B. of Whitehaven, *Lmtd.*	73,	38,	506,	617,		176,		9,
5	Liverpool Comml., *Lmtd.*	350,	201,	783,	1,333,	977,	—	206,	150,
6	„ Union	450,	238,	1,765,	2,453,	2,162,	—	256,	35,
7	Nat. of Liverpool, *Lmtd.*	449,	58,	323,	830,	739,	—	71,	21,
8	N.-Western, *Ld.*, L'pool.	405,	54,	715,	1,174,	1,041,	—	100,	33,
9	N. & S. Wales, Liverpool.	300,	160,	2,816,	2,776,	1,785,	991,		—

* Half-

Here and at pp. 136 to 145 are printed tables of English provincial balance sheets for 1870 and 1873, London and provincial balance sheets for 1873, and Scotch balance sheets for 1866 and 1870. These tables may be useful for comparison with those of Section II.

Sheets for 1870, *with Analysis, Dividends, Prices, and Yield.*
thus 225 – 225,000*l.*, except in Col. 9.]

9	10	11	12	13	14	15	16	
Analysis.								
Net Profits, less Charges.	Ratio per Cent. of Net Profits to Total Resources.	Government Securities, Cash, &c.	Ratio per Cent. of Government Securities, Cash, &c., to Liabilities to Public.	Dividend per Cent. per Annum.	Amount per Share Paid.	Market Price, January, 1871.	Yield per Cent. per Annum at Market Price.	Number.
£	Per cent.	£	Per cent.	Per cent.			£ s. d.	
13,7	2⅘	—	—	20	5	15	6 13 4	1
27,4	1⅞	386,	33	12	12½	28	5 7 2	2
16,8	3	—	—	20	12½	39	6 8 2	3
13,2	2⅙	250,	49	16¼	10	30	5 8 4	4
32,7	2½	206,	26	10	10	16	6 5 –	5
70,3	2⅞	256,	14	10	15	22	6 16 4	6
12,7*	3	71,	21	5⅚	15	12	7 5 10	7
36,1	3	100,	14	5½	7½	7	5 17 10	8
52,8	1⅞	991,	42	20	10	24	8 6 8	9

year's profits.

TABLE XLVI.—*English Provincial Joint Stock Bank Balance Sheets*

| | | 1 | 2 | 3 | 4 | 5 | 6 | 7 | 8 |
| | | Liabilities. | | | | Assets. | | | |
Num-ber.	Bank.	Paid-up Capital.	Reserve and Undivided Profit.	Money Lodged and other Liabilities to Public.	Total Re-sources.	Bills and Advances.	Government and other Securities.	Cash &c.	Property Account.
		£	£	£	£	£	£	£	£
10	Parr's B. C., *Ld.*, Wrgtn.	100,	48,	1,093,	1,241,	932,	76,	227,	6,
11	Manchr. County, *Lmtd.*	600,	226,	2,963,	3,789,	3,756,	—	—	33,
12	Union of Manchr., *Lmd.*	417,	100,	885,	1,402,	1,189,	—	197,	16,
13	Bradford Bkg. Company	220,	235,	1,323,	1,778,	1,773,			5,
14	„ Coml. J. S. Bk.	165,	123,	308,	596,	578,			18,
15	„ Dist. Bk., *Lmd.*	195,	63,	335,	593,	586,			7,
16	„ Old Bk., *Lmtd.*	386,	131,	733,	1,250,	1,054,	118,	58,	20,
17	Bank of Leeds, *Limited*	151,	22,	352,	526,	496,		20,	10,
18	Yorkshire Banking Co....	250,	67,	1,746,	2,063,	1,923,	100,	—	40,
19	Sheffield Bkg. Company	292,	97,	1,097,	1,486,	1,465,			21,
20	„ and Hallamsh..	183,	53,	427,	663,	658,			5,*
21	„ and Rotherham	161,	79,	993,	1,233,	1,218,			15,
22	„ Union	120,	23,	248,	391,	387,			4,
23 {	Burton, Uttoxeter,&c., Union	130,	59,	1,092,	1,281,	928,	347,		6,
24	Nottingham J.S.Bk.,Ld.	79,	15,	472,	566,		560,		6,
25 {	Stamford, Spalding, &c., Banking Compy.	105,	67,	886,	1,058,	645,	218,	179,	16,
26	Staffdsh. J. S. Bk., *Lmtd.*	174,	45,	432,	651,	589,	14,	41,	7,
27 {	Lloyd's Bkg. Co., *Ld.*, Birmingham	305,	86,	2,549,	2,940,	2,593,	56,	249,	41,
28	Brmnghm. J. S. Bk., *Ld.*	204,	216,	1,225,	1,645,	1,303,	226,	98,	19,
29	„ Bkg. Co., *Ld.*	109,	41,	839,	989,	832,	40,	94,	23,
30	„ Town & Dist.	157,	28,	436,	621,	537,	37,	34,	14,
31	Dudley & W. Bromwich	85,	7,	560,	652,	533,	113,	—	7,
32	Wrcstr. City & Coty., *Ld.*	250,	107,	794,	1,150,	956,	55,	112,	28,
33	Bucks & Oxon Un., *Lmtd.*	80,	10,	522,	612,		600,		12,
34	W. of Eng. & S. Wales Dis.	750,	105,	2,726,	3,581,	2,912,	308,	276,	85,
35	Devon and Corn. Bkg. Co.	128,	66,	1,320,	1,514,	1,514,			
	Totals	8,180,	3,055,	34,752,	45,989,	29,266,	11,751, 1,602,	2,612,	762,

* Half-year's profits.   † This summation is arrived at by doubling the

for 1870, *with Analysis, Dividends, Prices, and Yield—Contd.*

9	10	11	12	13	14	15	16	
Analysis.								
Net Profits, less Charges. [00's omitted.]	Ratio per Cent. of Net Profits to Total Resources.	Government Securities, Cash, &c.	Ratio per Cent. of Government Securities, Cash, &c., to Liabilities to Public.	Dividend per Cent. per Annum.	Amount per Share Paid.	Market Price, January, 1871.	Yield per Cent. per Annum at Market Price.	Number.
£	Per cnt.	£	Per cnt.	Per cnt.			£ s. d.	
32,7	$2\frac{5}{8}$	303,	28	8	10	18	4 8 10	10
41,9*	$2\frac{1}{4}$	—	—	9	15	24	5 12 6	11
44,7	$3\frac{1}{8}$	197,	22	$10\frac{3}{4}$	11	15	7 17 8	12
48,3	$2\frac{3}{4}$	72,	5	$22\frac{1}{2}$	40	119	7 11 3	13
28,2	$4\frac{3}{4}$	—	—	18	20	45	8 – –	14
11,6*	4	—	—	6	30	40	4 10 –	15
21,0*	$3\frac{3}{8}$	176,	24	$11\frac{1}{4}$	20	37	6 1 7	16
12,5	$2\frac{3}{8}$	20,	5	5	25	22	5 13 7	17
32,6*	$3\frac{1}{8}$	100,	6	20	$12\frac{1}{2}$	39	6 8 2	18
38,1	$2\frac{5}{8}$	—	—	$12\frac{3}{4}$	140	255	7 – –	19
21,3	$3\frac{1}{4}$	—	—	$11\frac{5}{8}$	25	44	6 12 1	20
31,2	$2\frac{1}{8}$	—	—	$16\frac{7}{8}$	32	72	7 10 –	21
15,0	4	—	—	$9\frac{3}{8}$	12	20	5 12 6	22
10,2*	$1\frac{5}{8}$	347,	31	14	10	23	6 1 8	23
8,0	$1\frac{3}{8}$	—	—	5	10	9	5 11 1	24
22,6	$2\frac{1}{8}$	397,	45	15	10	27	5 11 1	25
21,5	$3\frac{1}{4}$	55,	13	$7\frac{1}{2}$	20	21	7 1 10	26
24,0*	$1\frac{5}{8}$	305,	11	$12\frac{1}{2}$	$7\frac{1}{2}$	14	6 13 11	27
43,8	$2\frac{5}{8}$	323,	26	20	10	30	6 13 4	28
18,5	$1\frac{7}{8}$	134,	16	$6\frac{1}{4}$	5	10	3 2 6	29
15,7	$2\frac{1}{2}$	71,	16	$7\frac{1}{2}$	8	10	6 – –	30
4,3	$\frac{5}{8}$	113,	20	5	10	6	8 6 8	31
13,1*	$2\frac{1}{4}$	166,	21	$10\frac{1}{8}$	$12\frac{1}{2}$	19	6 18 2	32
15,7	$2\frac{5}{8}$	—	—	$16\frac{1}{2}$	5	—	—	33
65,1	$1\frac{3}{4}$	584,	21	8	15	17	7 1 2	34
18,0	$1\frac{1}{4}$	—	—	$12\frac{1}{2}$	32	70	5 14 3	35
1,102,4†	Average $2\frac{2}{3}$	5,623,	Average 22	—	—	—	Average 6 7 2	

profit in the case of those banks in which it is given for the half-year only.

TABLE XLVII.—*Scottish Bank Balance*

[000's omitted in all money columns

			1	2	8	4	5	6	7
						Liabilities.			
Num-ber.	Banks.	Date.	Paid-up Capital.	Reserve Fund and Balance Carried Forward.	Money Lodged.	Circu-lation of Notes.	Accept-ances.	Total Resources.
			£	£	£	£	£	£
1	Bank of Scotland	Feb., 1866	1,000,	275,	7,159,	604,	199,	9,238,
	Central Bank of Scotland	'66	100,	55,	898,	50,	—	1,103,
	B. of Scotld. with Central	„ '70	1,000,	304,	8,227,	614,	947,	11,092,
2	Royal Bank of Scotland {	Sept.,1865	2,000,	343,	8,128,	707,	200,*	11,378,
		„ '70	2,000,	437,	8,686,	673,	198,	11,994,
3	British Linen Company {	April,1866	1,000,	316,	7,322,	454,	382,	9,475,
		„ '70	1,000,	346,	7,283,	540,	293,	9,462,
4	Commercial Bank of Scotland .... {	Nov., 1865	1,000,	275,	7,089,	697,	350,	9,411,
		„ '70	1,000,	362,	7,533,	709,	333,	9,937,
5	National Bank of Scot-land .... {	Dec., 1865	1,000,	313,	7,016,	679,	500,*	9,508,
		„ '70	1,000,	406,	8,282,	629,	1,119,	11,436,
6	Union Bank of Scotland {	April,1866	1,000,	259,	8,299,	686,	341,	10,584,
		„ '70	1,000,	374,	8,296,	620,	148,	10,439,
7	Clydesdale Banking Company.................... {	Dec., 1865	900,	304,	4,579,	408,	164,	6,355,
		„ '70	900,	339,	5,293,	484,	172,	7,189,
8	City of Glasgow Bank {	June,1866	870,	228,	4,956,	642,	564,	7,259,
		„ '70	870,	312,	6,109,	697,	667,	8,653,
9	Aberdeen Town and County Bank .... {	Jan., 1866	156,	56,	1,401,	139,	—	1,752,
		„ '70	182,	25,	1,448,	153,	—	1,808,
10	North of Scotland Bank {	Sept.,1865	280,	82,	1,716,	223,	—	2,300,
		„ '70	320,	57,	1,862,	276,	—	2,516,
11	Caledonian Banking Company.................... {	June,1870	125,	43,	702,	70,	—	940,
		„ '70	125,	55,	741,	93,	—	1,015,
	Totals .... {	1865–66	9,431,	2,549,	59,263,	5,359,	2,699,	79,302,
		'69–70	9,397,	3,018,	63,758,	5,488,	3,878,	85,540,

* Estimated.

Sheets for Years 1856-66 *and* 1869-70.

except No. 12, in which 00's are omitted.]

8	9	10	11	12	13	14	15	16	
		Assets.				Analysis.			
Bills and Advances.	Government and other Securities.	Coin, Notes, &c.	Property Account.	Net Profits less Charges. [00's omitted.]	Ratio per Cent. of Net Profits to Total Resources.	Liabilities to Public.	Government Securities, Cash, &c.	Ratio per Cent. of Government Securities, Cash, &c., to Liabilities to Public.	Number.
£	£	£	£	£	Per cnt.	£	£		
6,317,	2,258,	532,	131,	128,6	1⅜	7,962,	2,790,	30	}1
522,	510,	53,	18,	20,0	1¾	948,	563,	—	
7,668,	2,775,	464,	186,	123,7	1⅛	9,788,	3,238,	33	
8,207,	2,565,	494,	112,	177,9	1½	9,035,	3,059,	34	}2
8,486,	2,708,	686,	113,	175,6	1⅞	9,556,	3,394,	36	
6,362,	2,720,	270,	123,	131,4	1⅜	8,158,	2,990,	30	}3
6,782,	2,160,	395,	124,	136,0	1½	8,116,	2,556,	34	
6,179,	2,622,	515,	95,	130,9	1⅘	8,137,	3,137,	39	}4
7,090,	2,203,	532,	112,	152,1	1⅘	8,575,	2,735,	32	
6,737,	2,076,	593,	101,	132,1	1⅜	8,195,	2,669,	32	}5
7,903,	2,905,	500,	128,	145,9	1⅘	10,030,	3,405,	34	
8,158,	1,413,	848,	165,	136,3	1½	9,325,	2,261,	24	}6
7,766,	2,110,	406,	157,	135,6	1½	9,065,	2,516,	28	
5,163,	621,	475,	96	112,1	1¾	5,150,	1,095,	21	}7
5,467,	1,043,	562,	16,	121,7	1⅞	5,949,	1,605,	29	
5,232,	1,182,	642,	202,	94,5	1¼	6,161,	1,824,	29	}8
6,236,	1,398,	803,	216,	94,2	1 1/11	7,471,	2,201,	30	
1,343,	251,	132,	26,	27,9	1½	1,539,	383,	25	}9
1,329,	276,	165,	38,	20,1	1⅛	1,600,	442,	25	
1,687,	610,		3,	35,7	1½	1,939,	610,	31	}10
1,742,	501,	252,	21,	34,5	1⅜	2,139,	753,	35	
{834,	216,}	89,	17,	17,0	1¼	771,	89,†	—	}11
676,		100,	23,	17,2	1⅛	835,	316,	38	
{55,908, 834,	16,218, 610,}	4,642,	1,089,	1,144,8	Average 1·44	66,873,	20,906,	31½	
61,145,	18,295,	4,866,	1,232,	1,157,2	1·35	73,124,	23,161,	31¾	

† Exact amount cannot be ascertained.

H

TABLE XLVIII.—*Scottish Banks. Dividend, Price, and Yield to Investor*, 1866 *and* 1870.

Banks.	Dividend per Cent. per Annum.	Amount per Share Paid.	Market Price. January, 1866.	Market Price. January, 1871.	Yield on Purchase Price, January, 1871.
		£ s.	£	£	£ s. d.
Bank of Scotland..............	11	Stock	218	—	—
Central Bank of Scotland	12½	Stock	—	—	—
B. of Scotld. with Central	11½	—	—	270	4 8 10
Royal Bank of Scotland {	7½	Stock	154	—	—
	8	—	—	180	4 8 10
British Linen Company {	11	Stock	231	—	—
	12	—	—	267	4 17 9
Commercial Bank of { Scotland	11	Stock	236	—	—
	14	—	—	282	4 19 6
National Bank of Scot- { land	11	Stock	220	—	—
	13	—	—	275	4 14 6
Union Bank of Scotland {	9	Stock	190	—	—
	12	—	—	242	4 19 4
Clydesdale Banking { Company	10	Stock	209¾	—	—
	12	—	—	227	4 17 10
City of Glasgow Bank.... {	7	Stock	140	—	—
	9	—	—	189	4 15 2
Aberdeen Town and { County Bank	10	6 -	13¼	—	—
	10	7 -	—	14	5 - -
North of Scotland Bank {	10	3 10	7 18/	—	—
	10	4 -	—	8	5 - -
Caledonian Banking { Company	10	2 10	5½	—	—
	12	—	—	6	5 - -
	Average				Average
Totals .... { 1865-66	10	—	—	—	—
'69-70	11¼	—	—	—	4 16 6

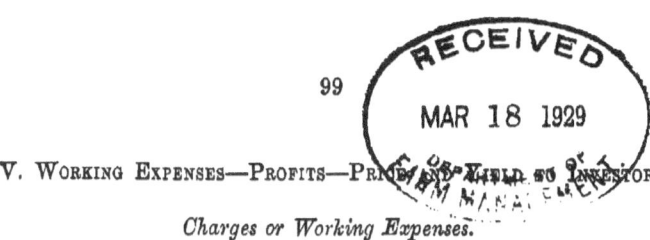

RECEIVED
MAR 18 1929

V. Working Expenses—Profits—Price and Yield to Investor.

Charges or Working Expenses.

In dealing with the column for charges and the columns of ratios based upon it, we must remember that perfect accuracy of comparison is rendered impossible by diversity of practice on the part of various banks. Some pay their dividends free of income tax, and the tax on the dividend then swells the expenses, but the chief diversity doubtless arises in the matter of rent. If a bank owning its premises does not debit charges with rent, its current expenses will show an unduly favourable comparison with those of a bank which either pays rent or debits its charges account with an equivalent sum.

In the tables two ratios have been calculated in reference to charges—first, their ratio to net profits, and second, their ratio to liabilities to the public. A third is supplied below, viz., their ratio to total resources.

The Scotch banks have not been in the practice of stating charges in their balance sheets, but the total amount of their charges for 1874 was returned at 888,458*l.* to the Committee on Banks of Issue.

The Irish banks' return of charges supplied to the committee omits one bank of issue, and is comparatively valueless, as the aggregate liabilities of the banks making the return are not known. Only three of the five Irish banks whose balance sheets I have tabulated give their charges in their published statements. As two of these three are banks of non-issue, I am enabled to supply the charges of the third non-issuing bank from the return furnished to the Parliamentary Committee.

The returns of charges furnished to the Committee by thirty-six English joint stock banks of issue, and by forty-five English joint stock banks of non-issue, are valueless for purposes of comparison, because in neither case are the aggregate liabilities of these banks either stated in the evidence or otherwise ascertainable. If we might assume that the thirty-six issuing English banks whose charges are stated in the Appendix to the evidence, at pp. 554 and 555, showing a total of 424,369*l.*, were the same thirty-six banks whose total deposits Mr. Palgrave was enabled to return as 42,342,294*l.* (Appendix, No. 14, p. 548), the ratio of their charges to their deposits would appear as 1 per cent., and this, it will be seen, approximates very closely to the ratio shown below for the twenty country banks whose charges are stated in the accounts summarised in Tables XXVII and XXVIII.

H 2

The subjoined table (No. XLIX) compares charges proportionally with net profit less charges, with liabilities to public and with total resources.

TABLE XLIX.— *United Kingdom Joint Stock Banks; Ratios per Cent. of Charges or Working Expenses*, 1874.

Locality.	To Net Profits, less Charges.	To Liabilities to Public.	To Total Resources.
	Per cent.	Per cent.	Per cent.
ENGLAND—			
Purely London—			
3 senior banks (no return for Union)	38·1	0·48	0·44
3 others	47·5	1·01	0·78
6 banks average	39·5	0·54	0·48
London and provincial—			
2 senior banks	92·8	1·14	1·06
5 others	74·0	1·60	1·30
7 banks average	88·7	1·22	1·10
Purely provincial, 20 banks	42·7	0·95	0·80
SCOTLAND—11 banks	62·2	0·96	0·84
IRELAND—4 banks	67·9	1·41	1·18

I find that generally the larger the number of branches, the higher are the expenses relatively to the ultimate net profit realised, and also that the ratio of expenses to liabilities to the public is smallest in those banks which show the largest average of liability at each office. This is precisely what might be expected. Where the rate of profit earned on the total resources is small, the expenses bear a correspondingly high ratio to the net profit earned.

Amongst the purely provincial English banks, the absolutely lowest ratio of expenses to liabilities to the public is 0·55 in the case of the Swaledale and Wensleydale Bank, a bank of issue. The highest ratio, excluding three exceptional banks, is 1·80, in the case of the Worcester City and County Bank, Limited.

Profits.

For some years past the "Economist" has published half-yearly analyses of the London joint stock bank balance sheets, and in order to arrive at the net business profit earned on the cash deposits, has deducted from the actual net profit earned 4 per cent. on the capital and reserve fund.

The *rationale* and *modus operandi* of the calculation arc stated by the " Economist " as follows :—

" The profits of banking aro derived from two sources, first from the income obtained by the investment of the paid up capital and the reserve of undivided profits; and, secondly, from the profits arising from the employment of funds belonging to customers—that is to say, deposits and balances of current accounts— supplemented by commissions for agency business transacted for country and foreign banks, for acceptances given on behalf of customers and correspondents against securities of various kinds lodged by the parties as collateral guarantee. The first may be called investment, and the second, business profits. It is reasonable to suppose that the banks realise quite 4 per cent. per annum on the investment of their paid up capital and reserves, and if the amount representing this interest be deducted from the total sum which remains at credit of profit and loss, *after* providing for bad debts, for interest allowed on deposits and credit balances, for depreciation and repair of premises and property, for rebate on current bills held under discount, the figures which remain will of necessity represent the amount of profits yielded by the business apart from the invest- ment of capital and reserves; and the most satisfactory mode of exhibiting the ultimate result will be by calculating the percentage of the business profits on the amount of the cash deposits. It is clear, for example, that a bank employing its deposits chiefly in the discount of bills of the highest class, in the purchase of securities of the most solid and most marketable character, and deriving but little profit for commissions on acceptances and credit, will exhibit a smaller *percentage* of profit on deposits than the case of banks managed on principles less rigid."

Now it seems to me that this calculation of net profit on cash deposits is entirely fallacious as a basis of comparison between bank and bank, unless it happens that the figures of the banks bear very nearly the same proportional relations to one another. If the calculation be applied to two banks the proprietors' funds of which are in one case 50 per cent., and in the other case 10 per cent. of the money lodged, the results will be very misleading. If the pro- prietors' funds are large relatively to the liabilities, they will naturally and legitimately be partially employed in the ordinary business of the bank, and will thus earn, on the average, more than 4 per cent., and whatever they earn beyond 4 per cent. would go to swell fallaciously the profits apparently earned on the deposits; whereas if the proprietors' funds are small relatively to liabilities they may earn considerably less than 4 per cent. overhead, and whatever they earn less than that rate would, on the " Economist's " basis of calculation, serve to diminish the rate apparently earned on cash deposits.

This fallacy in the " Economist's " system was completely over- looked by Mr. Charles Gairdner, one of the Scotch witnesses before the Committee on Banks of Issue, 1875, when he put in the following calculation :—

Percentage of net business profits :—

	£	s.	d.
On cash deposits of 21 English provincial banks	1	13	2 per cent.
„ 11 Scotch banks	1	1	11
Difference	– 11	3	,,

And from this difference, assuming the English provincial deposits at 200,000,000*l.*, he calculated there would be "a gain of 1,125,000*l.* " to the people of provincial England by the adoption of the Scotch " margin of banking profit." Mr. Gairdner omitted the working expenses from his calculation, but this is immaterial, as it is found by Table XLIX that they bear very nearly the same ratio to liabilities in provincial England as in Scotland; but it was a most unwarrantable straining of the "Economist's " mode of calculation to treat its results as an index of the comparative cost of banking to the public; and it was pertinently pointed out by Mr. Rae in his evidence, that as all the Scotch banks are bound by one scale of interest, discount, and charges, the very return upon which Mr. Gairdner's estimate was based exposed the fallacy of his reasoning, for it showed the net profit on deposits of the British Linen Company to be 1*l.* 7*s.* 10*d.* per cent., whilst that of the City of Glasgow Bank was only 17*s.* 2*d.* per cent. a difference of 10*s.* 8*d.* per cent. between two banks whose terms of business to the public are identical.

I have not adopted the "Economist's " basis of calculation, because it would be misleading when applied to banks differing widely in position and characteristics.

Ratio of Net Profits to Total Resources.

Believing the best test of a bank's annual profits to be the ratio they bear to the total resources employed in its business, I have calculated that ratio in the various tables ; but it must not be supposed that the rate of profit affords any reliable index to the comparative cost of banking to the public.

It will be interesting to compare the annual ratio as shown by the joint stock banks of the different districts :—

Locality of Banks.	Number of Banks.	Rate of Net Profit on Total Resources.
		Per cnt.
Purely London	7	1·22
London and provincial	7	1·24
Purely provincial	49	2·07
Scotch	11	1·35
Irish	5	1·66

Amongst the London banks the absolutely highest rate of profit is 1·92, shown by the Alliance Bank, and the lowest ·84, shown by the City Bank.

The three senior banks show great equality in the rate of their profit, viz., 1·2 per cent.

Amongst the London and provincial banks the absolutely highest rate of profit, 2·09 per cent., is shown by the Consolidated Bank.

Amongst the purely provincial English banks, the lowest rate of profit earned on the resources is 1·44, for the North and South Wales Bank and the Hampshire Banking Company, and the highest, 4·22, for the Bradford Commercial Banking Company, Limited. The rate of the Manchester and Liverpool District Bank, the largest of the purely provincial banks, is 1·5 per cent.

The rate of profit earned on the total resources will naturally be modified by local circumstances, but, speaking generally, we may expect it to depend in a great measure on (1) the character and activity of the business, (2) the proportion of proprietors' funds to liabilities to the public, (3) the proportion of the resources held in cash or in a readily convertible shape, and (4) the working expenses.

Where rediscounting customers' bills is practised, the rate of profit will necessarily be increased. Where the proprietors' funds are large relatively to the money lodged, the profits should be correspondingly enhanced. On the other hand, where large reserves are held at unremunerative rates, the rate of profit must necessarily be diminished. Where not only all the proprietors' funds, but also a considerable proportion of the money lodged, are held in cash and low-interest-bearing securities, the profit will be comparatively smaller than where not only all the money lodged, but likewise a portion of the proprietors' funds, are employed at a banking profit in accommodating the customers with discounts and advances.

The working expenses naturally tend to increase with the number of branches.

Table L places in juxtaposition the net profit earned on the total resources, the ratio of proprietors' funds to liabilities to public, the ratio of cash and surplus funds to liabilities to public and to proprietors' funds, and the number of branches and sub-branches, in the case of the London and provincial and purely provincial English joint stock banks.

TABLE L.—*London and Provincial and Purely Provincial English Joint Stock Banks ; Rate of Profit Earned,* 1874.

Number.	London and Provincial and Purely Provincial English Banks. [Banks of Issue in *Italics*]	Rate of Net Profit earned on Total Resources.	Number of Branches and Sub-Branches.	Ratio of Proprietors' Funds to Liabilities to Public.	Ratio of Cash and Surplus Funds to Liabilities to Public.	Ratio per Cent. of Cash and Surplus Funds to Pro-prietors' Funds.
	LONDON AND PROVINCIAL.	Per cnt.	No.	Per cnt.	Per cnt.	Per cnt.
1	National Provincial Bank of England	1·28	137	9·0	42·4	471
2	London and County Bank..................	1·00	148	8·9	33·2	371
3	Consolidated Bank, *Limited*	2·09	3	27·3	30·6	111
4	Midland Banking Company, *Limited*	1·62	27	24·1	16·0	66
5	London and South-Western Bk., *Limd.*	1·48	26	19·6	28·4	144
6	„ Provincial Bank, *Limited*	1·46	54	13·6	42·3	310
7	* „ Yorkshire Bank, *Limited*	0·88	10	29·4	14·1	48
	PURELY PROVINCIAL.					
	I. Cumberland and Northumberland.					
1	*Carlisle and Cumberland Bank*..........	2·28	5	28·0	—	—
2	*Cumberland Union Bkg. Co., Limited*	2·10	17	16·6	26·2	158
3	*Carlisle City and District Bank*	2·50	4	25·4	—	—
4	*Bank of Whitehaven, Limited*	2·21	3	30·5	14·4	47
5	*North-Eastern Bank, Limited*	1·80	16	107·3	27·9	26
	II. Liverpool.					
6	*Adelphi Bank, Limited*	3·02	1	71·7	17·8	25
7	Liverpool Commercial Bkg. Co., *Lmtd.*	2·45	0	45·2	7·4	16
8	„ Union Bank	2·17	0	22·8	33·7	147
9	National Bank of Liverpool, *Limited*	2·94	2	82·0	16·3	20
10	North-Western Bank, *Limited*	2·04	0	37·4	10·4	28
11	North and South Wales Bank	1·44	36	14·8	30·7	207
	III. Manchester District.					
12	Manchester and Liverpool District	1·50	51	11·7	33·9	290
13	„ County Bank, *Limited*	1·90	26	17·4	—	—
14	Union Bank of Manchester, *Limited*	2·90	20	32·6	14·0	43
15	*Lancashire and Yorkshire, Limited*	2·14	8	45·4	24·4	53
16	Manchester Joint Stock Bank, *Limited*	2.92	1	43·3	—	—
17	Parr's Banking Company, *Limited*	2·09	16	12·9	48·2	373
	IV. Yorkshire.					
18	*Swaledale and Wensleydale Bkg. Co.*	1·78	3	12·1	29·4	243
19	*Bradford Banking Company*	2·51	0	31·7	—	—
20	„ *Comml. Joint Stock Bank*	4·22	0	60·5	—	—
21	Bradford District Bank, *Limited*	3·08	1	47·4	—	—
22	„ Old Bank, *Limited*	3·25	2	45·5	—	—
23	Bank of Leeds, *Limited*	2·27	0	45·8	7·7	11½
24	*Halifax Comml. Banking Co., Limited*	2·92	1	47·7	—	—
25	*Yorkshire Banking Company*	3·05	21	15·5	—	—
26	*Sheffield Banking Company*	2·77	3	26·8	—	—
27	„ *and Hallamshire Bank*	3·44	0	41·8	—	—
28	„ *and Rotherham Bank*	1·63	4	14·8	—	—
29	Sheffield Union Banking Company	3·33	3	50·2	—	—

* For note see next page.

TABLE I.--*London and Provincial and Purely Provincial English Banks.—Contd.*

Number.	London and Provincial and Purely Provincial English Banks. [Banks of Issue in *Italics.*]	Rate of Net Profit earned on Total Resources.	Number of Branches and Sub-Branches.	Ratio of Proprietors' Funds to Liabilities to Public.	Ratio of Cash and Surplus Funds to Liabilities to Public.	Ratio per Cent. of Cash and Surplus Funds to Proprietors' Funds.
	V. Derby, Notts, &c.	Per cnt.	No.	Per cnt.	Per cnt.	Per cnt.
30	*Burton, Uttoxeter, &c., Union Bank....*	1·89	2	15·9	—	—
31	*Nottingham Joint Stock Bank, Limited*	1·52	5	22·2	—	—
32	*Stamford, Spalding, and Boston Bank*	2·01	18	23·1	47·3	204
33	*Leicestershire Banking Company*	2·13	10	24·1	35·3	147
	VI. Black Country.					
34	Staffordshire Joint St. Bank, *Limited*	2·29	7	34·3	17·1	50
35	County of Stafford Bank	2·38	0	22·5	25·8	114
36	Lloyd's Banking Company, *Limited*	1·61	35	9·6	—	—
37	Birmingham Joint Stock Bank, *Limited*	2·37	2	25·9	23·8	92
38	„ Bkg. Company, *Limited*	2·21	1	24·7	25·8	104
39	„ Town and District Bank	2·62	7	23·4	11·7	50
40	*Wolverhampton and Staffordshire*........	1·49	0	15·8	—	—
	VII. W. and S. Counties.					
41	*Stourbridge and Kidderminster Bank*	2·16	13	15·8	25·7	163
42	*Worcester City and County, Limited*	2·42	13	34·3	22·2	64
43	Bucks and Oxon Union Bank, *Limited*	2·26	8	14·0	—	—
44	*W. of Engld. and S. Wales Dist. Bank*	2.33	42	19·9	20·4	102
45	Devon and Cornwall Banking Comp.	1·45	14	12·6	—	—
46	*Three Towns Banking Co., Limited	2·67	0	109·9	9·3	8½
47	*Wilts and Dorset Banking Company....*	1·55	49	12·8	62·2	485
48	Hampshire Banking Company	1·44	29	9·0	39·5	438
49	*North Kent Bank, Limited..................	1·82	1	29·9	13·7	46

* Banks indicated thus are exceptional, either in consequence of their recent establishment, or of the small extent of their business.

In this, as in the other tables, the names of the banks of issue are printed in italics. On comparing their rate of profit with that of the non-issuing banks, I cannot find that the results are much, if at all, different.

The National Provincial Bank and the London and County earn net profits of 1·28 and 1 per cent. respectively, with very small proportions of proprietors' funds, a very large number of branches, and handsome proportions of cash and other reserves.

Amongst the Cumberland banks the smallest rate of profit on total resources is earned by the Cumberland Union Bank, whose cash and surplus funds exceed its proprietors' funds by 58 per cent.

Amongst the purely Liverpool banks the highest rate of profit is earned by the National Bank, with the highest ratio of proprietors' funds, and a moderate reserve of cash and surplus funds.

Amongst the banks of the Manchester district, the lowest rate of profit ($1\frac{1}{2}$ per cent.) is earned by the Manchester and Liverpool District Bank, with the smallest ratio of capital to liabilities, a large number of branches, and large cash and other reserves, of which a great proportion is in English Government securities, yielding of course a comparatively feeble profit; whilst the highest rate of profit (2·9 per cent.) is earned by the Union Bank of Manchester, with a large proportion of proprietors' funds, and apparently small proportions of cash and other reserves.

The Yorkshire banks generally present by far the highest rate of net profit, along with such very large proportions of proprietors' funds, as go far to account for their exceptionally high return. The highest rate of profit in this group, and indeed in the whole table, is earned by the Bradford Commercial Joint Stock Bank, with the unusually large ratio of $60\frac{1}{2}$ per cent. of proprietors' funds to liabilities to the public. The smallest rate of profit but one in the group is earned by the Swaledale and Wensleydale Banking Company, with a moderate ratio of proprietors' funds to liabilities to the public, and very handsome proportions of cash and reserves. The Yorkshire banks, as a rule, do not state their cash and reserves, and the very high rates of profit which in many cases their resources yield, though no doubt accounted for, to some extent, by the generally high proportion of their proprietors' funds and by the great activity of trade in the district, suggest the inference that in these cases the reserves employed at unremunerative rates are small, and that in some instances the profits may be enhanced by recourse to the practice of rediscounting. None of them, except the Yorkshire Banking Company, have numerous branches.

Amongst the black country banks, Lloyd's Banking Company, Limited, with by far the smallest ratio of capital, and by far the greatest number of branches, shows all but the smallest rate of profit.

Amongst the banks of the western and southern counties, omitting two exceptional instances, the highest rate of profit is shown by the Worcester City and County Bank, with the highest ratio of proprietors' funds, whilst the lowest rate of profit is shown by the Hampshire Banking Company, with the smallest ratio of proprietors' funds, twenty-nine branches, and a very goodly proportion of reserves. Similarly the small return of 1·55 per cent. of profit shown by the Wilts and Dorset Bank, is doubtless due to its moderate ratio of proprietors' funds, 13 per cent., its numerous branches, forty-nine, and its enormous ratio of cash and reserves, 62 per cent. to liabilities to public, and no less than 485 per cent. to proprietors' funds.

TABLE LI.—*Scotch and Irish Joint Stock Banks, Rate of Profit Earned*, 1874.

Banks.	Rate of Net Profit on Total Resonrces.	Number of Branches and Sub-Branches.	Ratio of Proprietors' Funds to Liabilities to Public.	Ratio of Cash and Surplus Funds to Liabilities to Public.	Ratio of Cash and Surplus Funds to Proprietors' Funds.
SCOTCH BANKS.	Per cnt.	No.	Per cnt.	Per cnt.	Per cnt.
1. Bank of Scotland	1·22	76	10·8	30·5	282
2. Royal	1·41	106	21·3	31·7	148
3. British Linen Co.	1·58	67	15·5	30·5	197
4. Commercial	1·39	100	13·0	32·2	248
5. National	1·29	91	11·0	28·2	249
6. Union	1·30	116	12·8	32·5	254
7. Clydesdale	1·56	79	19·4	34·6	178
8. City of Glasgow	1·12	122	14·2	27·8	195
9. Aberdeen Town and Cy.	1·42	38	18·1	24·0	134
10. North of Scotland	1·37	46	14·6	32·1	220
11. Caledonian	1·38	21	16·2	87·0	230
Averages	1·35	76	14·6	30·8	211
IRISH BANKS.					
1. Hibernian	2·42	31	44·3	11·4	26
2. Munster, *Limited*	1·47	39	21·1	16·9	80
3. *National*	1·62	112	16·7	42·6	255
4. Royal	2·02	4	27·4	25·7	93
5. *Ulster*	1·26	43	14·6	25·8	177
Averages	1·66	46	20·2	32·0	158

That there should not be so much variation of the rate of profit amongst the Scotch banks as amongst the English provincial banks, is quite to be expected from the similarity of the characteristics and local circumstances of the former. The highest rates of profit are 1·58 and 1·56, shown by the British Linen Company and the Clydesdale, whilst the lowest rates are 1·12 and 1·22, shown by the City of Glasgow Bank and the Bank of Scotland.

In Ireland the highest rate of profit is 2·42 per cent., shown by the Hibernian Bank, which has a very large proportion of proprietors' funds relatively to liabilities to public; and the lowest rate of profit is 1·26, shown by the Ulster Bank.

The following table compares the rate of net profit earned on the total resources in the various territorial divisions collating the principal conditions by which it is modified :—

TABLE LII.—*United Kingdom Joint Stock Banks. Rate of Net Profit on Total Resources, and the Features which tend to Modify the same.*

Joint Stock Banks.	Ratio of Net Profit to Total Resources.	Ratio of Proprietors' Funds to Liabilities to Public.	Average Number of Offices per Bank.	Average Amount per Office of Liabilities to Public. [000's omitted.]	Ratio of Cash and Surplus Funds to Liabilities to Public.	Ratio of Cash and Surplus Funds to Proprietors' Funds.	Ratio per Cent. of Working Expenses to Total Resources.
	Per cnt.	Per cnt.	No.	£	Per cnt.	Per cnt.	Per cnt.
ENGLAND—							
Purely London	1·22	11·0	5	2,475,	26·2	238	0·48
London and provincial........... }	[1·24	10·9	59	135,	36·7	335	1·10
Purely provincial .	2·07	21·1	11	148,	30·9	148	0·80
SCOTLAND	1·85	14·6	79	106,*	30·8	211	0·84
IRELAND	1·66	20·2	47	100,	32·0	158	1·18

* Taking the figures shown in Table LXXVII, Progress of Scotch Banking, the average liability to public per office would be 101,000l.

In the case of the London banks the large average liability per office, and the consequently small ratio of working expenses, should enhance the profit, whilst the small ratio of proprietors' funds to liabilities to the public depresses it. The profit of the London and provincial banks is depressed by their large proportions of cash and surplus funds to liabilities to the public, by their comparatively high rate of working expenses, and by the small proportion of their proprietors' funds to their liabilities.

The profit of the purely provincial English banks shows the highest rate of all, which is accounted for in great measure by the larger proportion of their proprietors' funds, and their satisfactory average liability per office as compared with the Scotch and Irish figures. The average sustains also a very appreciable increase from the enhanced rate of profit earned by those banks which rediscount their customers' bills. The English provincial working expenses compare most favourably with the Scotch, when it is considerd that the scale of salaries is very appreciably higher in England than in Scotland.

The Scotch working expenses are, indeed, singularly low, when the enormous extension of their system of branches is considered. It may be estimated that so far as the public are concerned, some 400 of their branches are superfluous. Reckoning the average cost of these at the low rate of 600l. per office, it would appear that the total cost to the banks of their superfluous offices amounts to 240,000l. per annum, which if added to their profit for 1874, would bring the rate of that profit on the total resources to 1·58 per cent. The large sums very prudently held by the Scotch banks in

English Government securities tends to depress the rate of profit which they earn.

Market Price and Yield to Investors.

The market price of bank shares and their yield to the investor are regulated by a variety of circumstances:—

1st. Public opinion as to the safety of the bank, the nature of its business, and the soundness of its management.

2nd. The amount of reserve fund which is designed to protect the proprietors against great fluctuations of dividend and possible loss of capital.

3rd. The actual amount of dividend and bonus paid.

4th. The prospects of increased dividend. If the actual amount of the profits much exceeds the amount of the dividend and bonus paid, investors are encouraged to expect an increased distribution, and this expectation is discounted in the market price.

5th. In the case of recently established banks, the market price naturally represents the dividends expected rather than those realised.

Table LIII is designed to illustrate some of these points.

TABLE LIII.—*London and Provincial and Purely Provincial English Joint Stock Banks ; Profit, Dividend, Price, and Yield per Cent. to Investor, January,* 1875.

	London and Provincial and Purely Provincial English Banks. [Banks of Issue in *Italics*.]	Ratio per Cent. of Reserve Fund to Paid-up Capital.	Profit per Cent. per Annum on Paid-up Capital.	Dividend and Bonus per Cent. per Annum.	Premium per Cent. of Shares in Market, January, 1875.	Yield per Cent. Per Annum at Market Price.
		Per cnt.	Per cnt.	Per cnt.	Per cnt.	£ s. d.
	LONDON AND PROVINCIAL.					
1	National Provincial Bank of England	57	24·4	23	300	5 15 —
2	London and County Bank	52	18·6	20	228¾	6 1 8
3	Consolidated Bank, *Limited*	15	11·2	10	72	5 16 4
4	Midland Banking Company, *Limited*	15	9·6	9	37½	6 10 11
5	London and S.-Western Bank, *Limd.*	8	9·8	7½	12½	6 13 4
6	„ Provincial Bank, *Limited*	20	14·7	10	65	6 1 3
7	* „ Yorkshire „	2	4·0	4	discount	6 — —
	PURELY PROVINCIAL. I. Cumberland and Northumberland.					
1	*Carlisle and Cumberland Bank*	138	25·0	22	297½	5 10 8
2	*Cumberland Union Bkg. Co., Limited*	37	20·3	18	220	5 12 6
3	*Carlisle City and District Bank*	113	26·6	20	252	5 13 7
4	*Bank of Whitehaven, Limited*	93	18·3	20	285	5 3 10
5	*North-Eastern Bank, Limited*	31	4·6	5½	12¼	4 12 5
	II. Liverpool Banks.					
6	*Adelphi Bank, Limited*	4	7·5	5	discount	5 11 1
7	Liverpool Commercial Bank, *Limited*	58	12·5	12½	80	6 18 10
8	„ Union Bank	27	14·9	10	45	6 17 11
9	National Bank of Liverpool, *Limited*	20	7·9	6¾	8½	6 3 1
10	North-Western Bank, *Limited*	25	9·4	7	30	5 7 8
11	*North and South Wales Bank*	55	17·3	20	210	6 9 —

* For note see next page.

TABLE LIII.—*London and Provincial and Purely Provincial English Banks.—Contd.*

	London and Provincial and Purely Provincial English Banks. [Banks of Issue in *Italics*.]	Ratio per Cent. of Reserve Fund to Paid-up Capital.	Profit per Cent. per Annum on Paid-up Capital.	Dividend and Bonus per Cent. per Annum.	Premium per Cent. of Shares in Market, January, 1875.	Yield per Cent. per Annum at Market Price.		
	III. Manchester District.	Per cnt.	Per cnt.	Per cut.	Per cnt.	£	s.	*d.*
12	Manchester and Liverpool District....	63	23·3	20	255	5	12	8
13	,, County Bank, *Limited*	53	18·2	15	180	5	7	1
14	Union Bank of Manchester, *Limited* ..	30	15·3	11⅓	94⅛	5	16	7
15	*Lancashire and Yorksh. Bank, *Limited*	14	7·8	6	35	4	8	10
16	Manchester Joint Stock Bank, *Limited*	21	6·0	10	87½	5	6	8
17	Parr's Banking Company, *Limited*	29	23·7	15	162½	5	14	3
	IV. Yorkshire.							
18	*Swaledale and Wensleydale Bkg. Co.*	52	25·2	20	Shares very rarely change hands.			
19	*Bradford Banking Company*...............	65	17·7	25	285	6	9	10
20	,, *Commel. Joint Stock Bank*	84	20·7	18	192½	6	3	1
21	Bradford District Bank, *Limited*	50	14·2	10½	104⅞	5	2	10
22	,, Old ,, ...	35	14·0	13¾	150	5	10	–
23	Bank of Leeds, *Limited*	28	9·2	7	27	5	10	3
24	*Halifax Commercial Bkg. Co., Limited*	59	14·2	14	138⅞	5	17	3
25	*Yorkshire Banking Company*	59	36·1	24	300	6	–	–
26	*Sheffield* ,, ...	36	18·0	17	95⅝	8	13	8
27	,, *and Hallamshire Bank*	30	15·2	15	99	7	10	9
28	,, ,, *Rotherham Bank*	53	19·5	18¾	161	7	3	8
29	Sheffield Union Banking Company	28	12·7	12½	75	7	2	10
	V. Derby, Notts, &c.							
30	*Burton, Uttoxeter, &c., Union Bank*...	53	21·1	20	170	7	8	2
31	Nottingham Joint Stock Bank, *Limited*	34	11·2	8½	50	5	13	4
32	*Stamford, Spalding, and Boston*	51	16·2	17	236¼	5	1	1
33	*Leicestershire Banking Company*	36	15·0	13¾	125	6	2	2
	VI. Black Country.							
34	Staffordshire J. Stock Bank, *Limited*	35	12·1	8¾	41¼	6	3	11
35	*County of Stafford Bank*	58	20·5	18	220	5	12	6
36	Lloyd's Banking Company, *Limited*	37	25·2	20	262½	5	10	4
37	Birmingham Town and Dist. Bk., *Lim.*	107	28·9	20	240	5	17	7
38	,, J. Stock Bank, *Limited*	78	19·9	13¾	200	4	11	8
39	,, Bkg. Company, *Limited*	38	19·1	11¼	103⅛	5	10	8
40	*Wolverhampton and Staffordshire*	41	15·5	10	80	5	11	1
	VII. W. and S. Counties.							
41	*Stourbridge and Kidderminster*...........	86	29·5	20	150	8	–	–
42	*Worcester City and Coty. Bk. Co., Ltd.*	41	13·3	12⅜	102	6	2	9
43	Bucks and Oxon Union Bank, *Limited*	23	22·6	20	250	5	14	3
44	*W. of Engld. and S. Wales Dist. Bank*	20	16·8	14	128½	6	5	4
45	Devon and Cornwall Bkg. Company....	68	21·7	16½	134⅞	7	–	9
46	Three Towns Bkg. Company, *Limited*	2	5·2	5	discount		—	
47	*Wilts and Dorset Banking Company*..	62	22·1	22	300	5	10	–
48	Hampshire Banking Company	27	22·2	13	180	5	13	–
49	*North Kent Bank, *Limited*..................	7	8·5	8	par	8	–	–

* Banks indicated thus are exceptional, either in consequence of their recent establishment, or of the small extent of their business.

VI. ATTEMPTED ESTIMATE OF TOTAL BANKING LIABILITIES AND ASSETS OF THE UNITED KINGDOM.

Liabilities already Ascertained, and those Remaining to be Estimated.

The tables give substantially the capital and liabilities of all the London banks, of all the London and provincial banks, of all the Scotch banks, of forty-nine out of ninety-seven English purely provincial banks, and of five out of nine Irish banks. The aggregate deposits of all the Irish banks are given by Dr. Hancock, from figures furnished to him by the various banks, as 31,700,000*l.* at 31st December, 1874. The average Irish circulation of the four weeks ending 26th December, 1874, was 7,151,000*l.*, making the total liabilities to the public of the Irish banks 38,851,000*l.* If, therefore, we can estimate the liabilities of the forty-seven English purely provincial banks, whose balance-sheets we have not had access to, and of the private banks, provincial and London, we shall be in a position to attain an approximate estimate of the grand total of the banking liabilities of the United Kingdom.

Purely Provincial English Joint Stock Banks.

The forty-nine English purely provincial joint stock banks in Table XXVII show paid-up capital 11,940,000*l.*, liabilities to public 81,404,000*l.*

Other forty-four English purely provincial banks are known to have a paid-up capital of 7,422,400*l.*, and estimating them to have liabilities in the aggregate in the same proportion to paid-up capital as the forty-nine banks whose liabilities are ascertained, the amount of their liabilities would be 50,600,000*l.* There are three other banks whose capital is not stated, and whose liabilities we cannot estimate at more than 1,000,000*l.*

This gives an aggregate liability to the public for the purely provincial joint stock banks of 133,000,000*l.*

The calculation may be verified by other methods, thus :—

The forty-nine purely provincial banks in Table XXVII show five hundred and forty-nine offices, with aggregate liabilities to the public of 81,403,700*l.*, or 148,000*l.* per office. At the same rate per office, the other two hundred and seventy-four offices of the English provincial joint stock banks should show an aggregate liability to the public of 40,600,000*l.*, making a total for the English purely provincial banks of 122,000,000*l.* against 132,000,000*l.*, found by the calculation based on the capital.

But this calculation calls for some rectification. The 49 banks with 549 offices, show an averge of 11¼ offices per bank, whilst the remaining 48, or really 47 banks, as one does not do banking business, having 273 offices, show an average of 5¾ offices per bank. It is found generally that the fewer the offices per bank the larger the liabilities per office. Amongst the 49 banks whose liabilities are ascertained, the 25 which have fewer than 6 offices per bank, show an average liability per office of 400,000*l.* Deducting from these the 7 largest with 1 office each, the average liability of the remaining banks is 270,000*l.* per office. If the average liability per office of the 47 banks whose liabilities we seek to estimate were taken at 250,000*l.* per office, the total would be 68,000,000*l.*, which added to the ascertained liabilities of 49 banks, would yield a total for the 96 banks of 150,000,000*l.*

Again, calculating roughly by the number of banks:—

		£
49 show liabilities of	....	81,400,000
Deduct the 5 largest with liabilities of	....	31,900,000
Leaving .... 44 with liabilities of	....	49,500,000
In the same ratio per bank		
47 would have liabilities of	....	53,000,000
Making .... 96 with liabilities of	....	134,400,000

Let us see how far these conclusions are verified by the figures published in the Appendix (No. 18) to the evidence given to the Banks of Issue Committee, 1875. The table there given I have here reprinted.

TABLE LIV.—*United Kingdom Joint Stock and Private Banks. Returns Capital and Deposits supplied to Committee on Banks of Issue—Sess 1875.*
[Reprinted from Appendix No. 18 to the Committee's Report and Evidence.]

Banks.	Number.	Returns.		Capital.	
		Sent.	Not Sent.	Subscribed.	Paid-up.
London banks—				£	£
Joint stock	29*	19	10	37,723,600	13,805,074
Private	60†	19	41	—	—
Total London banks.	89	38	51	37,723,600	13,805,074
Country banks—					
Joint stock, England........	99	88	11	60,329,805	13,750,257
„ Scotland........	12	11	1	—	9,697,000
„ Ireland	9	8	1	8,000,000	5,190,000
Private, England	189	143	46	—	—
„ Ireland................	3	—	3	—	—
Total country banks.	312	248	64	68,329,805	28,637,257
Grand totals	401	286	115	106,053,405	42,442,331

* This number evidently includes discount companies and London and provincial banks.
† This number includes bill brokers, and other houses not properly speaking bankers.

TABLE LIV.— *United Kingdom Joint Stock and Private Banks—Contd.*

Banks.	Rest or Reserve of Undivided Profits.	Deposits.		
		From Public.	From Banks.	Total.
London banks—	£	£	£	£
Joint stock	4,033,410	108,235,092	6,623,366	114,858,458
Private	—	31,803,561	7,164,820	38,968,381
Total London banks.	4,033,410	140,038,653	13,788,658	153,826,839
Country banks—				
Joint stock, England	8,942,418	118,053,863	1,708,617	119,762,480
„ Scotland	1,134,000	—	—	78,401,000
„ Ireland	2,326,135	31,781,747	296,125	32,077,872
Private, England	—	60,525,661	147,806	60,673,467
„ Ireland...............	—	—	—	—
Total country banks.	12,402,553	210,361,271	2,152,548	290,914,819
Grand totals	16,435,963	350,399,924	15,940,734	444,741,658

Note.—This return must be looked upon as to some extent conjectural, as the missing Irish returns may possibly have been sent in anonymously and posted in England, so that the postmark would give no indication of their origin.

The total deposits of eighty-eight of the English country joint stock banks are here shown to be 119,762,480*l.*, or an average of 1,360,000*l.* per bank. Eleven banks gave no return, but as we have found the total number of English purely provincial joint stock banks to be ninety-seven in 1874 (not ninety-nine, as stated in the Committee's return), and as one of these was ascertained to exist only as a bank of issue, I will calculate the remaining eight, at the same rate per bank as those which furnished figures to the chairman of the Committee, though this may be rather an over estimate. The calculation will then stand thus :—

England and Wales Joint Stock Country Banks, 1874.

£

Ascertained deposits of 88 banks 119,762,000
Estimated, at same rate per bank, 8 banks   10,890,000
Circulation of 54 banks............................... 2,276,000
Acceptances... 2,100,000

Total estimated liabilities to public 135,028,000

These figures amply confirm the calculations already arrived at, quite independently, by the present inquiry; and I adopt

I

134,000,000*l.* as my estimate of the liabilities to the public of the purely provincial English joint stock banks.

English Provincial Private Banks.

The calculation by offices enables us to attempt an approximate estimate of the liabilities of the private bankers in the provinces. I have stated the number of the offices of the private banks in the English provinces as five hundred and twenty-three. As the number of the offices of these private banks per bank is only two and three-quarters as against eight and a-half offices per bank in the case of the purely provincial joint stock banks, and as we find that in the joint stock banks which have not more than three branches the average liability to the public per office is 436,000*l.*, I confess I should have thought it quite possible that the average liabilities of the private country banks might be reckoned as high as 250,000*l.* per office; but this estimate so very much exceeded that of Mr. Palgrave for 1871, viz., an average of 130,000*l.* per office for capital and deposits of all the country banks, joint stock and private, that I at once decided to reject it, and preferred to assume the average liability per office of the private banks to be only a little more than that of the joint stock banks, or say 160,000*l.* per office. This would yield a total liability to the public for the private country banks of 84,000,000*l.*

I have endeavoured to verify this approximation by a calculation based on the amount of note issues. From Mr. Palgrave's valuable evidence of 1875, it appeared that in thirty-six joint stock banks of issue the proportion of circulation to deposits was 4 per cent. in 1874. The average circulation of the one hundred and sixteen private banks of issue was in 1874 2,600,000*l.* If the note circulation were 5 per cent. of their deposits, the latter would show a total of 52,000,000*l.* or 450,000*l.* per bank. At the same rate per bank, the money lodged of the eighty private country banks of non-issue would show a total of 36,000,000*l.*, and the calculation would stand thus:—

England and Wales Private Country Banks, 1874.

	£
116 issuers—circulation	2,600,000
,, money lodged	52,000,000
80 non-issuers	36,000,000
Total	90,600,000

The table of the Committee on Banks of Issue furnishes another and a surer means of testing the estimate of the liabilities of the private country banks. It gives the number of private provincial banks as one hundred and eighty-nine, I make them one hundred and ninety-six. It gives the deposits of one hundred and forty-three as 60,673,467*l.*, which is equal to an average of 424,000*l.* per bank. Reckoning the deposits of the remaining fifty-three at the same rate, they should amount in the aggregate to 22,472,000*l.*, and the account would stand thus :—

England and Wales Private Country Banks, 1874.

		£
Ascertained deposits	143 banks	60,673,000
Estimated ,,	53 ,,	22,472,000
Note circulation		2,540,000
Total estimated liabilities		85,685,000

Here again my own independent estimates are strikingly confirmed by the statistics furnished to the chairman of the Committee. I adopt therefore 85,000,000*l.* as a reasonable estimate of the liabilities to the public of the private country bankers.

London Private Banks.

Following the "Banking Almanac," I have in Table VIII set down the number of London private bankers as fifty-five, but the list will be found to include many houses which are bill-brokers, exchange and bullion dealers, or merchants, and I find on sifting it that there are in the city fourteen, and in the west end twelve, private bankers strictly so called. After inquiry and reflection, I estimate their money lodged at 60,000,000*l.*, their acceptances at 10,000,000*l.*, and the proprietors' capital employed in their business at 10,000,000*l.*, equal to a total of 80,000,000*l.*; as against Mr. Palgrave's estimate for 1871, endorsed by Mr. Newmarch, of 75½ millions. (See "Notes on Banking," by R. H. Inglis Palgrave; London, John Murray, 1873, p. 2.) Mr. Palgrave stated this as an under estimate, and there must have been some increase of money lodged with the private banks, as we have found there has been with the joint stock banks since 1871. Mr. Richard Seyd, in his instructive "Estimates of Amounts of Capital engaged in the "City of London Wholesale and International Commerce," sets down the capital of twenty-two London private bankers as 15,000,000*l.*, and their deposits as 90,000,000*l.*; but the latter sum seems to be quite an over-estimate.

The table of the Committee on Banks of Issue already referred to does not unfortunately supply the means of testing any estimate of the money lodged with the London private bankers. It states the number of these to be sixty, and thus necessarily includes bill brokers and others, not in strictness entitled to be ranked as bankers. Of these it states the deposits of nineteen as amounting to 38,968,381*l.*, which is equal to an average of 2,051,000*l.* per bank; but as it is probable that several of the private bankers did not make any return, the figures of the table are valueless as a basis for a calculation of the total money lodged of the London private banks properly so called.

Discount Houses and Bank of England.

From the "Commercial History and Review" of 1874, I find that the capital and liabilities of the three discount companies therein tabulated are :—

	Capital.	Reserve.	Deposits.
	£	£	£
Three London Discount Co.'s....	2,600,000	685,000	16,947,000

The author of that publication reckons the other discount houses to have in the aggregate resources amounting to 47,210,000*l.* These may, I assume, be distributed thus :—

	Capital and Reserve.	Deposits.
	£	£
Other discount houses	4,000,000	43,210,000

At 30th December, 1874, the figures of the Bank of England stood thus :—

[000's omitted.]

	Capital.	Rest.	Deposits.	Active Circulation and Bills.
	£	£	£	£
Bank of England........	14,550,	3,090,	26,500,	26,140,

Synopsis of Results.

From these various data I am enabled, with the assistance of the percentages of items to totals estimated in Table XLIV for liabilities and Table XLV for assets, to construct the following table* of the estimated total liabilities and assets of the banks of the United Kingdom :—

Estimated Total Amount of Bills in Circulation.

It may here be incidentally remarked that the figures in col. 9 of the table* quite corroborate the calculation of the

* See pp. 118 and 119.

total amount of bills in circulation made by Mr. Palgrave by au entirely different method. In his "Notes on Banking," Mr. Palgrave computed that "the aggregate of bills in circulation is probably " not more than 300 to 350 millions at one time, including foreign " bills."

Col. 9 of our national banking balance sheet gives the total amount of bills under discount as 274,300,000l. From this there must be deducted say 30 millions for bills which being rediscounted appear twice in the total, and there must be added at least 80 millions for bills held by foreign and colonial banks, and undiscounted in private hands, and say 20 millions for bills held collaterally against advances and acceptances; making a total of 344 millions.

Previously to Mr. Palgrave in 1871, Mr. Newmarch had estimated the bills current for Great Britain at 180 to 200 millions for 1856, and at 116 millions for 1843–46, whilst Mr. Leatham's figures were for the United Kingdom 132 millions, for 1839, and 89 millions for 1832. [See *Statistical Society's Journal*, vol. xiv, part 2, pp. 160 and 167, and Mr. Palgrave's "Notes on Banking," p. 36.]

It may be further remarked that col. 9 affords the means of estimating the amount of the loan fund ordinarily available in the London market for the discount of bills, thus—

	Bills Estimated. £
London discount houses	49,800,000
Bank of England (say in London)	6,000,000
London and provincial banks, say about one-half of their total bills }	10,000,000
Purely London banks, joint stock and private	39,400,000
	105,200,000
English provincial, Scotch and Irish banks, without intervention of bill brokers }	20,000,000
	125,200,000

If we reckon the average currency of these bills at seven weeks, the average amount maturing each week would be 17,900,000l., and the average amount maturing in each of the forty-two business days of these seven weeks would be very nearly 3 millions. I feel quite sure I am well within the mark in estimating that there are 3 millions of bills taken off the London market by discount daily, on the average of the business days of the year.

Mr. Newmarch's estimate for 1850, of the average amount of bills under discount in London at one time, was 78 millions.

His estimates did not include Ireland, and compare thus with mine, less the Irish figures. [See p. 120.]

TABLE LV.—*Estimated Total Liabilities and Assets*

LIABILITIES.

[00,000's omitted, thus 6,8 = 6,800,000*l*.]

	1	2	3	4	5	6	7	8
	Paid-up Capital.	Reserve Fund.	Proprietors' Funds.	Money Lodged.	Note Circulation.	Acceptances.	Liabilities to Public.	Total.
ENGLAND—	£	£	£	£	£	£	£	£
Purely London—								
Joint stock	6,8	2,5	9,3	68,7	—	15,4	84,1	93,4
Private	—	—	10,0	60,0	—	10,0	70,0	80,0
Total London	—	—	19,3	128,7	—	25,4	154,1	173,4
London and Provincial	4,3	1,7	6,0	50,3	—	4,1	54,4	60,4
Purely Provincial—								
Joint stock, 49 banks	11,9	5,3	17,2	79,2	0,9	1,3	81,4	98,6
„ 47 „	7,4	3,9	11,3	50,4	1,4	,6	52,6	63,9
Total joint stock	19,3	9,2	28,5	129,6	2,3	2,1	134,0	162,5
Private	—	—	8,5	82,5	2,5	—	85,0	93,5
Total purely provincial }	—	—	37,0	212,1	4,8	2,1	219,0	256,0
Total England	30,4	13,4	62,3	391,1	4,8	31,6	427,5	489,8
SCOTLAND	9,7	3,8	13,5	80,7	6,6	5,1	92,4	105,9
IRELAND	6,8	2,7	9,5	31,7	7,2	—	38,9	48,4
Total	46,9	19,9	85,3	503,5	18,6	36,7	558,8	644,1
BANK OF ENGLAND	14,5	3,1	17,6	26,8	25,9	,3	53,0	70,6
Three London discount companies }	2,6	,7	3,3	16,9	—	,5	17,4	20,7
Other London discount houses }	—	—	4,0	43,2	—	—	43,2	47,2
Total London discount houses }	—	—	7,3	60,1	—	,5	60,6	67,9
GRAND TOTAL	64,0	23,7	110,2	590,4	44,5	37,5	672,4	782,6

Note.—The figures ascertained are in common type,

of Banks of United Kingdom, December, 1874.

ASSETS.

[00,000's omitted, thus 91,2 = 21,200,000l.]

9	10	11	12	13	14	15	
Bills Dis-counted.	Loans and Over-drafts.	Total Lent to Customers	Govern-ment and Other Securities.	Cash, &c.	Total Cash and Surplus Funds.	Property Account.	
£	£	£	£	£	£	£	ENGLAND—
							Purely London—
21,2	49,6	70,8	8,6	13,5	22,1	,5	Joint stock
18,2	42,6	60,8	7,2	11,6	18,8	,4	Private
39,4	92,2	131,6	15,8	25,1	40,9	,9	Together
							London and Provincial—
19,7	19,6	39,3	8,7	11,3	20,0	1,1	Joint stock
							Purely Provincial—
} —	—	—	—	—	—	—	
—	—	—	—	—	—	—	
—	—	—	—	—	—	—	
92,8	92,8	185,6	24,8	42,2	66,5	3,9	Total purely provincial
151,9	204,6	356,5	48,8	78,6	127,4	5,9	Total England
45,7	30,5	76,2	22,2	6,3	28,5	1,2	SCOTLAND
20,0	13,4	33,4	7,7	6,3	14,0	1,0	IRELAND
217,6	248,5	466,1	78,7	91,2	169,9	8,1	Total
6,9	3,9	10,8	37,3	21,5	58,8	1,0	BANK OF ENGLAND
—	—	—	—	—	—	—	{ Three London discount houses
—	—	—	—	—	—	—	{ Other London discount houses
49,8	6,8	56,6	—	—	11,2	,1	London discount houses
274,3	259,2	533,5	—	—	239,9	9,2	GRAND TOTAL

thus—23,4. Those estimated are in block type, thus—**203,4.**

Estimated Bills under Discount in Great Britain.

[000's omitted.]

Bills under Discount.	Mr. Newmarch, 1850.	Percentages.	Present Inquiry 1874.	Percentages.
In London	78,000,	78	125,000,	48
Locally	22,000,	22	135,000,	52
Total	100,000,	100	260,000,	100

Even allowing for a possible under-estimate of the amount of bills discounted locally in 1850, these figures indicate the very large increase in the banking resources and commercial business of Scotland and the English provinces.

Total Banking Liabilities—Comparison with Previous Investigations.

The total liabilities shown by the above approximate banking balance sheet of the United Kingdom may without exaggeration be characterised as stupendous. The amount, including the capital employed in the business, reaches a grand total of 782,600,000*l.*, or 7 millions more than the present amount of the national debt, and about 173 millions more than the total capital, including loans, of the railway system of the United Kingdom. It should be observed that the amount does not include foreign and colonial banks, which hold in England, and especially in London, an amount of capital and resources which, if it could be approximately estimated, would add many millions to the large total shown in the preceding table.

It will be instructive to compare the results of the present inquiry with those of previous investigations. The only complete estimates previously made are, I believe, that of Mr. Newmarch for 1850, that of Mr. Palgrave for 1871, and that of Mr. T. B. Moxon, of Stockport, 1873.

Mr. Moxon's able research, entitled, "The Banks of the United "Kingdom, their Resources and Reserves," and published for private circulation, in March, 1875, proceeds in so many respects upon methods identical with, or akin to those which I have adopted, that I owe it to myself to say that my own work was far advanced, and the method of it laid down in every part some time before Mr. Moxon's succinct little pamphlet came into my hands.

In collating the figures of the various investigations for comparison in the subjoined table, such alterations have been made in the mode and order of statement of each as were requisite to reduce them all to one common form.

TABLE LVI. — *United Kingdom. Capital and Liabilities of Private and Joint Stock Banks, 1850, 1871, 1873, and 1874.*

[000,000's omitted.]

	Mr. Newmarch, 1850.	Pro-portions to Total.	Mr. Palgrave, 1871.	Pro-portions to Total.	Mr. Moxon, 1873.	Pro-portions to Total.	Present Inquiry, 1874.	Pro-portions to Total.
	Mln. £	Per cnt.	Mln. £	Per cnt.	Mln. £	Per cnt.	Mln. £	Per cnt.
London banks	64,	25	174,	26	211,	29	234,	30
Country ,, ...	97,	37	210,	32	246,	33	256,	33
Together	161,	62	384,	58	457,	62	490,	63
Bank of England	36,	14	67,	10	70,	10	70,	9
London discount houses—capital and deposits	10,	4	78,	12	67,	9	68,	8
Total England	207,	80	529,	8c	594,	81	628,	80
Scotch banks	36,	14	92,	14	95,	13	106,	14
Irish ,, ...	17,	6	41,	6	43,	6	48,	6
Total United Kingdom	260,	100	662,	100	732,	100	782,	100

In this comparison my total for the London banks includes the London and provincial banks, some at least of which are certainly included as country banks in the estimates of Mr. Newmarch and Mr. Palgrave.

Relative Weight of Bank of England in the Money Market.

The great alteration in the relative weight of the Bank of England in the money market, is but faintly indicated by the fall in the percentage of its figures to the total in Table LVI, from fourteen per cent. in 1850, to nine per cent. in 1874.

The figures of the Bank of England in the above comparison include the bullion held, Government securities in both departments, and other securities, which last figure for 21,200,000*l.* in the total. It is, however, well known that a very large proportion of the item of "other securities" in the Bank of England returns consists of investments rather than banking loans or discounts, and cannot practically be reckoned as money "on the market."

It appears from a table in Mr. Palgrave's instructive "Analysis of the Transactions of the Bank of England," London, E. Stanford, 1874, that on the average of the year 1872, the "other securities" consisted of—

	£
Bills discounted	6,900,000
Temporary advances	3,900,000
More permanent advances and investments	10,600,000
Total " other securities "	21,400,000

In this proportion I have distributed the total of the "other "securities" between cols. 9, 10, and 12 of Table LV.

In order, therefore, to arrive at a just estimate of the feebleness of the normal power of the Bank of England in the money market, it is necessary to turn to that Table, where in col. 11 the total sum lent by the banks of the United Kingdom to their customers appears by estimate to be 533,500,000l., of which the Bank of England is reckoned to lend 10,800,000l., or 2 per cent. of the whole. Taking bills under discount merely, the Bank of England is reckoned to hold only 2½ per cent. of the total amount of 274,300,000l., estimated as held by the entire banks of the United Kingdom, exclusive of foreign and colonial banks. Again, the purely London, and London and provincial banks and discount houses, are reckoned to hold a total in bills discounted of 115,800,000l., and the proportion of that amount with the Bank of England is barely 6 per cent.

Once more, restricting the comparison to purely London banks alone, the Bank of England's discounts in London and country are less than one-third of those of the London joint stock banks, and less than one-seventh of those of the London discount houses and bill brokers.

Including loans and discounts, the Bank of England lends less than one-sixth of the amount lent by the London joint stock banks, and less than one-fifth of the amount lent by the London bill brokers.

Two of the purely London joint stock banks, two of the London and provincial banks, and probably one of the London discount companies, hold bill cases individually equal in amount to or greater than that of the Bank of England.

Finally, reckoning the average amount of bills daily discounted in London at 3,000,000l., the Bank of England's share in the amount, assuming the average currency of their bills at only four weeks, is only 250,000l., or only 8 per cent. of the total.

All these striking figures, about the approximate accuracy of which there can be no doubt, prove beyond the possibility of controversy that whatever may have been the relative power of the Bank of England in the money market prior to 1844, the present extent of its transaction in discounts and ordinary banking loans is so small as virtually to place it in a secondary position as a lending bank in ordinary times, and thus to take quite out of its hands the control of the money market. Hence it occurs that of late years there has been between the Bank of England official minimum and the open market rate a divergence which tends so to increase both in amount and in frequency, that there is much reason to fear that it must impede seriously the action of the Bank of England rate upon the foreign exchanges, the control of which by means of the rate of discount is of such prime importance in the maintenance of the bullion reserve.

The position is briefly this—rightly or wrongly, the Bank of England is charged with the maintenance of the bullion reserve for the entire United Kingdom, and yet the instrument by which chiefly that vital trust can be fulfilled is now virtually beyond its control.

Money Lodged by the Public.

In order to arrive at a fair estimate of the total money lodged with the banks by the public, it is necessary to deduct bankers' balances in the hands of other banks and discount houses.

Mr. Palgrave estimated for 1871 that three-fifths of the deposits of the London discount houses were deposited by bankers. This would cause a deduction of 36,000,000*l.* According to Table LIV, London banks and bankers holding money lodged of 153,827,000*l.*, held 13,789,000*l.* of it from other banks, but the return includes some bill brokers, and I reckon the total bankers' balances held by the London private and joint stock banks at 20,000,000*l.*, and the total held by the purely provincial banks at 3,000,000*l.*, and assuming the bankers' balances in the Bank of England at 10 millions, we have :—

Estimate of Deposits by Private and Joint Stock Banks with Discount Houses and other Banks.

	£
With discount houses	36,000,000
With London banks, private and joint stock, and with London and provincial banks	20,000,000
With country banks	3,000,000
Bank of England	10,000,000
	69,000,000

The savings banks' deposits (old and post office) amounted at December, 1874, to 64½ millions.

In order to estimate the total money lodged by the public with the banks of the United Kingdom, we must make the following additions and deductions :—

		£
Total money lodged as stated in Table	....	590,400,000
Deduct deposits by banks		69,000,000
		521,400,000
Add savings banks' deposits		64,500,000
Total money lodged by the public with the banks of the United Kingdom, exclusive of Foreign and Colonial banks	}	585,900,000

This enormous total yields striking evidence of the wealth of the country.

Total Banking Liabilities Resting on Bank of England Reserve.

In his valuable "Notes on Banking," Mr. Palgrave makes an estimate of the banking liabilities resting on the reserve of notes and gold in the Bank of England, practically the ultimate bullion reserve of the entire kingdom.

Side by side with his figures I have, for comparison, placed those of the present inquiry.

TABLE LVII.—*Estimate of Banking Liabilities Resting ultimately on the Reserve of the Banking Department of the Bank of England.*

Banking Liabilities.	Mr. Palgrave, 1871.	Present Inquiry, 1874.
	Mln. £	Mln. £
Deposits of Bank of England..................	34	27
Liabilities to Public— Of English banks, London and country.	335	427½
Discount Houses— Two-fifths of deposits (say)	32	24
Liabilities to Public— Of Scotch banks .... „ Irish „	82 34½	92½ 39
Foreign and Colonial Banks— Liabilities in this country (say)	18	25
	535½	635

The banks cannot be assumed to hold ordinarily a larger amount of legal tender than they require for till money, and in a period of pressure they naturally seek to strengthen their tills. The bullion reserve in the Bank of England is thus the basis upon which rests the enormous superstructure of credit calculated by Mr. Palgrave at 535,000,000*l.*, and by myself at 635,000,000*l.* Let us see what this basis at present amounts to.

The total bullion held by the Bank of England in both departments was, at 8th December, 1875, 23,000,000l., but of this 12,000,000l. was tied up by the Act of 1844 to secure the notes in circulation beyond the amount of 15,000,000l. issued under the Act against securities. The free bullion reserve was thus only 11,000,000l., or somewhat under 1¾ per cent. of the liabilities which practically rest upon it. Even making the largest possible allowance for such proportion of these liabilities as may not be payable at call, the utter inadequacy of the bullion reserve cannot be contemplated without a shudder. Two days' panic in the City and it would vanish, leaving behind it the shameful alternatives of the infraction of the Act of 1844, or of the suspension of the Bank of England, and of every banker and trader in the kingdom.

Constitution of our Monetary System.

It must be confessed that our monetary system is a very peculiar one.

Our whole scheme of credit and banking may be likened to the familiar peg-top of the schoolboy, which gyrates upon a small metallic point sufficient to support it so long as it spins with rapidity, but inadequate to the task when the rotatory force is relaxed. Credit is the rotatory force of our financial system. So long as this force is unimpaired the system spins merrily on, but when it fails the insufficiency of the small metallic basis becomes only too apparent, and the fabric topples to its fall. Metaphor apart, the case stands thus : bankers hold a certain amount of deposits, which I have estimated at about 600,000,000l. With part of these they accommodate the customers who discount bills with or take advances from them. Another part—generally a fourth or a third—they hold in Government or other good securities, and in cash at call or short notice with other bankers or bill brokers. The country banks keep balances with the London banks and with the bill brokers. The London banks and bill brokers trade with these balances, reserving in their turn a fourth or a third, and keep accounts with the Bank of England. The Bank of England, whose deposits are thus composed in a great measure of bankers' balances, trades with these balances, maintaining a reserve of notes to meet liabilities ; and this is the sole ultimate legal tender reserve of the entire country.

Panics.

Such is the development of credit in this country, that it has been roughly calculated that 97 per cent. of the money transactions of the nation are ordinarily effected by cheques, bills, and other expedients of credit, about 2½ per cent. by bank notes, and about one-half per cent. by coin.

But periodically it is found that credit has been over-stretched. Distrust usurps the place of confidence. All who have commercial engagements to meet—merchants, manufacturers, brokers, bankers, alike—strive to strengthen their position. The mercantile world draws upon its reserve of money lodged or credit with the banker. The banker draws upon his reserves in London to strengthen or maintain his cash balances—perhaps to meet a run upon him by his depositors. As the crisis intensifies, bills and cheques, the ordinary instruments of exchange, are looked upon with suspicion, and Bank of England notes come into rapidly increased demand. Cautious or timid bankers and others seek to obtain increased supplies, and a great pressure on the Bank of England for advances is the result. The natural consequence is, that the reserve of notes in the Bank suffers an alarmingly rapid diminution, and the panic rages with fearfully augmented intensity as the monetary barometer is seen rapidly to fall towards zero. Then Government is implored to suspend the Act. No other course seems open, and the Act is suspended by authorising the extension of the issues against security—a measure which at once allays the severity of the panic.

When it is found that in every panic since the Act was passed —alike in 1847, in 1857, and in 1866—it has been necessary to suspend its operation, it is no matter for surprise that the onus of the break-down should be very generally laid upon the Act itself. So far as I can judge, however, it is in the one-reserve system of the country, and in the management of the banking department under that system, rather than in the provisions of the Act itself, that the causes of its periodical suspension are to be sought. The Act serves the all-important purpose of providing an undoubted security for the perfect convertibility of the legal tender notes, except in the unlikely event of the public ceasing to hold them to the extent of 15,000,000*l.*

The simple reason why the Act was suspended in 1847, 1857, and 1866, was that, no other banks in the country holding bullion reserves, the reserve in the banking department had been permitted to fall in the first case to 2,000,000*l.*, in the second to 581,000*l.*, and in the third to 1,200,000*l.*; and as the Bank directors either could not or would not take steps to increase it, the banking department was practically unable to continue its business, and might at any moment have been compelled to suspend payments by a demand from two or three of the leading London banks for the repayment of their deposits.

It certainly cannot be good management which brings the

leading bank of the kingdom—the pattern bank as it ought to be
—periodically to such abject straits, that it is only saved from
the crowning disgrace of failure by the arbitrary suspension of the
law of the land. Whilst the Bank directors have no control whatever over the self-regulating issue department, they have unfettered
control over the banking department. Is it not clear that they are
bound to administer that department in such wise that in all calcu-
lable contingencies, however adverse, it shall continue, without
assistance from the State, to carry on its transactions and meet the
claims of its customers as usual? The directors know the nature
of the business they conduct; they know by experience the pressure
to which their resources are subjected in times of crisis; they know
the state of panic which is produced as their reserve is seen to
dwindle down towards a miserable million, and yet time after time
they have permitted the Bank to drift into a crisis utterly unprovided
against exigencies which stare them in the face. A commercial crisis
overtakes them with no more—perhaps less—than their usual reserve
of one-third of their liabilities. Beyond raising the rate of discount
they stir no finger to maintain or increase their resources. They
want notes. They cannot obtain them by the sale of English Government securities, for in a crisis there is generally no buyer of such
securities, certainly no large buyer. They can have notes in
exchange for bullion. They import no bullion, for they hold no
foreign securities to give them the command of bullion in the
European markets. Nay, more, they continue to trade with their
deposits, which may be withdrawn from them at any moment.
They drift towards the abyss of suspension with the happy con-
sciousness that Government will interfere at the supreme moment,
to avert, in the interests of the country, the consequences of their
mismanagement.

Would not the management of any other joint stock bank
be condemned if, when a crisis came, it was unable to carry
on its business without the assistance of a loan from Government? Why, then, should the Bank of England be exonerated
by State intervention from the natural results of its own mismanagement? Is there anything exceptional about the Bank
which should render it exempt from the duty common to all bankers
of maintaining at all times ample provision for the claims which are
likely to be made upon it? On the contrary, does not its position as the leading bank of the kingdom, the banker of the State,
the bank of the bankers, tend only to render in its case that duty
all the more imperative?

The Bullion Reserve must be Augmented.

But it will be said, What would you have the Bank to do?

When a crisis is imminent it cannot restrict its advances; it must deal liberally with its customers and the public, or panic would be precipitated, and unless its advances are to be restricted the reserve must dwindle to a dangerously low point. How is this to be avoided? I reply, that the very occurrence of exhaustion proves that the reserve which becomes so rapidly spent by the strain of the crisis must have been inadequate at the outset. Since, then, the customary minimum reserve of one-third is found insufficient, why cannot the Bank habitually maintain a much larger reserve—say equal to one-half of its liabilities, and when it falls below that proportion raise the rate, and, if needful, import gold, so as to readjust the balance?

If the Bank could work habitually with a very much larger reserve, steadily maintained by means of the rate of discount, and when necessary by the importation of gold through the realisation of foreign securities, the frequency and intensity of the fluctuations in the official rate would be diminished, and the Bank would be enabled to support the banking and mercantile interests in times of pressure at least as freely as heretofore, without that exhaustion of its resources which has on past occasions superinduced monetary panic on commercial distrust.

It will at once, however, be perceived that this policy would involve a great sacrifice of profit on the part of the Bank.

The Bank is a joint stock trading company, and it is the duty of its directors to secure the best possible dividends for their shareholders. The habitual maintenance of even so small an additional bullion reserve as 5,000,000l. would diminish the dividend by about 1½ per cent. per annum. The directors may very naturally shrink from a policy which would entail such results.

The private interests of the Bank as a dividend-earning company are thus antagonistic to its supposed public duties as the custodian of the ultimate bullion reserve of the country. The directors are in the equivocal position of having to serve two masters—the public, who cry for reserves; the shareholders, who call for dividends.

The Leading London Banks should keep their own Legal-Tender Reserves.

If the directors of the Bank of England, out of a natural and excusable regard for the dividends of their shareholders, persistently decline or omit to keep an adequate bullion reserve, it is quite clear that the instinct of self-preservation should compel those chiefly interested in the maintenance of banking credit to take the duty into their own hands.

The leading London joint stock and private banks are the

parties who are primarily imperilled by the maintenance of an inadequate bullion reserve. They habitually keep their reserve balances with the Bank of England. They do so only as a matter of convenience. They get no interest for these balances. If they were to withdraw them and hold them in notes or bullion in their own vaults, the Bank of England would lose, say 8,000,000l. of its deposits and 8,000,000l. of its reserve. This, at 8th December, 1875, would alter the position of the account as follows:—

Banking Department.		[000's omitted.]	
	£	£	£
Liabilities	26,025,	− 8,000,	= 18,025,
Reserve	10,795,	− 8,000,	= 2,795,
Proportion of reserve to liabilities 41½ per cent.		15½ per cent.	

leaving the Bank with less than 3,000,000l. of bullion wherewith to supply its tills and satisfy all demands for additional accommodation.

This course would probably compel the Bank of England to add to its reserve at least 4 millions, thus securing a total bullion reserve in London of 15,000,000l. instead of 11,000,000l., which would be a very important step in the right direction.

It will not surely be urged that the large London banks, joint stock and private, would not like to cut themselves adrift from the Bank of England, as they might require support from that institution at a time of panic. I should be very sorry to hear such a plea of weakness put forth. These banks are, several of them, much larger daily lenders in the market than the Bank of England, and in the aggregate their transactions and their liabilities greatly exceed those of the banking department in Threadneedle Street. If these large institutions, the depositaries of 150 millions of money, the London agents of scores of country banks, are to conduct their business with an *arrière pensée* of reliance on the Bank of England, I have no hesitation in saying that they are unworthy of the confidence which they enjoy.

It cannot be too strongly insisted upon, it cannot be too urgently repeated, that we have now to deal with a set of circumstances entirely different from those of 1844. The tables of this inquiry show the stupendous growth of deposit banking, and consequently of banking liabilities, since that date. Can those who are responsible for the maintenance of our banking, and, I may add, our international credit, calmly contemplate, nay glory in that growth, and yet shut their eyes to its fearful peril when they know that it is unaccompanied by any appreciable growth of the bullion reserve upon which it is based?

The danger must be firmly and honestly faced if we are to hope at all for a timely remedy. The subject is no longer confined to the region of speculation. It is eminently and intensely practical, and urgently demands the prompt and earnest attention of practical men. It was prominently brought forward by Mr. Palgrave in his " Notes on Banking " and his " Analysis of the Transactions of the " Bank of England." It was mooted by B, an eminent authority, in the "Economist," on 5th December, 1874, and again on 15th January, 1876; but no action has as yet ensued. It is to be hoped that the leading London banks, joint stock and private, will rouse themselves to grapple with the question ere it be too late. It is to be hoped that setting aside all private and conflicting interests, they will meet and discuss it, and come /to the determined resolution to secure at all hazards and in the face of all obstacles, an adequate bullion reserve for the gigantic banking liabilities of the country. It is to be hoped that if the Bank of England declines, as it is probable it may, to bear the burden, they will resolve to undertake it themselves. I venture to think that if they took the initiative they might rely upon the co-operation of the country banks, who next to themselves are most vitally interested in the matter.

After all it may fairly be urged that the banking fraternity which reaps large profits from its enormously extended liability for money lodged, should not in justice seek to shunt upon the Bank of England the cost and the responsibility of keeping the bullion reserve which is necessary to sustain that liability.

The vastly altered circumstances of these present times drive us irresistibly to the conclusion that the artificial one-reserve system which was possible, and might be safe, when banking liabilities were but a fraction of what they are now, and when the Bank of England was a triton amongst minnows, has ceased to be any longer either safe or possible. It should be remembered that the one-reserve system is neither a condition nor a corollary of the Act of 1844. Engendered by the old monopoly of the Bank of England, it has survived its ill-omened sire by half a century; but its days are surely numbered. The free bullion reserve which safety demands should now be kept in this country cannot be placed at a less sum than 25,000,000*l.*, which indeed would be equivalent to only 4 per cent. of the banking liabilities ultimately resting upon it. This will be admitted to be a burden far too heavy to be borne by the Bank of England or by any other individual banking company. The artificial one-reserve system is thus in fact an anachronism, and must now give place to the natural system of a plurality of reserves, each leading bank bearing its fair share.

But it will be asked what guarantee should we then have that the necessary aggregate reserve would be maintained ? What is every body's business is nobody's business. By relieving the Bank of England from a duty which it now partially acknowledges and

partially fulfils, we should lose a certainty which, however inadequate, is still so far a certainty, and we should gain an uncertainty
which might as likely as not prove when put to the test, equally if
not more inadequate. Here then legislation must step in. Parliament should require every bank to make a monthly return of its
average stock of legal tender at the close of each week. The publication of such a return should, with the aid of public opinion
and public criticism, secure the maintenance of a sufficient
bullion reserve, and it would effectually put a stop to the pernicious
practice which is said to prevail with some London joint stock
banks, of accumulating large cash reserves at the close of each
half-year, for the purpose of parading in their balance sheets a
show of strength which they do not normally maintain. It should
also be considered whether every bank, joint stock or private,
should not be required by law to make a periodical return for
publication of the amount of its liabilities to the public.

All this, and it is much, could be done without any alteration of
the Bank Act; but the leading banks which shared with the Bank
of England the burden of bearing the bullion reserve, would of right
claim a voice in fixing the official rate of discount, which is the
regulator of the reserve.

Possible Legislation.

Many people consider, however, that no material change for the
better can be made without an alteration of the Bank Act.

It has been proposed by some that the separation of the issue
department from the banking department, decreed in 1844, should
be repealed, and that no portion of the bullion held by the Bank
should be specially set apart to secure the note; that, in fact, the
status quo ante 1844, should be reverted to. This, I understand,
is the course advocated by Mr. Newmarch, who strongly insists
that exclusive protection of the note holder is only attainable
by *pro tanto* damaging the depositor. There is no authority
in the country whose opinion on such matters is entitled to greater
respect than Mr. Newmarch, and it is therefore with great diffi-
dence that I venture to differ from him. If the Bank of England
note were not legal tender his position would be unassailable; but
the State, in 1833, decreed the Bank of England note to be legal
tender. By thus making it imperative upon the creditor to accept
that note in payment of his debt, the law virtually invested it
with the national guarantee. It accordingly became needful to
provide a more tangible safeguard for its absolute convertibility
than the mere prudence of a board of fallible directors. The
Bank of England had allowed its stock of bullion to dwindle in
1825 to the dangerously low figure of 1,000,000*l.*, and again in

K 2

1839 to 2,400,000*l.*, as against liabilities in circulation and deposits to the amount of about 25,000,000*l.* ; and it is quite clear that a run for payment of notes, even to a very moderate extent, would in these circumstances have caused the Bank to suspend payments and its notes to be discredited. The prime merit of the Act of 1844 is that it provides effectually for the maintenance of the convertibility of the legal tender note.

We cannot now afford to dispense with a legal tender note. We cannot face the possibility of having to return to the use of coin for large payments whenever it may suit the whim of a creditor to decline payment in any other shape. We must also have the convertibility of the legal tender note absolutely secured, and therefore we cannot, I think, return to the *status quo ante* 1844.

It has been contended by some that the suspension in times of pressure of the restrictive clause of the Bank Act should be legally provided for under certain prescribed conditions. In 1873 Mr. Lowe, then Chancellor of the Exchequer, proposed the following provisions in his " Bank of England Notes Bill : "—" Whenever " the First Lord of Her Majesty's Treasury and the Chancellor of " the Exchequer, after communicating with the Governor and " Deputy-Governor of the Bank of England, are satisfied : (1) That " the minimum rate of interest then being charged by the Governor " and Company of the Bank of England on discounts and tem- " porary advances is not less than 12 per cent. per annum ; " and (2) That the foreign exchanges are favourable to this " country ; and (3) That a large portion of the existing amount of " Bank of England and other bank notes in circulation is rendered " ineffective for its ordinary purpose by reason of internal panic ; " they may, by order under their hands, empower the issue depart- " ment of the Bank of England to make, in excess of the authorised " issue, a special and temporary issue of Bank of England notes by " delivering the same into the banking department in exchange for " and on the credit of an equal amount of Government securities " to be transferred to the issue department." As the Bill was withdrawn it is unnecessary now to criticise the conditions of suspension which it imposed. It is sufficient to state that any suspensory power, whether exercised as heretofore at the sole discretion of the Government, or prospectively legalised by Act of Parliament, can be viewed in no other light than as an empirical and delusive remedy for the defects of the existing system. It

" Will but skin and film the ulcerous place,
Whiles rank corruption, mining all within,
Infects unseen."

It, in fact, offers a premium to that spirit of improvidence which is the great vice of our financial system. Everybody, from the Bank of England downwards, is tempted to speculate on the

suspensory power coming into operation to relieve them from the
effects of their own improvidence; and those banks and merchants
who, in the face of the temptation have, at a heavy cost, persistently maintained adequate reserves over a period of years find,
when the pressure comes at last, that the suspensory power deprives
them of the legitimate fruits of their self-denying forethought and
enables their less provident neighbours to ride through the storm
as securely as themselves. Again, the suspensory power must
always be unjust in its incidence. If it come into operation to-day
it will save the merchant or banker whose bills fall due to-morrow;
while the unfortunate individual, no less worthy of assistance,
whose bills fell due yesterday has been compelled to succumb.

Proposed State Department of Issue.

Probably the best, if not the only practicable, legislative
solution of the pressing difficulty would be the transference of the
issue department to Government, coupled with a provision for a
monthly return of the average stock of legal tender held weekly by
each bank.

Under this arrangement the State Department of Issue would hold
securities for 15,000,000l., and gold coin and bullion for the excess
of issue beyond that sum. It might also with advantage act as a
bank of deposit receiving from the bankers sums in notes or gold of
not less than say 100,000l. at any one time, and inscribing these to
their credit, to be drawn out also in sums of not less than 100,000l.
at any one time. The securities and bullion would thus always
equal the sum of the notes in circulation and the bankers' balances.

Accounts might be published weekly in some such form as
this :—

	£		£
Notes issued	30,000,000	Securities	15,000,000
Bankers' balances	10,000,000	Gold coin and bullion.	25,000,000
	40,000,000		40,000,000

When notes were paid in, either an equivalent of coin or bullion
would be taken out, or an equivalent increase would be made to the
bankers' balances. When gold was paid in, either notes would be
issued for the amount, or the sum would be added to the bankers'
balances. When gold was taken out, either the notes issued or the
bankers' balances would be correspondingly diminished.

This would involve no interference with the principle of the Act
of 1844, and would effectually cause the Bank of England, and all
other leading banks to rely upon their own reserves, without resting
upon that hope of assistance from the State in a period of pressure
which, already three times realised, constitutes in a great measure
the vice and perpetuates the weakness of the present system.

The result would be that in the aggregate a much larger bullion reserve would be held, and the duty of supporting banking and general credit by liberal advances in time of crisis, instead of being concentrated as hitherto upon one institution with an inadequate reserve, would be distributed amongst several large institutions each holding a substantial reserve.

The official rate of discount might from time to time be fixed by a committee of the clearing banks, under the presidency of the governor of the Bank of England, as suggested by " B " in his recent letter to the " Economist."

If it be contended that this scheme would be most uneconomical of capital, it may be replied that is its very merit. We are now suffering the serious inconveniences and incurring the grave dangers of a system in which economy of capital is carried to a point far beyond the limits of prudence. The loss of interest involved in the alteration of that system to one of ampler reserves will count as nothing compared with the advantage of placing the enormous financial and banking engagements of this great commercial country upon a thoroughly sound and adequate basis of bullion.

Here, however, it should be observed that the largest possible bullion reserves will avail nothing if credit be stretched beyond its proper limits. This is a matter that bankers have pretty much in their own hands. They are the chief administrators of credit. Truly it is a grave trust, but it is satisfactory to know that their own best interests lie in its steadfast fulfilment.

An authority so eminent as Mr. Bagehot having declared emphatically against the transference of the issue department to the State, it is necessary to inquire into the grounds of his objection. These are embodied as follows in his evidence before the Committee on Banks of Issue, 1875 :—" I think that in time of " panic, if a State issue was the sole legal tender, there might be " extreme and very dangerous pressure on the Government to lend " money to persons to whom it ought not to be lent." "At present " the loans are made by the Bank of England in time of panic, and " the Bank of England knows how to manage, because it is a " trader in the market ; but if the Government once began to lend, " I do not know whether it would have the same discretion. I am " quite sure it would never be thought to be equally impartial, " because the Prime Minister or the Chancellor of the Exchequer " might be member for a great commercial community, for London " or Liverpool, and the public would never believe that his con- " stituents did not get a benefit. For these reasons, under a Parlia- " mentary Government like ours, I think a State issue would be " exceedingly dangerous."

Mr. Bagehot's objection is based on the assumption that Government would be called upon to lend notes, and would lend notes, in a

time of panic; but surely that is a groundless assumption. Is Government called upon to make advances, and does Government make advances in gold because the Mint is a department of the State? Certainly not. And the functions of a State department of issue would necessarily be as purely mechanical as those of the Mint. Under existing circumstances, pressure is put on the Bank of England for loans in a time of panic, because it is a lending bank as well as the source of legal-tender issue. The combination of these two functions in the Bank is in fact one of the prime causes of the unsatisfactory operation of the existing system. If these functions were completely dissevered by the transference of the purely mechanical issue department to the State, the Bank of England and all other banks would be constrained, as I have indicated, to rely, in a time of pressure, upon their own reserves, and not upon any empirical and temporary addition to the legal-tender issues of the State.

Very probably some of the suggestions which I have hazarded may be considered crude and impracticable. Perhaps they are; but they are thrown out in the conviction that the subject urgently demands investigation and discussion in all its bearings.

That a question so momentous should continue year after year to be shirked, as it has been, is scarcely creditable to the vaunted prudence of bankers, to the discernment of Her Majesty's advisers, or to the wisdom of Parliament, and it will be well for the country if it be not some day rudely awakened from its ignorant indifference to the subject by a commercial and banking collapse totally unparalleled by any previous experience.

Precautions suggested for Present Adoption.

Parliamentary inquiry will no doubt come, but legislation will linger, and meanwhile it seems to be before all needful that instead of looking to and leaning upon the Bank of England, no longer *primus inter pares*, those who in the centre of our national and international finance are the most deeply interested in the permanent maintenance of banking credit should themselves hold the command of such supplies of bullion as may suffice to stem the rising tide of distrust on the first symptoms of danger. The means thereto are plain. Let the great London banks hold, besides their reserves of bullion in their own vaults and their securities immediately convertible in the London market, such funds in readily available shape, money at call, short bills, saleable securities, in the chief money markets of Europe, as shall ensure by their realisation a free and immediate flow to London of that bullion which is so needful when "distrust asleep," as credit has been well styled, threatens to awake and put on the fearful aspect of panic.

TABLE LVIII.—*Purely Provincial English Joint Stock*

[000's omitted in columns

Number.	Purely Provincial Banks. [Banks of Issue in *Italics*.]	1 When Established.	2 Date of Balance, 1873.	3 Subscribed Capital.	4 Uncalled Capital.	5	6
						Liabilities.	
						Paid-up Capital.	Reserve, including Balance of Profit Carried Forward.
				£	£	£	£
1	*Carlisle and Cumberland Bank* ...	1836	Dec.	300,	225,	75,	102,
2	*Cumbld. Union Bkg. Co., Limd.*....	'29	„	540,	315,	225,	78,
3	*Carlisle City and District Bank*....	'37	,,	160,	80,	80,	86,
4	*Bank of Whitehaven, Limited*	'37	,,	220,	146,	74,	42,
5	Adelphi Bank, Limited	1861	Dec.	260,	130,	130,	2,
6 {	Liverpool Commercial Banking Company, Limited.................	'32	,,	700,	350,	350,	204,
7	Liverpool Union Bank	'35	,,	600,	75,	525,	210,
8 {	National Bank of Liverpool, Limited	'63	,,	750,	300,	450,	77,
9	North-Western Bank, Limited	'64	,,	1,080,	675,	405,	92,
10	*North and South Wales Bank*	'36	June	300,	—	300,	170,
11	Parr's Banking Company, Limited	1865	Dec.	1,000,	850,	150,	46,
12 {	Manchester and County Bank, Limited	'62	,,	4,400,	3,740,	660,	321,
13 {	Union Bank of Manchester, Limited	'36	June	947,	531,	417,	107,
14 {	Lancashire and Yorkshire Bank, Limited	'72	Dec.	485,	243,	243,	29,
15	*Bradford Banking Company*	1827	Dec.	550,	330,	220,	260,
16	„ Commercial J. S. Bk....	'33	,,	680,	510,	170,	126,
17	Bradford District Bank, Limited	'62	,,	650,	455,	195,	103,
18	„ Old Bank, Limited	'64	,,	983,	590,	393,	136,
19	Bank of Leeds, Limited	'64	·,,	605,	454,	151,	37,
20	Yorkshire Banking Company	'43	,,*	500,	250,	250,	121,
21	Sheffield Banking Company	'31	,,	419,	126,	293,	104,
22	*Sheffield and Hallamshire Bank*...	'36	June	733,	550,	183,	55,
23	„ *Rotherham* „	'36	Dec.	502,	341,	161,	85,
24	Sheffield Union Banking Company	'43	June	250,	100,	150,	38,
25	*Burton, Uttoxeter, &c., Union Bank*	1839	Dec.	260,	130,	130,	68,
26	Nottingham J. S. Bank, Limited...	'65	,,	470,	376,	94,	29,
27	*Stamford, Spalding, &c., Bkg. Co.*	'32	,,	200,	—	200,	104,
28	Leicestershire Banking Company..	'29	,,	750,	525,	225,	87,

* Including bills

Banks. *Balance Sheets of Forty-Four Banks,* 1873.

headed £, thus 300 = 300,000*l.*]

7	8	9	10	11	12	13	14	15	
Liabilities.			Assets.						
Money Lodged, including Dividend Due.	Circulation of Notes.	Acceptances.	Total Resources.	Bills and Advances.	Government and other Securities.	Cash, &c.	Property Account.	Authorised Issue.	Number.
£	£	£	£	£	£	£	£	£	
558,	—	—	735,	—	727,	—	8,	25,610	1
1,791,	34,	—	2,128,	1,534,	65,	489,	39,	35,395	2
703,	—	—	869,	—	864,	—	5,	19,972	3
626,	28,	—	770,	628,	62,	73,	8,	32,681	4
178,	—	—	310,	258,	—	31,	22,	—	5
1,209,	—	—	1,763,	1,438,	—	175,	150,	—	6
2,895,	—	601,	4,231,	3,264,	—	930,	36,	—	7
740,	—	41,	1,309,	918,	—	366,	25,	—	8
950,	—	350,*	1,797,	1,644,	—	120,	32,	—	9
3,286,	59,	108,	3,924,	2,910,	1,014,		—	63,951	10
1,972,	—	—	2,168,	1,285,	101,	771,	12,	—	11
6,378,	—	—	6,359,	—	6,326,	—	33,	—	12
1,300,	—	47,	1,871,	1,550,	—	298,	28,	—	13
499,	—	—	770,	609.	—	160,	1,	—	14
1,668,	50,	—	4,198,	—	4,193,	—	5,	49,292	15
512,		—	808,	—	794,	—	14,	30,084	16
574,	—	—	871,	—	857,	—	4,	—	17
1,141,	—	—	1,669,	—	1,649,	—	20,	—	18
361,	—	58,	608,	539,	—	59,	10,	—	19
2,262,	119,	—	2,751,	—	2,703,	—	48,	122,532	20
1,596,	—	—	1,994,	—	1,972,	—	22,	85,843	21
567,	—	—	805,	—	800,	—	5,	23,524	22
1,562,	—	—	1,807,	—	1,793,	—	15,	52,496	23
359,	—	—	547,	—	543,	—	5,	—	24
1,289,	—	—	1,487,	—	1,466,	—	21,	60,701	25
558,	—	—	681,	—	670,	—	10,	—	26
1,100,	53,	—	1,457,	858,	301,	278,	20,	55,721	27
1,282,	64,	—	1,659,	1,185,	265,	244,	15,	86,060	28

rediscounted 214,823*l.*

TABLE LVIII.—*Purely Provincial English Joint Stock*

[000's omitted in columns

		1	2	3	4	5	6
							Liabilities.
Number.	Purely Provincial Banks. [Banks of Issue in *Italics*.]	When Established.	Date of Balance, 1873.	Subscribed Capital.	Uncalled Capital.	Paid-up Capital.	Reserve, including Balance of Profit Carried Forward.
				£	£	£	£
29	Staffordshire J. S. Bank, Limited..	1864	Dec.	874,	700,	174,	55,
30	*County of Stafford Bank*	'36	,,	120,	60,	60,	32,
31	Lloyd's Banking Company, Limited	'65	,,	2,030,	1,726,	305,	128,
32	Birmingham J. S. Bank ,,	'61	,,	2,039,	1,835,	204,	215,
33	,, Banking Co. ,,	'66	June	1,491,	1,342,	149,	106,
34	,, Town and District...	'36	,,	400,	240,	160,	49,
35	Dudley and W. Bromwich B. Co..	'33	Dec.	426,	341,	85,	6,
36	*Wolverhptn. & Staffdsh. B. Co.*	'32	,,	500,	400,	100,	36,
37	*Worcester City and Coty., Limtd.*	1840	Dec.	1,000,	750,	250,	105,
38	Bucks and Oxon Union B., Lmtd.	'66	,,	400,	320,	80,	16,
39	*W. of Engld. & S. Wales. Dist. B.*	'34	,,	1,000,	250,	750,	129,
40	Devon and Cornwall Banking Co.	'32	,,	400,	272,	128,	80,
41	Three Towns' Banking Co., Limited	'63	,,	100,	50,	50,	1,
42	*Wilts and Dorset Banking Co.* ...	'35	,,	375,	125,	250,	155,
43	Hampshire Banking Company	'34	,,	—	—	150,	41,
44	North Kent Bank, Limited	'64	,,	65,	43,	22,	1,

* Including cash

TABLE LIX.—*London and Provincial Joint*

[000's omitted in columns

		1	2	3	4	5	6
							Liabilities.
Number.	Purely Provincial Banks.	When Established.	Date of Balance, 1873.	Subscribed Capital.	Uncalled Capital.	Paid-up Capital.	Reserve, including Balance of Profit Carried Forward.
				£	£	£	£
1	National Provincial Bank of England .... CAPITAL. 10,000 shares at 100*l.* = 1,000,000*l.* 77,500 ,, 20*l.* = 1,550,000*l.*	1833	Dec.	2,550,	1,200,	1,350,	650,
2	London and County Bank	'36	,,	3,000,	1,800,	1,200,	624,
3	Midland Banking Co., Limited	1868	Dec.	1,500,	1,200,	300,	49,
4	London and South-Western Bank, Limited	'62	,,	831,	665,	166,	11,
5	London and Provincial Bank, Limited	'64	,,	254,	127,	127,	17,
6	London and Yorkshire Bank, Limited	'72	,,	674,	576,	98,	1,
	Totals	—	—	8,809	5,568	3,241	1,352

of Forty-Four Banks—Contd.

]

10	11	· 12	13	14	15	
		Assets.				
Total Resources.	Bills and Advances.	Government and other Securities.	Cash, &c.	Property Account.	Authorised Issue.	Number.
£	£	£	£	£		
867,	739,	28,	96,	5,	—	29
499,	368,	35,	88,	8,	9,418	30
4,671,	3,770,	—	852,	49,	—	31
1,985,	1,598,	235,	138,	19,	—	32
1,320,	1,080,	55,	160,	24,	—	33
1,017,	847,	45,	106,	19,	—	34
1,100,	976,*	117,	—	7,	37,696	35
855,	827,	—	24,	4,	35,378	36
1,367,	1,140,	54,	144,	28,	6,848	37
713,	—	701,	—	12,		38
5,088,	4,040,	507,	452,	88,	83,535	39
1,847,		1,847,			—	40
96,	87,		4,	5,		41
3,162,	1,471,	1,272,	378,	40,	76,162	42
2,041,	1,300,	331,	374,	35,	—	43
106,	90,	—	14,	2,	—	44

Sheets for Year 1873.

)00l.]

9	10	11	12	13	14	
		Assets.				
cept-ces.	Total Resources.	Bills and Advances.	Government and other Securities.	Cash, &c.	Property Account.	Number.
£	£	£	£	£	£	
547,	24,496,	14,569,	5,215,	4,299,	413,	1
970,	24,142,	16,835,	1,817,	5,209,	281,	2
—	1,766,	1,575,	—	168,	22,	3
36,	1,021,	799,	—	199,	23,	4
—	1,196,	700,	227,	247,	21,	5
—	349,	304,	—	81,	14,	6
353,	52,970,	34,782,	7,259,	10,153,	774,	

TABLE LX.— *Analysis of Balance Sheets of Forty-Four*

[00's omitted in Cols. 1 and 3, thus 19,2 = 19,200*l*.]

Number.	Purely Provincial Banks. [Banks of Issue in *Italics*.]	1 Net Profit, less Charges	2 Ratio per Cent. per Annum of Net Profits to Total Resources.	3 Charges.	4 Ratio per Cent. of Charges to Net Profits.	5 Ratio per Cent per Annum of Charges to Liabilities to Public.	6 Number of Branches.
		£	Per cnt.	£	Per cnt.	Per cnt.	No.
1	*Carlisle and Cumberland Bank*	19,2	2·62	—	—	—	5
2	*Cumbld. Union Bkg. Co., Limd.*.....	44,6	2·10	14,2	31·81	0·77	12
3	*Carlisle City and District Bank*...	21,4	2·46	—	—	—	4
4	*Bank of Whitehaven, Limited*	18,1	2·35	8,7	20·58	0·56	3
5	Adelphi Bank, Limited	4,2*	2·70	2,9*	69·04	3·24	1
6 {	Liverpool Commercial Banking Company, Limited................ }	44,1	2·50	—	—	—	—
7	Liverpool Union Bank	74,8	1·76	—	—	—	—
8 {	National Bank of Liverpool, Limited .... }	13,3*	2·03	—	—	—	1
9	North-Western Bank, Limited ...	40,3	2·25	—	—	—	—
10	*North and South Wales Bank*	70,3	1·79	33,7	47·95	0·97	27
11	Parr's Banking Company, Limited	42,7	1·97	15,9	37·19	0·80	9
12 {	Manchester and County Bank, Limited .... }	66,0*	2·08	17,5*	26·53	0·64	17
13 {	Union Bank of Manchester, Limited .... }	52,0	2·78	19,7	37·99	1·46	12
14 {	Lancashire and Yorkshire Bank, Limited .... }	8,3*	2·15	4,3*	51·81	1·72	4
15	*Bradford Banking Company*	67,9	3·09	—	—	—	—
16	,, *Commercial J. S. Bk.*	34,9	4·32	—	—	—	—
17	Bradford District Bank, Limited....	15,6*	3·58	3,5*	22·15	1·22	1
18	,, Old Bank, Limited	28,7	3·44	—	—	—	2
19	Bank of Leeds, Limited	15,1	2·48	3,2	20·93	1·52	—
20	Yorkshire Banking Company	43,5*	3·16	—	—	—	14
21	Sheffield Banking Company............	58,4	2·92	—	—	—	3
22	*Sheffield and Hallamshire Bank*....	26,4	3·28	—	—	—	—
23	,, ,, *Rotherham* ,, ...	37,5	2·07	—	—	—	4
24	Sheffield Union Banking Company	20,4	3·73	—	—	—	2
25	*Burton, Uttoxeter, &c., Union Bank*	14,3*	1·92	—	—	—	2
26	Nottingham J. S. Bank, Limited....	13,7	2·02	4,7	33·94	0·84	4
27	*Stamford, Spalding, &c., Bkg. Co.*	29,6	2·03	—	—	—	9
28	*Leicestershire Banking Company*	36,1	2·18	—	—	—	8
29	Staffordshire J. S. Bank, Limited...	22,4	2·58	—	—	—	7
30	*County of Stafford Bank*..............	13,4	2·68	—	—	—	—
31	Lloyd's Banking Company, Limited	79,8	1·71	—	—	—	14
32	Birmingham J. S. Bank, Limited....	49,4	2·49	—	—	—	1
33	,, Banking Co., Limited	25,4	1·93	—	—	—	—

* For half

Purely Provincial English Joint Stock Banks, 1873.

[000's omitted in Cols. 8, 9, 10, and 13.]

7	8	9	10	11	12	13	14	
Number of Sub-Branches.	Average Liabilities to Public at each Office, ex Subs.	Liabilities to Public.	Proprietors' Funds.	Ratio per Cent. of Proprietors' Funds to Liabilities to the Public.	Ratio per Cent. of Uncalled Capital to Liabilities to Public.	Government Securities, Cash, &c.	Ratio per Cent. of Government Securities, Cash, &c., to Liabilities to Public.	Number.
No.	£	£	£	Per cnt.	Per cnt.	£	Per cnt.	
—	93,	558,	177,	31·62	40·29	—	—	1
4	140,	1,825,	303,	16·61	17·26	554,	30·38	2
—	140,	703,	166,	23·66	11·40	—	—	3
—	164,	655,	116,	17·57	22·35	135,	20·48	4
—	89,	178,	132,	73·89	72·88	31,	17·27	5
—	1,209,	1,209,	554,	45·85	28·96	175,	14·47	} 6
—	3,496,	3,496,	735,	21·02	2·14	930,	26·61	7
—	391,	782,	527,	67·44	38·38	366,	46· 2	} 8
—	1,300,	1,300,	497,	38·20	51·91	120,	9·26	9
5	123,	3,454,	470,	13·61	—	1,014,	29·36	10
5	197,	1,972,	196,	9·93	43·09	872,	44·20	11
7	299,	5,878,	981,	18·24	69·54	—	—	} 12
4	104,	1,347,	524,	38·88	39·39	293,	21·72	} 13
1	100,	499,	271,	54·45	48·65	160,	32·09	} 14
—	1,218,	1,718,	480,	27·92	19·21	—	—	15
—	512,	512,	296,	57·82	99·55	—	—	16
—	287,	574,	298,	51·86	79·29	—	—	17
—	380,	1,141,	529,	46·35	51·69	—	—	18
—	419,	419,	189,	45·02	108·25	59,	14·11	19
7	159,	2,380,	371,	15·58	10·50	—	—	20
—	399,	1,596,	397,	24·90	7·87	—	—	21
—	567,	567,	238,	42·02	97·00	—	—	22
—	312,	1,562,	246,	15·72	21·87	—	—	23
—	120,	359,	188,	52·29	27·82	—	—	24
—	430,	1,289,	198,	15·36	10·09	—	—	25
—	111,	558,	123,	22·05	67·48	—	—	26
9	115,	1,153,	304,	26·39	—	579,	50·19	27
2	152,	1,347,	312,	23·17	38·99	509,	37·79	28
—	80,	638,	229,	35·88	109·72	123,	19·35	29
—	406,	406,	92,	22·76	14·77	122,	30·14	30
9	282,	4,238,	433,	10·22	40·73	852,	20·10	31
—	783,	1,567,	419,	26·72	117·16	372,	23·77	32
—	1,064,	1,064,	255,	23·97	12·61	215,	20·22	33

year only.

TABLE LX.—*Analysis of Balance Sheets of Forty-Four*

[00's omitted in Cols. 1 and 3, thus 19,2 = 19,200*l.*]

Num'er.	Purely Provincial Banks. [Banks of Issue in *Italics.*]	1 Net Profit, less Charges.	2 Ratio per Cent. per Annum of Net Profits to Total Resources.	3 Charges.	4 Ratio per Cent. of Charges to Net Profits.	5 Ratio per Cent. per Annum of Charges to Liabilities to Public.	6 Number of Branches.
		£	Per cnt.	£	Per cnt.	Per cnt.	No.
34	Birmingham Town and District	24,2	2·38	—	—	—	—
35	Dudley and W. Bromwich B. Co....	5,7	0·52	—	—	—	4
36	*Wolverhptn. & Staffdsh. B. Co.*	14,0	1·64	—	—	—	—
37	*Worcester City and Coty., Limtd.*.	20,7*+	3·03	9,8*	47·12	1·93	9
38	Bucks and Oxon Union B., Limtd.	18,0	2·52	—	—	—	8
39	*W. of Engld. & S. Wales Dist. B.*	118,4	2·33	51,8	43·73	1·23	37
40	Devon and Cornwall Banking Co.	27,4	1·48	—	—	—	14
41	Three Towns' Banking Co.,Limited	2,6	2·71	1,7	65·39	3·77	—
42	*Wilts and Dorset Banking Co.*	55,5	1·75	29,9	53·94	1·08	41
43	Hampshire Banking Company	15,1*	1·48	14,5*	96·02	1·56	24
44	North Kent Bank, Limited............	9*	1·63	—	—	—	1

* For half year only.

TABLE LXI.—*London and Provincial Joint Stock*

[00's omitted in Cols. 1 and 3, thus 397,1 = 397,100*l.*]

Number.	Purely Provincial Banks.	1 Net Profit, less Charges.	2 Ratio per Cent. per Annum of Net Profits to Total Resources.	3 Charges.	4 Ratio per Cent. of Charges to Net Profits.	5 Ratio per Cent. per Annum of Charges to Liabilities to Public.	6 Number of Branches.
		£	Per cnt.	£	Per cnt.	Per cnt.	No.
1	National Provincial Bank of England..................... CAPITAL. 10,000 shares at 100*l.* = 1,000,000*l.* 77,500 „ 20*l.* = 1,550,000*l.*	397,1	1·62	—	—	—	134
2	London and County Bank	148,7*	1·23	117,9*	79·25	1·05	148
3	Midland Banking Co., Limited	16,0*	1·82	11,6*	72·35	1·63	21
4	London and South - Western Bank, Limited	8,1*	1·59	11,1*	136·88	2·63	23
5	London and Provincial Bank, Limited	10,8*	1·80	13,9*	—	2·64	46
6	London and Yorkshire Bank, Limited	3,1	0·89	7,6	245·16	3·03	7
	Totals	—	—	—	—	—	379

* For half

Purely Provincial English Joint Stock Banks—Contd.

[000's omitted in Cols. 8, 9, 10, and 13.]

7	8	9	10	11	12	13	14	
Number of Sub-Branches.	Average Liabilities to Public at each Office, ex Subs.	Liabilities to Public.	Proprietors' Funds.	Ratio per Cent. of Proprietors' Funds to Liabilities to the Public.	Ratio per Cent. of Uncalled Capital to Liabilities to Public.	Government Securities, Cash, &c.	Ratio per Cent. of Government Securities, Cash, &c., to Liabilities to Public.	Numb
No.	£	£	£	Per cnt.	Per cnt.	£	Per cnt.	
—	808,	808,	209,	25·85	29·71	150,	18·60	34
—	204,	1,009,	91,	9·01	33·76	—	—	35
—	719,	719,	136,	18·90	55·60	—	—	36
4	101,	1,012,	355,	35·11	74·13	199,	19·66	37
—	68,	617,	96,	15·56	51·86	—	—	38
4	111,	4,209,	879,	20·88	5·94	960,	22·81	39
—	109,	1,639,	208,	12·69	16·59	—	—	40
—	45,	45,	51,	112·42	110·85	4,	8·47	41
8	66,	2,757,	405,	14·54	4·53	1,651,	59·30	42
—	74,	1,849,	191,	10·34	—	705,	38·13	43
—	41,	82,	24,	29·04	52·37	14,	16·61	44

† Without deduction of rebate.

Banks. Analysis of Balance Sheets, 1873.

[000's omitted in Cols. 8, 9, 10, and 13.]

7	8	9	10	11	12	13	14	
Number of Sub-Branches.	Average Liabilities to Public at each Office, ex Subs.	Liabilities to Public.	Proprietors' Funds.	Ratio per Cent. of Proprietors' Funds to Liabilities to the Public.	Ratio per Cent. of Uncalled Capital to Liabilities to Public.	Government Securities, Cash, &c.	Ratio per Cent. of Government Securities, Cash, &c., to Liabilities to Public.	Numbe
No.	£	£	£	Per cnt.	Per cnt.	£	Per cnt.	
2	167,	22,496,	2,000,	8·88	5·33	9,514,	42·29	1
—	150,	22,318,	1,824,	8·16	8·06	7,026,	31·48	2
4	64,	1,416,	349,	24·66	84·76	168,	11·89	3
—	35,	814,	177,	20·95	78·76	199,	23·54	4
—	22,	1,052,	144,	13·66	12·06	474,	45·08	5
—	31,	250,	99,	39·53	230·33	31,	12·47	6
—	—	18,376,	4,593,	—	—	17,411,	—	

year only.

TABLE LXII.—*Dividends and Prices of Forty-Four Purely Provincial English Joint Stock Banks*, 1873.

Number.	Purely Provincial Banks. [Banks of Issue in *Italics*.]	1 Dividend per Cent. per Annum, including Bonus.	2 Amount per Share Paid.	3 Market Price, January, 1874.	4 Premium per Cent.	5 Yield per Cent. at Purchase Price. £	s.	d.
1	*Carlisle and Cumberland Bank*	22	5	19	280	5	15	9
2	*Cumbld. Union B. Co., Limd.*	16	12½	37½	200	5	6	8
3	*Carlisle City and District Bank*	22	12½	43½	248	6	6	5
4	*Bank of Whitehaven, Limited*	22½	10	38½	285	5	16	10
5	Adelphi Bank, Limited	Nil	10	7½	Dis.	—		
6	Liverpool Commercial Banking Company, Limited	11¼	10	17¾	77½	6	6	9
7	Liverpool Union Bank..................	10	17½	25½	45 5/7	6	17	3
8	National Bank of Liverpool, Limited	6⅜	15	14¼	Dis.	6	17	11
9	North-Western Bank, Limited	7	7½	8¾	16⅔	6	–	
10	*North and South Wales Bank*	17½	10	31	210	5	12	10
11	Parr's Banking Company, Limited	15	15	38	153⅓	5	18	5
12	Manchester and County Bank, Limited	13¾	15	42	180	4	18	2
13	Union Bank of Manchester, Limited	10¾	11	18¾	70 6/11	6	6	1
14	Lancashire and Yorkshire Bank, Limited	6	10	12	20	5	–	–
15	*Bradford Banking Company*	25	40	150	275	6	13	4
16	,, *Commercial J. S. Bk.*....	18	20	59	195	6	2	–
17	Bradford District Bank, Limited	8½	30	57½	91⅔	4	8	8
18	,, Old Bank, Limited	13¾	20	46	130	5	19	6
19	Bank of Leeds, Limited	7	25	32	28	5	9	4
20	Yorkshire Banking Company	22⅘	12½	49	292	5	16	3
21	Sheffield Banking Company	17	140	270	92 6/7	8	16	3
22	*Sheffield and Hallamshire Bank*....	14	25	47½	90	7	7	4
23	,, *and Rotherham* ,, ...	20	32	83	159⅜	7	14	2
24	Sheffield Union Banking Company	11¼	12	20½	76⅝	6	11	8
25	*Burton, Uttoxeter, &c., Union Bank*	17	10	26½	165	6	8	4
26	Nottingham J. S. Bank, Limited	8½	10	14	40	6	1	5
27	*Stamford, Spalding, &c., B. Co.*	16	20	64	220	5	–	–
28	*Leicestershire Banking Company*	13½	40	80	100	6	5	
29	Staffordshire J. S. Bank, Limited	8¾	20	23½	17½	7	8	11
30	*County of Stafford Bank*	18	5	15½	210	5	16	1
31	Lloyd's Banking Company, Limited	20	7½	21½	186⅔	6	19	6
32	Birmingham J. S. Bank, ,,	20	10	35	250	5	14	3
33	,, Banking Co., ,,	11¼	5	13	160	4	6	6
34	,, Town and District	10	8	13½	68¾	5	18	6
35	Dudley and W. Bromwich B. Co.	6¾	10	13	30	5	3	10
36	*Wolverhptn. and Staff'dsh. B. Co.*	10	10	16	60	6	5	–

TABLE LXII.—*Dividends and Prices of Forty-Four Purely Provincial English Joint Stock Banks—Contd.*

Number.	Purely Provincial Banks. [Banks of Issue in *Italics*.]	1 Dividend per Cent. per Annum, including Bonus.	2 Amount per Share Paid.	3 Market Price, January, 1874.	4 Premium per Cent.	5 Yield per Cent. at Purchase Price. £ s. d.
37	*Worcester City and County, Limd.*	12⅜	12½	21½	72	7 3 10
38	Bucks and Oxon Union, Limited	20	5	16½	230	6 1 2
39	*W. of Engld. and S. Wales Dist. B.*	14	15	30	100	7 – –
40	Devon and Cornwall Banking Co.	15⅝	32	74	131¼	6 15 1
41	Three Towns' Banking Co., Limited	5	25	—	—	—
42	*Wilts and Dorset Banking Co.*	22	10	49½	395	4 8 10
43	Hampshire Banking Company	13	10	—	—	—
44	North Kent Bank, Limited...........	8	10	par	—	8 – –

TABLE LXIII.—*London and Provincial Joint Stock Banks. Dividends and Prices,* 1873.

Number.	Purely Provincial Banks.	1 Dividend per Cent. per Annum, including Bonus.	2 Amount per Share Paid.	3 Market Price, January, 1874.	4 Premium per Cent.	5 Yield per Cent. at Purchase Price. £ s. d.
1	National Provincial Bank of of England .... CAPITAL. 10,000 shares at 100*l.* = 1,000,000*l.* 77,500 „ 20*l.* = 1,550,000*l.*	25	42	157½	275	6 13 4
2	London and County Bank	20	20	62	210	6 9 –
3	Midland Banking Co., Limited	9	20	26½	32½	6 15 10
4	London and South-Western Bank, Limited	6½	20	16½	Dis.	7 17 6
5	London and Provincial Bank, Limited	9½	5	7¾	55	6 2 6
6	London and Yorkshire Bank, Limited	4	7½	5½	Dis.	5 9 1
	Average	—	—	—	—	6 11 3

VII. NON-LEGAL-TENDER NOTE CIRCULATION.

Introduction.

The intrusion into Cumberland of branches of a Scotch bank, which occurred in February, 1874, has directed the attention of the public and of Parliament to the question of the non-legal-tender note issues. In 1875 Mr. Goschen introduced into the House of Commons a Bill, the object of which was to confine the banking operations of the Scotch banks to their own country, under the penalty of losing their privilege of issue in Scotland. This Bill was met at the instance of the Government by the appointment of a

Select Committee of the House " to consider and report upon the " restrictions imposed and the privileges conferred by law on " bankers authorised to make and issue notes in England, Scotland, " and Ireland respectively." This committee has examined twenty-six witnesses, whose evidence has been printed in a voluminous blue book, with a short report to the effect that the committee " have not had time to prepare a report in the present session, and " consequently recommend their reappointment next year."

Much controversy has thus been revived on the vexed but important question of note issues.

In order to the clear understanding of the case I propose to state :—

1. The statutory conditions of note issues in England, Scotland, and Ireland, and their effects.

2. The distribution and actual position of the note circulation in each of the three kingdoms.

3. The various lines of policy proposed.

4. The bearing of these lines of policy on the question of the intrusion of the Scotch banks into England.

Statutory Conditions of Non-Legal-Tender Note Issue in England and Wales, and their Operation.

The statutory conditions of note issue by banks in England and Wales other than the Bank of England are :—

1. By Act of 1826, 7 Geo. IV, cap. 6, notes under 5*l.* are prohibited.

2. By Act of 1826, 7 Geo. IV, cap. 46, which authorised the establishment of joint stock banks of issue, they are prohibited from having any house of business or establishment as bankers in or within sixty-five miles of London.

The remaining conditions are prescribed by the Act of 1844.

3. No bank not a bank of issue on 6th of May, 1844, shall make or issue bank notes in any part of the United Kingdom.

4. A bank ceasing to issue its notes may not resume.

5. Each bank must make a weekly return of the daily amount of its notes in circulation, showing the weekly average, and the return at the end of each fourth week must show the average for the four weeks, such average being the aggregate of the notes in circulation on every business day of the four weeks divided by the number of such business days.

6. No bank shall have in circulation upon an average of four weeks a greater amount of notes than the amount of its authorised issue, under the penalty of forfeiting a sum equal to the excess.

7. Private banks on amalgamation may retain the aggregate authorised issues of the separate banks, provided the number of

partners in the united bank do not exceed six. No joint stock bank can add to its authorised issue by amalgamation with any other bank of issue, joint stock or private; and the issues of banks which are absorbed by a joint stock bank are *eo ipso* forfeited. This provision places joint stock banks of issue at an unjust disadvantage with private banks of issue.

8. The Commissioners of Stamps and Taxes have power, with consent of the Treasury, to cause the books of banks containing accounts of their note circulation to be inspected, under a penalty of 100l. for every refusal to permit such inspection. This power has never, I believe, been exercised.

9. The Bank of England may arrange to allow any bank of issue a composition of 1 per cent. per annum on the amount of Bank of England notes which such bank may issue and keep in circulation, as a consideration to that bank for the relinquishment of its right of issue, such composition not exceeding 1 per cent. per annum on the amount of authorised circulation relinquished.

10. Her Majesty in Council may from time to time authorise the Bank of England to increase the amount of its issues against securities to the extent of not more than two-thirds of the lapsed issues of other banks. In virtue of this provision the issues of the Bank of England against securities have been successively increased from 14 millions in 1844, to 15 millions at the present time.

Several of these conditions were manifestly designed to promote the absorption of the country issues, and it will be instructive to trace how far they have operated in that direction.

The following table shows the number of banks of issue in England by the Act of 1844, with the amount of their authorised issue, the number and amount of issues lapsed, and the amount of those remaining.

TABLE LXIV.—*England and Wales. Issues Authorised by Act of 1844, since Lapsed, and now Remaining, December,* 1875.

Authorised Issues.	Private Banks.		Joint Stock Banks.		Together.	
	Number.	Authorised Issue.	Number.	Authorised Issue.	Number.	Authorised Issue.
		£		£		£
By Act of 1844	207	5,153,407	72	3,495,446	279	8,648,853
Since ceased to issue	89	1,345,415	18	842,453	107	2,187,868
Amalgamated without loss of issue.... }	6	—	—	—	6	—
	95	—	—	—	113	—
Remaining	112	3,807,992	54	2,652,993	166	6,460,985

The diminution in the number of issuers since 1844 is 43 per cent. of the private issuers, 25 per cent. of the joint stock, and 38 per cent. of the total.

Twenty-five per cent. of the total amount of issue authorised by the Act of 1844, has lapsed in thirty-one years; 26 per cent. being the proportion lapsed in the case of the private banks, and 24 per cent. in the case of the joint stock banks. The average authorised issue per bank was in

	Private Banks.	Joint Stock Banks.
	£	£
1844	24,895	48,548
'75 (December)	34,000	49,130

It will be interesting to tabularise the lapsed issues according to the causes of their forfeiture, and this is done in the following table, compiled from the Banking Almanacs :—

TABLE LXV.—*England and Wales. View of Lapsed Issues,* 1844-75, *Classified according to the Causes of their Forfeiture.*

[Compiled from the Banking Almanacs.]

Cause.	Private Banks.			Joint Stock Banks.			Together.		
	Number of Issuers.	Amount of Authorised Issue.	Percentage of Total Lapsed Authorised Issue.	Number of Issuers.	Amount of Authorised Issue.	Percentage of Total Lapsed Authorised Issue.	Number of Issuers.	Amount of Authorised Issue.	Percentage of Total Lapsed Authorised Issue.
		£	Per cnt.		£	Per cnt.		£	Per cnt.
1. Bankrupt or stopped payment	33	547,321	41	2	48,101	6	35	595,422	27
2. Closed or dissolved	10	84,741	6	7	169,589	20	17	254,330	12
Together	43	632,062	47	9	217,690	26	52	849,752	39
3. Ceased to issue (no reason named)	6	82,592	6	—	—	—	6	82,592	4
4. Arranged to issue Bank of England notes	12	194,992	15	—	—	—	12	194,992	9
5. Opened in London	—	—	—	1	442,371	52	1	442,371	20
6. Amalgamated or transferred business	28	435,759	32	8	182,392	22	36	618,151	28
	89	1,345,405	100	18	842,453	100	107	2,187,858	100

It will be seen from this table that of the total amount of issues lapsed, 39 per cent. have been extinguished by bankruptcy or dissolution ; 9 per cent. have been relinquished by arrangement with the Bank of England ; 4 per cent. have been given up without reason assigned ; 20 per cent. have been forfeited by a joint stock bank, the National Provincial, opening in London, and 28 per cent. have been forfeited by amalgamation.

It will also be seen that of the amount of joint stock issues lapsed, 74 per cent. have been compulsorily forfeited under the Act, and 26 per cent. by bankruptcy or dissolution ; whilst of the amount of private bank issues lost, 32 per cent. have been forfeited compulsorily under the Act ; 21 per cent. have been given up voluntarily, and 47 per cent. have lapsed by bankruptcy or dissolution. These figures show that even with the disadvantage under which they rest in respect of amalgamation, there has been greater permanency in the issues of the joint stock than in those of the private banks.

The amount of authorised issue lapsed in each period of five years since 1844, and in the two years 1874-75, has been as follows :—

Years.	Date.	Authorised Issue Lapsed.
		£
5	1844–48......................	423,410
5	'49–53......................	282,981
5	'54–58......................	234,174
5	'59–63......................	173,212
5	'64–68......................	753,814*
5	'69–73......................	157,099
2	'74–75......................	163,178
		2,187,868

* Including National Provincial Bank of England, 442,371*l.*

It is most improbable that the issues would continue to lapse at the same rate, because when the weaker have been eliminated the stronger will show greater permanency ; but even if the same rate be assumed it would take ninety-three years to clear off the issues now remaining. This shows a stability on the part of the English country issues which, could he have foreseen it, might have materially modified Sir Robert Peel's views.

Statutory Conditions of Note Issue in Scotland.

The conditions under which the Scotch banks enjoy the privilege of issue are :—

1. They retain the 1*l*. note abolished in England in 1826.

2. They have, by the Act of 1844, a monopoly of issue in Scotland.

3. Banks amalgamating retain the aggregate fixed issues of the separate banks.

4. Banks may exceed the amount of their fixed issue to any extent on condition of holding at their head office gold and silver coin equal in amount, on the average of each four weeks, to the average excess of their note circulation during these four weeks —silver coin held in excess of one fourth of the gold coin held not being reckoned as a basis for any excess of fixed issues.

5. A weekly return is required of (1) the amount of notes in circulation at the close of business on Saturday. (2) The amount of gold and silver coin held at head office at the close of business on each day of the week. (3) The total amount of gold and silver coin in Scotland held by the bank at the close of business on Saturday. Every fourth week must be added (1) the average of the amount of notes in circulation at the close of business on each of the four Saturdays. (2) The average of the amount of coin held at the head office on each of the four Saturdays.

6. For any issues in excess of the provisions of the Act, the penalty is the forfeiture of a sum equal to the excess.

7. Bank of England notes are not a legal tender in Scotland.

8. The Commissioners of Stamps and Taxes have power, with consent of the Treasury, to cause the bank's books containing accounts of notes in circulation and of coin held to be inspected, under a penalty of 100*l*. for refusal.

The variations in the number and amount of the fixed issues under the Act of 1845 have been as under :—

Authorised Issues.	Number of Banks.	Amount of Fixed Issues.
		£
By Act of 1845	19	3,087,209
Reduction by amalgamation	6*	—
,, failure of Western Bank, which included issue of Ayrshire Bank	2	337,938
	8	
Remaining, December, 1875...............	11	2,749,271

* The fixed issue of these six banks retained, notwithstanding amalgamation, amounted to 373,800*l*.

Statutory Conditions of Note Issue in Ireland.

The statutory conditions under which the banks of issue enjoy that privilege in Ireland are as follows:—

1. The Act of 1844 prevents the establishment of any new bank of issue.

2. Notes under 5*l.*, abolished in England in 1826, are retained in Ireland.

3. The notes of each bank are payable in gold at every one of its branches.

4. The Bank of England note is not a legal tender in Ireland.

5. Banks amalgamating retain the aggregate fixed issues of the separate banks.

6. Banks may issue to any extent beyond the amount of their fixed issue on holding at their head offices or principal places of issue, on the average of each four weeks, gold and silver coin equal in amount to such excess of issue, not reckoning silver coin to a greater extent than one-fourth of the gold coin held.

7. The returns of circulation and coin held are the same as those required from the Scotch banks, but the head offices or principal places of issue at which coin held may be reckoned against circulation may be not more than four for each bank, of which not more than two shall be situated in the same province.

8. The power of inspection by the Commissioners of Stamps and Taxes, and the penalty upon excess of circulation beyond the provisions of the Act, are the same as in Scotland.

The number of banks of issue in Ireland, eight in 1845, has been diminished to six by amalgamation, but the amount of authorised fixed credit issue remains as it was in 1845, 6,354,494*l.*

Advantages of Scotch and Irish Banks of Issue over English Country Banks of Issue.

The advantages which the Scotch and Irish banks of issue possess over the English country banks of issue may be thus briefly summarised:—

1. Notes under 5*l.* are prohibited in England but permitted in Scotland and Ireland. In Scotland the 1*l.* note constitutes 66 per cent. of the total circulation. In Ireland where notes of 3*l.* and 2*l.* as well as 1*l.* are used, the small notes form 45 per cent. of the total note circulation. (See Mr. Palgrave's tables.) This gives especially to the Scotch banks and to the Scotch nation a great economy of coin in circulation not enjoyed in England.

2. The issues of Scotland and Ireland are not subjected to the competition of the legal tender notes of any State bank, whilst the country issues of England have to hold their ground side by side

with the notes of the Bank of England, which being legal tender are practically obligations of the State.

3. An English bank cannot under a penalty allow its average daily circulation for each four weeks to exceed the amount of its authorised issue, whilst a Scotch or an Irish bank can issue to any extent, provided merely it holds coin equal to the excess of its authorised issue. This is a tremendous advantage, and gives all the Scotch and several of the Irish banks the benefit of a permanent excess of their fixed issues, as well as the command of an unlimited amount of till money at their numerous branches in their own notes, on which they suffer no loss of interest and pay no stamp duty. The amount of till money so held in Scotland at the eight hundred and eighty-four offices of the banks cannot be less than 6,000,000l. An English bank of issue, whose circulation is nearly or quite up to its authorised amount has little or no command of till money in its own notes.

Moreover, the coin held by the Scotch and Irish banks in conformity with the requirements of the law is in no way hypothecated as a security for excess of issues, and in the event of failure must be applied as any ordinary asset towards payment of all the liabilities of the bank. In the course of his evidence before the Committee on Banks of Issue, 1875, Mr. Readman, manager of the Clydesdale Banking Company, in reply to Mr. Backhouse's question, "Would you think it desirable that less gold should be "retained in Scotland if they were not obliged to keep gold against "their excess of issue?" said, "We should not, I think, keep less "gold than we do even if we were not obliged by Act of Parliament "to keep gold against the excess of issue." The total liabilities to the public of the Scotch banks are 92½ millions. They hold 4,000,000l. in coin, which is equal to 4⅓ per cent. of their liabilities. This, it will be admitted, is a very moderate legal tender reserve against such enormous liabilities. Yet it is permitted to do duty, not only as a reserve, but also as the basis, and a most illusory basis it is, for an excess amounting on the average of 1874 to 3,150,000l. beyond the fixed or credit issue.

In Ireland the total liabilities of the banks of issue were at 31st December, 1874, 42,500,000l. The average amount of coin held by them in 1874 was 2,798,000l., or 6½ per cent. of their liabilities. Their authorised issue being so very large compared with that of the Scotch banks, their excess of issue is always very much less than the excess in Scotland. The fact that their notes are by law payable in coin at all their branches amply accounts for the much larger proportion of coin which they hold in comparison with the Scotch banks. It will be seen from the following table that the coin held beyond the legal requirements is only 958,000*l.* in Scotland, against 2,384,000*l.* in Ireland, and that the coin held bears the ratio to the excess of credit issue of 130 per cent. in Scotland, and 676 per cent. in Ireland.

TABLE XLVI.—*Scotch and Irish Banks, Average Excess of Issue, and Coin Held,* 1874.

1874.	Scotch.	Irish.
	£	£
Average actual circulation	5,900,000	6,769,000
Authorised or credit circulation	2,749,271	6,354,494
Average excess of issue	3,150,000	414,000
,, coin held	4,108,000	2,798,000
Coin held beyond legal requirements	958,000	2,384,000
	Per cnt.	Per cnt.
Ratio of coin held to excess of issue	130	676

4. The English banks have to return their circulation on the basis of a monthly average of *daily* amounts. The Scotch and Irish banks have the benefit of a monthly average of *weekly* amounts; and as the return is made at the close of business on Saturday, on which day exchanges of notes take place between the banks all over Scotland, the Scotch circulation is then at its minimum. Mr. Readman gave it in evidence before the Committee on Banks of Issue, 1875, that the circulation of the Clydesdale Bank being 717,000*l.* before the exchange, would be reduced by probably 200,000*l.* at the exchange; and in answer to Mr. Backhouse's question—" May I conclude from that answer that if we had the " circulation of all the Scotch banks before the exchange, it would " amount to something like 2,000,000*l.* more than is shown after " the exchange?" he said, " It would amount to a very considerably " larger sum at the half-yearly terms in May and November." There is in fact no doubt that the Scotch banks have the use in circulation of a sum in notes exceeding one third of their average annual circulation, without either paying stamp duty on such sum, or being required to hold coin in respect of it. Of course these notes are not in the hands of the ordinary public. They are in the hands of the other banks awaiting exchange, and if the banks went to the trouble and expense of having an exchange of notes at the close of business each day, they might work without this temporary additional excess of issues. The law, however, saves them this trouble and expense by giving them, on five days of the week, the power of unlimited issue without regard to amount of coin held, and without payment of stamp duty on the excess. There is very little doubt that, including unexchanged notes in the hands of other banks, the

normal amount of the Scotch circulation is actually on five days of the week in excess of the sum of the fixed issue and the amount of coin held.

5. In England the restrictions upon amalgamation of issues have operated to prevent the consolidation of issues, and have led, as has been shown, to the forfeiture of an appreciable proportion of the authorised circulation. In Scotland and Ireland there are no such restrictions ; and in both, but more extensively in Scotland, amalgamations have been effected without diminution of the amount of authorised issue, an advantage to the banks and the public not possessed in England. In Scotland the six banks incorporated with the eleven existing banks had a fixed credit issue amounting to 373,800*l*., and it is certain that but for the privilege of amalgamating issues, the greater portion of that sum of credit issue would have been lost to the banks and the country. In England, whilst it is curious to observe in passing, that one bank, the Ludlow and Tenbury Bank, has had the ingenuity to retain its existence as a bank of issue, notwithstanding the transference of its ordinary banking business to the Worcester City and County Bank, it is found that the authorised issue lost by amalgamations amounts to 618,151*l*., or 7 per cent. of the issue originally authorised by the Act of 1844. It may further be held as certain that many banking amalgamations would have taken place in England but for the penalty of loss of circulation, and thus the natural and desirable consolidation of the country bank system has been repressed and hampered by this pernicious provision of the law.

6. In Scotland the monopoly of issue has practically produced a monopoly of banking in favour of the existing banks. No such monopoly of banking exists in Ireland, where there are three joint stock banks of non-issue ; nor in England, where there are amongst the purely provincial banks, eighty-three private and forty-three joint stock banks, which are not banks of issue. Several of the Scotch members of the committee, and notably Mr. Orr Ewing, argued in questions put to various witnesses that the actual monopoly of banking in Scotland must arise not from the monopoly of issue, but from the undoubted stability of the banks, the complete manner in which they covered the ground with their branches, and the liberal terms on which they conducted their business ; because under similar circumstances in Ireland three joint stock banks of non-issue were carried on successfully side by side with the six privileged banks of issue.

In reply to this argument it may be stated that the privileges of the Irish banks of issue, though similar to those of the Scotch banks, are not so valuable. Their notes being by law payable at all their branches, they have to hold a stock of coin at every office, a condition from which the Scotch banks are exempt. Again, there were in Scotland in 1844 no established banks of non-issue, whereas in Ireland, the Hibernian Bank, established in 1825, and the Royal Bank of Ireland, established in 1836, were successfully carrying on business as banks of non-issue, when the monopoly of issue was decreed in 1844.

Distribution and Actual Position of Non-Legal-Tender Note Circulation in United Kingdom.

TABLE LXVII.—*Distribution of Non-Legal-Tender Note Circulation.*
[Based on Mr. Palgrave's Tables.]

Banks.	Authorised Circulation.	Average Authorised Circulation per Bank.	Average Circulation, 1874.	Average Circulation per Bank, 1874.
	£	£	£	£
ENGLAND AND WALES.				
113 private banks	3,845,908	34,034	2,600,000	23,009
54 joint stock banks	2,662,707	49,309	2,360,000	43,700
167 banks	6,508,615	38,973	4,960,000	29,640
SCOTLAND.				
11 joint stock banks	2,749,271	249,934	5,900,000	536,300
IRELAND.				
1 Bank of Ireland	3,738,428	3,738,428	2,879,000	2,879,000
5 other joint stock banks	2,616,066	523,213	3,890,000	778,000
6 joint stock banks	6,854,494	1,059,082	6,769,000	1,128,200

Even allowing for the absence of small notes in England, these figures show that in that division of the United Kingdom the right of issue is much more diffused and in smaller hands than in either Scotland or Ireland.

This discrepancy is purely the result of legislation. In Scotland from 1716 to 1844, banking, including the issue of small notes, was entirely unfettered by law. This freedom led to the establishment and development of joint stock banks on a large scale. In Ireland banking and issue were exclusively in private hands until the establishment of the Bank of Ireland, by statute of 1782, which conferred on that bank the monopoly of joint stock banking in Ireland—a monopoly continued until 1821, when powers of banking and issue were extended to any partnership in Ireland exceeding six persons, provided they had no place of business in Dublin or within a circuit of sixty-five English miles round that city. In 1844 issue was restricted to banks then exercising that function, but it appears that ere that time the issue of notes by private bankers in Ireland had died a natural death.

In England the monopoly of joint stock banking, conferred on the Bank of England, and jealously upheld till 1826, confined the country issues to private bankers having not more than six partners, and kept the country banking of England essentially local and comparatively weak, whilst the banking of Scotland was growing national and strong. In 1826 joint stock banking with the power of issue was legally sanctioned in England under certain restrictions which were somewhat relaxed in 1833. From that time till 1844, when Sir Robert Peel laid an iron hand on the country issues, joint stock banking had not time to develope itself in England, and the financial troubles of 1836 to 1840 contributed to retard its infant growth.

Thus it is that whilst in Scotland, and to a certain extent in Ireland also, the issues emanate from banks which are almost national in their importance as well as in the extent of their ramifications, in England, on the other hand, the issuing banks, since the National Provincial Bank of England ceased to belong to that class, are all such as restrict their operations, including the circulation of their notes, to districts more or less circumscribed. The following table will illustrate this:—

TABLE LXVIII.--*United Kingdom. Banks of Issue. Actual Circulation per Bank*, 1874.

Locality.	Lowest Actual Circulation per Bank.	Highest Actual Circulation per Bank.	Average Actual Circulation per Bank.
England and Wales—	£	£	£
Private	1,825	125,937	23,000
Joint stock	1,191	311,641	43,700
Together	1,191	311,641	29,640
Scotland	104,000	789,000	536,300
Ireland	476,000	2,879,000	1,128,200

These figures, as well as the following tables, are based upon copious tables prepared no less intelligently than laboriously by Mr. R. H. Inglis Palgrave for the Committee on Banks of Issue, and subsequently re-published in the "Bankers' Magazine" for 1875, and the "Banking Almanac" for 1876.

In Table LXIX the joint stock banks, and in Table LXX the private banks, are classified according to the amount of the actual circulation of each bank on the average of the year 1874.

TABLE LXIX.—*England and Wales. Joint Stock Banks of Issue, Classified according to Amount of Actual Average Circulation,* 1874.
[Compiled from Mr. Palgrave's Tables.]

Bank.	Authorised Issue.	Average Circulation, 1874
Under 10,000*l.*	£	£
1. Barnsley Banking Company	9,563	8,968
2. Chesterfield and North Derby	10,421	9,868
3. County of Stafford	9,418	9,047
4. Whitchurch and Ellesmere	7,475	4,371
5. Ludlow and Tenbury	10,215	8,769
6. Worcester City and County	6,848	1,191
7. Helston Banking Company	1,503	1,494
	55,443	43,708
Above 10,000*l. and not above* 25,000*l.*		
1. Carlisle City and District	19,972	19,857
2. „ and Cumberland	25,610	24,826
3. Bank of Westmoreland	12,225	10,611
4. Bradford Commercial	20,084	19,786
5. Halifax Joint Stock	18,534	17,391
6. „ Commercial, *Limited*	13,733	12,440
7. Wakefield and Barnsley Union	14,604	13,906
8. Sheffield and Hallamshire	23,524	22,748
9. Derby and Derbyshire	20,093	19,351
10. Coventry Union	16,251	15,034
11. „ and Warwickshire	28,734	16,581
12. Leamington Priors, &c.	13,875	11,417
13. Northamptonshire Banking Company	26,401	18,629
14. Wolverhampton and Staffordshire	35,378	18,333
	289,018	240,910
Above 25,000*l. and not above* 50,000*l.*		
1. Cumberland Union, *Limited*	35,395	33,967
2. Bank of Whitehaven, *Limited*	32,681	30,136
3. Whitehaven Joint Stock	31,916	28,546
4. Darlington District	26,134	25,592
5. Knaresborough and Claro	28,059	26,680
6. Bradford Banking Company	49,292	48,586
7. Hull Banking Company	29,333	28,897
8. Halifax and Huddersfield Union	44,137	37,243

TABLE LXIX.— *England and Wales. Joint Stock Banks of Issue—Contd.*

Bank.	Authorised Issue.	Average Circulation, 1874.
Above 25,000l. and not above 30,000l.— Contd.	£	£
9. Huddersfield Banking Company	37,354	35,551
10. West Riding Union	34,029	33,465
11. Sheffield Banking Company	35,843	35,530
12. Burton and Uttoxeter	60,701	46,257
13. Nottingham and Notts	29,477	25,603
14. Moore and Robinson's, *Limited*	35,813	30,587
15. Lincoln and Lindsay	51,620	49,778
16. Stamford, Spalding, &c. ....'.............	55,721	49,897
17. Stourbridge and Kidderminster	56,830	48,303
18. North Wilts Banking Company	63,939	37,982
	738,274	652,600
Above 50,000l. and not above 75,000l.		
1. North and South Wales	63,951	59,698
2. Lancaster Banking Company	64,311	59,342
3. Swaledale and Wensleydale	54,372	51,080
4. York Union	71,240	69,965
5. Sheffield and Rotherham	52,496	51,305
6. Pares's Leicestershire	59,300	54,043
7. Leicestershire Banking Company	86,060	65,786
8. Northamptonshire Union	84,356	58,172
9. Wilts and Dorset	76,162	73,356
	612,248	542,747
Above 75,000l. and not above 100,000l.		
1. York City and County	94,695	90,911
2. West of England and South Wales District........	83,535	81,256
3. County of Gloucester	144,352	91,615
	322,582	263,782
Above 100,000l.		
1. Yorkshire Banking Company	122,532	119,113
2. Stuckey's „	356,976	311,641
3. Gloucestershire „	155,920	144,145
	635,428	574,859

TABLE LXX.—*England and Wales.   Private Banks of Issue Classified according to Amount of Average Circulation*, 1874.
[Compiled from Mr. Palgrave's Tables.]

Local Name of Bank.	Name of Firm.	Authorised Issue.	Average Circulation 1874.
Under 10,000*l.*		£	£
1. Richmond Bank	Roper and Priestman	6.889	6,676
2. Loughborough Bank	Middleton and Co...........	7,359	6,876
3. Godalming Bank	Mellersh „	6,322	5,472
4. Faversham „	Hilton and Rigden	6,681	5,630
5. Bury St. Edmund's Bank	Worlledge and Co.	3,201	2,672
6. Penzance Bank	Batten „	11,405	8,208
7. Harwich „	Cox and Co.	5,778	4,133
8. Lynn R. and Norfolk Bank	Jarvis „	13,917	9;854
9. Wellington Bank, Somerset	Fox „	6,528	4,088
10. Yarmouth, Norfolk, and ⎱ Suffolk Bank.................... ⎰	Lacons „	13,229	8,378
11. Tavistock Bank	Gill, Sons, and Co.	13,421	8,158
12. Thornbury (Gloucester) Bk.	Harwood „	10,026	6,102
13. Macclesfield Bank	Brocklehurst and Co...........	15,760	9,525
14. Union Bank, Helston...........	Vivian, and Co., Helston.	17,003	9,781
15. Witney (Oxon) Bank...:.....⎰	J. Williams, Clinch, and ⎱ Sons ....⎰	11,852	6,553
16. Devonport Bank....................	Hodge and Co.	10,664	5,419
17. Lymington „	S. Barbe „	5,038	2;565
18. Royston „	J. G. Fordham and Sons.	16,393	8,015
19. Tiverton and Devonshire Bk.	Dunsford and Co.	13,470	6,157
20. Towcester Old Bank	Mercer and Co.	10,801	4.760
21. Oswestry Bank	Croxon „	18,471	7,603
22. Farnham „	J. Knight and Sons	14,202	5,662
23. Sittingbourne and Milton Bk.	Vallance and Co.	4,789	1,825
24. Winchester, Alresford, and ⎱ Alton .... ⎰	Bulpett and Co.	25,892	8,872
25. Wivilescombe	W. Hancock	7,602	2,365
26. Southampton Tn. and Cnty.	Maddison and Co.	25,359	7,620
27. New Sarum Bank	Pinckney Brothers...........	15,659	4,582
28. Wallingford „	Hedges and Co.	17,064	4,631
29. Rye Bank	Curteis „	29,864	7,231
30. Uxbridge Old Bank	Hull „	25,136	5,982
31. Devizes and Wiltshire Bank	Locke „	20,674	4,659
32. Barnstaple Bank....................	Marshall „	17,182	3,884
33. Salop Bank	Burton „	22,338	4,681
34. Monmouth Old Bank	Bromage „	16,385	2,720
		466,354	201,339
Above 10,000*l.* *and not above* 25,000*l.*			
1. Hull and Kingston-on-Hull	S. Smith Brothers and Co.	19,979	19,659
2. Scarborough Old Bank	Woodall and Co..............	24,813	24,331
3. Burlington and Driffield Bk.	Harding „	12,745	12,328
4. Whitby Old Bank	Simpson „	14,258	13,791
5. Miners' Bank	Willyams „	18,688	18,135
6. Thrapstone and Kettering...	Eland and Eland	11,559	11,030
7. Tring and Chesham	T. Butcher and Sons	13,531	12,254
8. Ashford Bank	Pomfret and Co...............	11,849	10,652
9. Knaresborough Old Bank	Harrison „	21,825	19,559
10. Derby Bank..........................	Evans „	13,332	11,073
11. Tonbridge Old Bank ....⎰	H. S., A. T., and A. ⎱ Beeching .... ⎰	13,183	10,886

TABLE LXX.—*Private Banks of Issue Classified—Contd.*

Local Name of Bank.	Name of Firm.	Authorised Issue.	Average Circulation, 1874.
Above 10,000l. and not above 25,000l.—Contd.	.	£	£
12. Kentish Bank	Wigan and Co.	19,895	16,132
13. Shrewsbury and Welchpool	Beck ,, ...	25,336	20,097
14. Guildford Bank	Haydon ,,	14,524	11,221
15. Warwick and Warwickshire	Greenway and Co.	30,504	22,919
16. Naval Bank, Plymouth	Harris and Co.	27,321	20,841
17. Leicester Bank ,, ...	T. and T. T. Paget...........	32,322	24,644
18. Kingston and Radnorshire	Davies and Co.	26,050	19,045
19. Ipswich Bank	Bacon ,, ...	21,901	15,195
20. Llandovery and Llandilo Bk.	D. Jones ,,	32,945	22,651
21. Weymouth Old Bank	Eliot ,,	16,461	11,150
22. Newark Bank	Godfrey and Riddell	28,788	19,654
23. Newmarket Bank	Hammond and Co.	23,098	15,254
24. Grantham ,, ...	Hardy and Co.	30,372	19,272
25. Buckingham ,, ...	Bartlett ,,	29,657	18,224
26. Canterbury ,, ...	Hammond and Co............	33,671	20,418
27. Brighton Union Bank	Hall, Lloyd, ,,	33,794	19,041
28. City Bank, Exeter	Milford, Snow, and Co. ...	21,527	11,631
29. Lewes Old Bank................	Whitfield and Co.	44,836	24,284
30. Broseley and Bridgnorth Bk.	Pritchard ,, ...	26,717	14,182
31. Reading Bank....................	Simonds ,, ...	37,519	19,881
32. Banbury ,, ...	J. C. and A. Gillett	43,457	22,098
33. Shrewsbury Old Bank	Rocke, Eyton, and Co. ...	43,191	22,123
34. Cambridge Bank................	Mortlock and Co.	25,744	12,784
35. Bicester and Oxfordshire Bk.	G. and H. Tubb	27,090	13,146
36. Colchester Bank	Round, Green, and Co.	25,082	11,885
37. Exeter ,, ...	Sanders and Co.	37,894	17,124
38. Aylesbury Old Bank	T. R. Cobb ,,	48,461	21,397
39. Baldock and Biggleswade Bk.	Wells, Hogge, and Co.	37,223	16,581
40. Stamford and Rutland Bank	Eaton and Co..................	31,858	12,402
41. Bristol Bank	Miles ,,	48,277	19,062
42. Saffron Walden and N. Essex	Gibson ,, ...	47,646	18,366
43. Newbury Bank, Berks	Matthews and Co.	36,787	12,247
44. Banbury Old Bank..............	Cobb and Son	55,153	16,751
		1,240,863	745,400
Above 25,000l. and not above 50,000l.		.	
1. Pease's Old Bank, Hull.......	Pease, Hoare, and Co.	48,807	48,515
2. Derby Old ,, ...	Crompton and Co.	27,237	26,684
3. Leeds Union ,, ...	Williams, Brown, and Co.	37,459	36,834
4. Nottingham ,, ...	S. Smith and Co.	31,047	30,029
5. Kendal Bank	Wakefield ,, ...	44,663	43,245
6. W. Riding Bank, Wakefield	Leatham, Tew, and Co.	46,158	43,345
7. Leighton Buzzard Bk. Beds	Basset and Co.	36,829	33,011
8. Bedford Bank	T. Barnard and Co.	34,218	29,795
9. Cambridge and Cambsh. Bk.	Foster and Foster	49,916	42,703
10. Oxford Old Bank	Parson and Co.	34,391	29,228
11. York Bank	Swann ,,	46,387	39,606
12. Newark and Sleaford Bank	Handley ,, ...	51,615	42,605
13. Derby Bank.......................	Smith ,, ...	41,304	32,969
14. Hitchin Bank, Herts	Sharples ,, ...	38,764	30,620
15. Dorchester Old Bank...........	Williams ,, ...	48,807	35,768

TABLE LXX.—*Private Banks of Issue Classified—Contd.*

Local Name of Bank.	Name of Firm.	Authorised Issue.	Average Circulation, 1874.
Above 25,000l. and not above 50,000l.—Contd.			
16. Brecon Old Bank	Wilkins and Co.	68,271	44,945
17. Yarmouth and Suffolk Bank	Gurneys ,,	53,060	34,463
18. Lynn R. and Lincolnsh. ,,	,, ,,	42,817	26,477
19. Wisbech and Lincolnsh. ,,	,, ,,	59,713	35,467
20. Reading Bank	Stephens ,,	43,271	25,018
21. Cornish ,,	Tweedy ,,	49,869	28,424
22. Ipswich and Needham Mrkt.	Alexanders and Co.	80,699	43,829
23. Bury and Suffolk Bank	Oakes and Co.	82,362	44,116
24. Colchester and Essex Bank	Mills ,,	48,704	25,664
25. Essex and Bishop Stortford	Sparrow ,,	69,637	36,255
26. Worcester Old Bank	Berwick ,,	87,448	44,441
27. Huntingdon Town and Cnty.	Veasey ,,	56,591	26,881
		1,360,044	960,937
Above 50,000l. and not above 75,000l.			
1. East Riding Bank	Beckett and Co.	53,392	52,071
2. Craven Bank	Birkbeck ,,	77,154	74,005
3. Boston ,,	Claypon, Garfit, and Co.	75,069	59,851
		205,615	185,927
Above 75,000l. and not above 100,000l.			
1. Darlington Bank	J. Backhouse and Co.	86,218	84,789
2. Lincoln ,,	Smith, Ellison, ,,	100,342	91,074
3. Norwich and Norfolk Bank	Gurneys and Co.	105,519	81,720
4. East Cornwall Bank	Robin ,,	112,280	81,131
		404,359	338,714
Above 100,000l.			
1. Leeds Bank	Beckett and Co.	130,757	125,937

The results of these two tables will be seen at a glance in Table LXXI, from which it may be calculated that 86 per cent. in number, and 58 per cent. in amount of the English issues are in sums of under 50,000l. each ; whereas the smallest actual circulation in Scotland is 104,000l., and the smallest in Ireland is 476,000l.

M

Table LXXI.—*England and Wales. Banks of Issue, Joint Stock, and Private. Actual Circulation of* 1874, *Classified according to Amount for each Bank.*

Classification.	Joint Stock.		
	Number of Banks.	Aggregate Authorised Issue.	Aggregate Average Issue.
Under 10,000*l.*	7	55,443	43,708
Above 10,000*l.* and under 25,000*l.*	14	289,018	240,910
„ 25,000*l.* „ 50,000*l.*	18	738,274	652,600
„ 50,000*l.* „ 75,000*l.*	9	612,148	542,747
„ 75,000*l.* „ 100,000*l.*	3	322,582	263,782
„ 100,000*l.*	3	635,428	574,899
	54	2,652,993	2,318,646
Average	—	49,129	42,938

Classification.	Private Banks.		
	Number of Banks.	Aggregate Authorised Issue.	Aggregate Average Circulation.
Under 10,000*l.*	34	466,354	201,339
Above 10,000*l.* and under 25,000*l.*	44	1,240,863	745,400
„ 25,000*l.* „ 50,000*l.*	27	1,360,044	960,937
„ 50,000*l.* „ 75,000*l.*	3	205,615	185,927
„ 75,000*l.* „ 100,000*l.*	4	404,359	338,714
„ 100,000*l.*	1	130,757	125,937
	113	3,807,992	2,558,254
Average	—	33,699	22,639

Classification.	Total.		
	Number of Banks.	Aggregate Authorised Issue.	Aggregate Average Issue.
Under 10,000*l.*	41	521,797	245,047
Above 10,000*l.* and under 25,000*l.*	58	1,529,881	986,310
„ 25,000*l.* „ 50,000*l.*	45	2,098,318	1,613,537
„ 50,000*l.* „ 75,000*l.*	12	817,863	728,674
„ 75,000*l.* „ 10,0000*l.*	7	726,941	602,496
„ 100,000*l.*	4	766,185	700,836
	167	6,460,985	4,876,900
Average	—	38,688	29,203

As the paid-up capital may be assumed to be a rough and ready test of the magnitude of a bank, I have prepared the following tables, in which the authorised circulation and the actual average circulation for 1874 as worked out by Mr. Palgrave, are brought into juxtaposition and comparison with the paid-up capital in the case of each bank.

TABLE LXXII.– *English Joint Stock Banks of Issue.* *Relation of Authorised Issues and Actual Circulation to Paid-up Capital,* 1874.

[Cols. 2 and 3 are compiled from Mr. Palgrave's Tables.]

		1	2	3	4	5	6	7
Number.	Name. [Banks printed in SMALL CAPITALS publish Balance Sheets.]	Authorised Issue.	Average Issue in 1874.	Ratio of Actual to Authorised Issue.	Number of Offices.	Paid-up Capital.	Ratio of Authorised Issue to Paid-up Capital.	Ratio of Actual Circulation to Paid-up Capital.
		£	£	Per cnt.	No.	£	Per cnt.	Per cnt.
1	CARLISLE CITY AND DIST.	19,972	19,857	99	6	80,162	25	25
2	CARLISLE AND CUMBLAND.	25,610	24,826	97	6	75,000	34	33
3	CUMBLAND. UNION Ltd.	35,395	38,967	96	18	225,000	16	15
4	B. OF WHITEHAVEN, Ltd.	32,681	30,136	92	4	98,530	33	31
5	Whitehaven Joint Stock	31,916	28,546	89	6	45,000	71	63
6	Bank of Westmoreland	12,225	10,611	87	2	25,680	47	41
7	N. AND S. WALES BANK	63,951	59,698	93	37	420,000	15	14
8	Lancaster Banking Co.	64,311	59,342	92	14	275,000	23	22
9	Darlington District Bank	26,134	25,592	97	8	68,000	38	38
10	SWALEDLE AND WENSLEYD	54,372	51,080	94	4	63,000	86	80
11	Knaresborough and Claro.	28,059	26,680	95	6 {	not stated	not known	not known
12	YORKSHIRE BKG. CO.	122,532	119,113	97	22	250,000	49	48
13	York City and County	94,695	90,911	96	15	125,000	76	73
14	York Union	71,140	69,965	98	10	132,000	54	53
15	Hull Banking Company	29,333	28,897	98	4	90,990	32	32
16	BRADFORD COMMERCIAL	20,084	19,786	98	1	193,500	10	10
17	BRADFORD BKG. CO.	49,292	48,586	98	1	408,000	12	12
18	Halifax Joint Stock Bank.	18,534	17,391	94	3	150,000	12	12
19	HALIFAX COMM., Limited.	13,733	12,440	90	2	120,000	11	10
20	Halifax and Hudders.	44,137	37,243	84	2	250,000	18	15
21	Huddersfield Bkg. Co.	37,354	35,551	95	4	382,500	10	9
22	West Riding Union Bank	34,029	33,465	98	3	200,000	17	17
23	Wakefield & Barnsley Un.	14,604	13,906	95	3	100,000	15	14
24	Barnsley Banking Co.	9,563	8,968	94	2	40,575	23	22
25	SHEFFIELD AND ROTHERM.	52,496	51,305	98	5	160,704	33	32
26	SHEFFIELD BANKING CO.	35,843	35,530	99	4	293,160	12	12
27	SHEFFIELD AND HALLAMSH.	23,524	22,748	97	1	183,200	13	12

TABLE LXXII.—*English Joint Stock Banks of Issue—Contd.*

Number.	Name. [Banks printed in SMALL CAPITALS publish Balance Sheets.]	1 Authorised Issue.	2 Average Issue in 1874.	3 Ratio of Actual to Authorised Issue.	4 Number of Offices.	5 Paid-up Capital.	6 Ratio of Authorised Issue to Paid-up Capital.	7 Ratio of Actual Circulation to Paid-up Capital.
		£	£	Per cnt.	No.	£	Per cnt.	Per cnt.
28	Chesterfield and N. Derby	10,421	9,868	94	1	35,000	30	28
29	Derby and Derbyshire........	20,093	19,351	96	3	62,500	32	31
30	BURTON AND UTTOXETER	60,701	46,267	76	3	130,000	47	36
31	Nottingham and Notts.......	29,477	25,603	87	8	203,500	14	12
32	Moore and Robinson's, *Ltd.*	35,813	30,587	85	1	127,000	28	24
33	Lincoln and Lindsey	51,620	49,778	96	12	87,500	59	57
34	STAMFORD, SPALDING, &c.	55,721	49,897	89	19	200,000	28	25
35	Pares's Leicestershire	59,300	54,043	91	6	310,000	19	17
36	LEICESTERSHIRE BKG. Co.	86,060	65,786	77	11	275,000	31	24
37	Coventry Union	16,251	15,034	92	2	56,000	29	27
38	Coventry and Warwicksh.	28,734	16,581	57	1	105,000	27	16
39	Leamington Priors and Warwickshire Bank	13,875	11,417	82	4	32,000	43	36
40	Northamptonshire Bk. Co.	26,401	18,629	71	4	78,000	34	24
41	Northamptonshire Un. Bk.	84,356	58,172	70	4	132,500	63	44
42	COUNTY OF STAFFORD	9,418	9,047	96	1	60,000	16	15
43 {	WOLVERHAMPTON AND STAFFORDSHIRE .... }	35,378	18,333	52	1	100,000	35	18
44 {	STOURBRIDGE AND KIDDERMINSTER BANK .... }	56,830	48,303	85	14	100,000	56	48
45	Whitchurch and Ellesmere	7,475	4,371	58	2 {	not stated	not known	not known
46	Ludlow and Tenbury Bank	10,215	8,769	86	1	,,	,,	,,
47 {	WORCESTER CITY AND COUNTY BANK, *Limited* }	6,848	1,191	17	14	250,000	3	0½
48	W. OF ENG. AND S. WALES	83,535	81,256	97	43	750,000	11	11
49	Helston Banking Company	1,503	1,494	99	2 {	not stated	not known	not known
50	Stuckey's Banking Co........	356,976	311,641	87	34	301,900	118	103
51	County of Gloucester Bank	144,352	91,615	63	12	181,000	80	51
52	Gloucestersh. Banking Co.	155,920	144,145	92	27	450,000	34	32
53	North Wilts Banking Co....	63,939	37,982	59	16	85,000	75	45
54	WILTS AND DORSET............	76,162	73,356	96	50	250,000	30	29
		1,652,993	2,318,646	87	489	8,816,901	For 50 Banks, 30	For 50 Banks, 26

TABLE LXXIII.—*Scotch Joint Stock Banks. Relation of Authorised Credit Issues and Actual Circulation to Paid-up Capital,* 1874.

[Cols. 2 and 3 are compiled from Mr. Palgrave's Tables.]

			1	2	3	4	5	6	7
Num-ber.	Name.	Esta-blish-ment.	Authorised Credit Issue.	Average Circula-tion in 1874.	Proportion of Circula-tion of 1874 to Authorised Issue.	Num-ber of Offices.	Paid-up Capital.	Ratio per Cent. of Authorised Issue to Paid-up Capital.	Ratio per Cent. of Actual Issue of 1874 to Paid-up Capital.
			£	£			£		
1	Bank of Scotland	1695	343,418	667,000	194	77	1,000,000	34	67
2	Royal B. of Scot.	1727	216,451	719,000	332	107	2,000,000	11	36
3	British Linen Co.....	'46	438,024	530,000	121	68	1,000,000	44	53
4	Commercial B. of S.	1810	374,880	774,000	207	101	1,000,000	37	77
5	National B. of S.	'25	297,024	587,000	198	92	1,000,000	30	59
6	Aberdeen Tn. and C.	1825	70,133	199,000	428	41	252,000	28	79
7	Union B. of S.	'30	454,346	789,000	174	117	1,000,000	45	79
8	North of Scotland....	'36	154,319	322,000	209	47	320,000	48	101
9	Clydesdale	'38	274,321	536,000	195	80	1,000,000	27	54
10	Caledonian...............	'38	53,434	104,000	195	22	150,000	36	69
11	City of Glasgow	'39	72,921	673,000	925	123	1,000,000	7	67
			2,749,271	5,900,000	214	875	9,722,000	28	61

TABLE LXXIV.—*Irish Joint Stock Banks of Issue. Relation of Authorised Credit Issues and Actual Circulation to Paid-up Capital,* 1874.

[Cols. 2 and 3 are compiled from Mr. Palgrave's Tables.]

			1	2	3	4	5	6	7
Num-ber.	Name.	Esta-blish-ment.	Authorised Credit Issue.	Average Circula-tion in 1874.	Proportion of Circula-tion of 1874 to Authorised Issue.	Num-ber of Offices.	Paid-up Capital.	Ratio per Cent. of Authorised Issue to Paid-up Capital.	Ratio per Cent. of Actual Issue of 1874 to Paid-up Capital.
			£	£			£		
1	Bank of Ireland	1783	3,738,428	2,879,000	77	50	2,769,230	135	104
2	Northern Bkg. Co.	1825	243,440	477,000	197	44	300,000	81	159
3	Provincial B. of I.	'25	927,667	885,000	95	44	540,000	172	164
4	Belfast Bkg. Co.	'27	281,611	476,000	169	36	250,000	112	190
5	National Bank	'35	852,269	1,366,000	160	106	1,500,000	56	91
6	Ulster Bkg. Co.	'36	311,079	686,000	221	44	250,000	124	274
			6,354,494	6,769,000	107	324	5,609,230	113	211

From these tables are drawn the following results :—

Nationality.	Ratio per Cent. of Actual Average Issue of 1874 to Authorised Issue.	Ratio per Cent. of Authorised Issue to Paid-up Capital.			Ratio per Cent. of Actual Average Issue of 1874 to Paid-up Capital.			Average Authorised Circulation per Bank of Issue.	Average Actual Average Circulation of 1874 per Bank of Issue.	Average Actual Circulation of 1874 per Office of Banks of Issue.
		Lowest.	Highest.	Average.	Lowest.	Highest.	Average.			
	Per cnt.	Per cnt.	Per cnt.	Per cnt.	Per cnt.	Per cnt.	Per cnt.	£	£	£
English	87	3	118	30*	0½	108	26*	49,129	42,938	4,742
Scotch ..	214	7	48	28	36	101	61	249,934	536,304	6,743
Irish	107	56	172	113	91	274	121	1,059,082	1,128,167	20,896

* For 50 of the 54 banks.

The above figures show how greatly in Scotland, and still more in Ireland, the .proportion of actual circulation to paid-up capital exceeds the like proportion in England. It will be seen that in Ireland, with one exception, the actual circulation of every bank is in excess of its paid-up capital.

Taking the average actual circulation of banks in Ireland at 100, the average circulation in Scotland is 48, and in England 4 per bank.

TABLE LXXV.—*English Joint Stock Banks of Issue, Classified according to Amount of Paid-up Capital.*

Capital.	Number of Banks.	Total Paid-up Capital.	Authorised Issue.	Actual Average Circulation, 1874.
		£	£	£
Not stated	4	—	47,252	41,314
„ above 50,000l.	5	178,255	78,000	69,410
Above 50,000l. and not above 100,000l.	15	1,204,682	482,636	410,751
„ 100,000l. „ 200,000l.	14	2,139,904	738,012	611,120
„ 200,000l. „ 300,000l.	9	2,471,660	500,765	451,131
„ 300,000l. „ 500,000l.	6	2,272,400	722,793	653,664
„ 500,000l.	1	750,000	83,535	81,256
Totals	54	8,816,901	2,652,993	2,318,646

A bank with a paid-up capital of only 100,000l. must be regarded as quite a small joint stock bank, yet we find that 44¼ per cent. in number and 22½ per cent. in amount of the joint stock issues in England emanate from banks whose paid-up capital does not exceed 100,000l.

Possible Legislation.

Such being the conditions under which the non-legal-tender circulation is conducted, and such its present position in the three kingdoms, it may now be considered what policy it would be practicable and at the same time judicious to adopt with regard to it.

The various lines of policy advocated seem to be as follows :—

1. To abolish all non-legal-tender issues and to confine the note circulation to the State or the Bank of England, or to the Bank of England for England, and similar State banks for Scotland and Ireland.

2. To reform the present system.

3. To reform and extend the present system.

Abolition of Non-Legal-Tender Issues.

This course would realise the ideas of Sir Robert Peel, who in introducing the Act which bears his name, avowed his intention of paving the way for the gradual absorption of all private issues. Sir Robert Peel had a prejudice, natural perhaps, but certainly mistaken, against private issues. He attributed to them a power for evil which they do not possess. He stated that being over-issued they became depreciated and produced speculation, inflation of prices, and consequently crisis. In fact he erroneously ascribed to a convertible note circulation the vices of an inconvertible note circulation, and to an over-issue of notes the calamities which really arose from the reckless advances and consequent losses made by bankers. In support of his arguments he gave the following table :—

TABLE LXXVI.—*Bankruptcies of Private Bankers in the Years* 1839-43.

	1839	1840	1841	1842	1843	Total.
Number of Bankruptcies...............	9	24	26	12	11	82
Of which were Banks of Issue...............	—	8	11	4	6	29

It would thus appear that out of eighty-two bankers who failed in the years 1839-43, only twenty-nine or 35 per cent. were issuing bankers. It seems certainly a stretch of imagination to ascribe these banking disasters to over-issues of notes when so preponderating a proportion of their number were failures of bankers who did not issue notes.

From a statement in the "Bankers' Magazine" of 1847, page 364, it would, however, seem that Sir Robert Peel's figures included a large number of fiats issued against joint stock bank proprietors, who were then styled bankers. The statement is as follows :—

Bankruptcies of Bankers, 1839-43.

Private banks of issue	27
„ non-issue	8
	—
Banks bankrupt	35
Duplicates of private bank fiats	2
Fiats issued against joint stock bank shareholders........	34
	—
	71

In fairness, it must be admitted that Sir Robert Peel's views have this plea for their partial justification, that at the period over which his experience extended, the desire to get their notes into circulation may have acted as a temptation to some bankers to make imprudent advances; but it is necessary to observe that there has been a remarkable alteration in the relative use of the various instruments of the banking trade since those days. The advances made by a bank of issue to its customers may and do increase largely without its note circulation being augmented by $5l$. In fact the part played by notes in the settlement of transactions is much more insignificant than it was five-and-thirty years ago. An overwhelming majority of the transactions of a bank are now made by cheque and by advice, without the intervention of coin or notes. Mr. Palgrave in his evidence before the Committee on Banks of Issue, submitted the following statement from a bank in Manchester: " In 1859 the cash payments, coin, and notes were about " 53 per cent. of the total turn over of the bank; in 1864 they " were about 42 per cent. of the total turn over; in 1872 they were " almost 32 per cent. In 1864 the coin was about 8 to 10 per cent., " and the notes 92 to 90 per cent. of the total payments in cash ; " in 1872 the coin was about 15 per cent. and the notes 85 per cent. " of the total payments in cash." Mr. Palgrave added, "The " progressive decline in the use of notes thus indicated is remark- " able." The fact is that the development of the system of cheques, and the admirable machinery of the clearing-house, have relegated the note circulation now more than ever to the position of being merely the small change of commerce. Even in Scotland and Ireland, where issues are practically unlimited, the note circulation bears the insignificant ratios of $6\frac{1}{4}$ and 15 per cent. respectively to the total resources wielded by the banks. Therefore, to speak now of our convertible note issues exercising any influence whatever on prices is a glaring absurdity. High prices are sometimes a cause, but never an effect of an increased circulation of convertible notes.

Again, so long as notes are paid in gold on demand they cannot be either over-issued or depreciated. The public take and keep out only such notes as they require for their minor payments and no more; and a note for which five sovereigns can be had in the next market town can never be said to be depreciated.

Banking is now in abler and stronger hands than it was five-and-thirty years ago, and thus the probability of abuse of country issues is much diminished, even if its possibility could be admitted still to exist.

It is, however, argued that note issue is in reality a function of the State as much as coinage, and should not be delegated to a multiplicity of private hands. This, however, is both theoretically and practically incorrect. Legal tender issue is certainly the proper function of the State, and if delegated should be delegated to only one State bank, or at most to one for each division of the United Kingdom, but it is not so with non-legal-tender issues. These are a form of credit which theoretically every one has a right to use; and practically that right should neither be restricted nor withdrawn, unless it be clearly proved that restriction or withdrawal is necessary in the interests of the community at large. The question is thus narrowed into one of expediency. Experience has demonstrated the expediency if not the necessity of restriction; but the expediency of withdrawal has not been, and as I shall venture to contend, cannot be proved.

Before considering what advantage would be derived from confining the note issues to a State bank, it should be observed that the security and convertibility of the Bank of England note are absolutely assured, for the State having decreed it to be legal tender is bound to provide for its payment if the State bank should fail to do so; and the Act of 1844 ensures convertibility, except in the unlikely event of the public ceasing to hold so much as 15,000,000*l.* of the bank's notes. No one can doubt the advantage of having an absolutely secure and convertible legal-tender note issue, and although Scotland and Ireland seem to get on well enough without any legal-tender note, yet if we had to choose in England between a system of one issue only, and that a legal-tender issue, and a system of plurality of issues, none of which were legal tender, our suffrages would, I think, be pretty unanimous in favour of legal tender and a single issue. But no such alternative is before us. No one proposes to abolish the legal tender issue of the State or the State bank. The alternative we have to consider is between a single issue which shall be legal tender, and a single legal tender issue supplemented by a plurality of non-legal-tender issues.

What, then, would be gained by the suppression of all non-legal-tender notes? This much certainly that there would no longer be in circulation in the country any note about the security

and ultimate convertibility of which there could for one moment be
any doubt whatever. That is an important advantage; but it is
the sole advantage, and it may be too dearly purchased.

It may be imagined that the State would derive some considerable profit from the transference of the country issues to the Bank
of England, and it may be well to estimate what this would amount
to. The average circulation of the Bank of England for the year
1874 was 26,264,000l., and the profit thereon paid to Her Majesty's
exchequer, exclusive of 60,000l. composition for stamp duty, was
138,578l., or a fraction over one-half per cent. per annum on the
amount of circulation. But the Act provides, sec. 9, that the public
are to have the net profits of any increase of authorised issue on
securities allowed in respect of lapsed country issues. If the English
country issues were suppressed, and the Bank were allowed under
the Act to increase its issues on securities by two-thirds of the
authorised issue of the country banks, the profit to the State might
be calculated thus :—

	£
Amount of authorised country issue suppressed...........	6,461,000
Two-thirds thereof added to Bank of England autho- rised issue on securities	4,300,000
Interest on 4,300,000l. securities at 3 per cent.............	129,000
Less Cost to Bank of notes and management at 12s. 7¼d. per cent.	27,100
	101,900
	£
Less loss to State of Stamp Duty on 5,000,000l. at 7s. per cent.	17,500
And loss of part of Licence Duty of 30l. per office, say..	15,000
	32,500
Net Profit to State	69,400

or barely 1⅖ per cent. on the amount of circulation suppressed, even
on the unlikely supposition that the Bank did not stipulate for a
more favourable arrangement.

It will not surely be seriously argued that a paltry profit to
the State of 69,000l. per annum would warrant the suppression of
the country issues, unless that step were called for on well-
established grounds of public policy. Moreover, justice forbids
that the country issues should be deprived of their circulation
without compensation.

The direct profit derived by the English country banks from
their issues may fairly be set down at 3 per cent. upon the amount
in circulation. The average English country circulation of 1874
was 4,980,000l. The profit thereon at 3 per cent. would be 149,400l.

but this sum by no means adequately represents the annual value of the circulation to the banks. The notes are not only a convenient and economical banking instrument, but they act as so many advertisements of the issuing bank ; they feed deposits ; and what is of still greater importance to the banks and the nation, when the authorised issue is not fully used they enable the bank to extend its branches to places where it would not otherwise pay to open a banking office. Therefore the actual value of their circulation to the English country issuers must be set down at very much more than 150,000*l.*

The following extract from Mr. Seebohm's thoughtful evidence before the Committee of 1875 will sufficiently illustrate this point. *Question :* " Will you explain the nature and value of local issues to " local issuing bankers ? " *Answer :* " The value to the country " issuing banker of the issue is not at all, as is often supposed, its " being a monopoly ; the country issuing bankers value their issue " far more than they would value a similar amount of deposits, " because by the abolition of the issue they would lose not only the " interest realised on the amount in actual circulation, after deducting " stamp duty, licences, and expenses, and also the interest saved on " the amount of unissued notes kept behind the counter ready for " issue, instead of coin or Bank of England notes ; but they would " also (and this is really the chief disadvantage) lose that power of " accommodating their customers and others in small transactions " which, especially in the rural districts, is intimately interwoven " with their business, and conducive to its success. If it had merely " been a monopoly of a certain amount, then probably it would be " simply a question of compensation in case of its withdrawal, but " seeing that it does enter into their mode of doing business, and " that it is so interwoven with it that it enables them to give facilities " to their customers which they could not otherwise give, the feeling " of the country bankers is, that if any change were made, at all " events all these points ought to be thoroughly taken into account, " and that no substitute for local issues would really be satisfactory " either to them or their customers, unless it afforded the same kind " of facilities as were now afforded by their local notes, and not only " as regards the larger transactions of trade, and the larger centres " of trade, but especially as regards the small transactions of busi- " ness in the agricultural and rural districts."

It is thus abundantly evident that any adequate pecuniary compensation to the issuers for the suppression of their circulation must entail a considerable permanent loss to the State.

It has, however, been hinted that to prevent injustice and to avoid pecuniary compensation, Parliament might fix a future date at which the right of private issue should cease and determine. If the privilege of private issue be worth ten, fifteen, or twenty years' purchase, Parliament might decree its prospective abolition at the close of such of these periods as might be determined upon. Just so. If land be worth thirty years' purchase, Parliament might decree that at the end of that time all the land in the United Kingdom should become the property of the State. But this would be confiscation. Yes, and the abolition of the private issues ten, fifteen, or twenty years hence without adequate compensation would likewise be confiscation. That Government would be bold indeed which should make any such proposal to Parliament.

What harm have the English country issues done, what harm are they likely to do that they should be suppressed? In thirty-one years only 12 per cent. of their number, and barely 7 per cent. of their amount as fixed in 1844, have lapsed by failure, whilst 60 per cent. of their number, and 75 per cent. of their amount as fixed in 1844, still remain to attest their stability and acceptability in spite of all the legislative provisions then designed to promote their forfeiture. Such remarkable stability and acceptability would surely seem to indicate that they are an institution worthy of retention. The utmost harm that can happen from their retention is that now and then a bank may fail, and the note holders may suffer loss. The note holder is generally an involuntary creditor, and as such seems quite entitled to some legislative protection; but this could readily be obtained for him without a measure so sweeping and unjust as the abolition of a system which can be shown to possess practical merits far outweighing this its only real defect.

These merits are:—

1 Ready convertibility.

2. Freedom from forgery.

3. Cheapening banking to the public.

4. Extending the benefits of banking over the country.

5. Relieving the Bank of England reserve of a periodical strain.

1. *Ready convertibility.*—Bank of England notes are payable only at the head office in London and at the place of issue from which they are dated. Thus although it circulates and is legal tender all over England and Wales, a Bank of England note issued at one branch of the bank is not only not payable, but is actually and systematically refused payment in gold at any other branch of the bank. It thus lacks the prime requisite of ready convertibility within the area of its circulation; and this defect cannot possibly be rectified except by the combination of two impracticable conditions: 1st. That the number of the country offices of the Bank, now only nine, be very largely increased; and, 2nd. That the notes issued at one office be payable in gold at every other office. The

non-legal-tender issues on the other hand do not circulate beyond the area occupied by the issuing bank's branches, and at these branches, though they may not be by law payable, they are never refused payment in gold. It must at the same time be admitted that change can be obtained at a railway station, a hotel, or a shop, for a Bank of England note more readily than for a local note which has strayed beyond the area of its circulation.

2. *Freedom from forgery.*—Mr. Seebohm made the following statements on this point to the Committee of 1875. " The freedom " of the local note from the risk of forgery is readily explained by " the fact that its genuineness can at once be determined by pre-" senting it at the issuing bank," or, it may be added, at one of its branches. " The forged notes would have to be circulated in the " very district where they would be most easily detected. Many " days could hardly pass before a forged note would find its way to " the local bank, and the public would be made aware that a forgery " had been committed ; but with a single issue that does not apply, " because the forged note would probably be circulated in an outlying " part most distant from the office where the forgery would be readily " detected. That is well known by the public, and the constant " practice of the public in the agricultural districts is that, whilst " they will take a local note without much scrutiny, and without " taking its number, they will always take the number of a Bank of " England note, and frequently write the name of the last holder " upon the back of it."

3. *Cheapening banking to the public.*—The possession of the power of issue enables a banker to do business on cheaper terms for the public. He can cash in his own notes free of commission cheques upon other towns, whilst on these a non-issuing banker must make a charge for collection. Sums paid to credit with a banker in his own notes are cash to him and to his customer the moment they are received. Sums similarly paid in Bank of England notes are not equivalent to cash if the till be already full. The banker must forward them to London or elsewhere before they can be cashed. Directly or indirectly the customer has to pay for the delay, the expense and the risk thus involved, whereas he would have nothing at all to pay in these respects if local notes were used. There is great economy of capital in local issues. They enable a bank to hold a considerable proportion of its till money in its own notes, instead of at a loss of interest in legal tender notes, and the customers of the bank reap the benefit in more moderate charges. The boasted cheapness of Scotch banking to the public is due in a very great measure to the Scotch system of issues.

Whilst then it might be possible at some cost to the taxpayer to compensate the English issuing bankers for the loss of their circulation, it would be quite impossible to compensate the public for the loss of the facilities which they derive from that circulation. In connection with this point I may cite the valuable testimony given before the Committee on Banks of Issue, by Mr. W. Bagehot, of Stuckey's Banking Company, the largest bank of issue in England. The chairman put to him the following question :—" If " I understand you rightly, you make advances or you give " facilities upon easier terms to very small people than you would " do if you had not the right of issue, and if you had not that right " of issue it would be a losing concern to you to give those " facilities. If you had received ten times the value of your issue, " once for all, I presume that you would still after a time desire to " conduct your business in what would be the most profitable way " to you, and that it would be impossible for Parliament to say you " ought to have done this or that with regard to this or that par- " ticular cow-keeper or withy-binder ?" Mr. Bagehot's reply was, " Of course it would be difficult, and, therefore, I think it is for " the consideration of Parliament whether by abolishing the country " issues it would be advisable to injure the public in this way."

4. *The power of private issue promotes the extension of the benefits of banking over the country.*—It enables a bank to plant branches in places where, if the till money had all to be held at a loss of interest, branches would not pay. How important a part the extension of banking over the length and breadth of the country plays in the development, economisation, and utilisation of the national resources, requires no demonstration. The great development of the branch system in Scotland would have been impossible but for the power of issue. Mr. Seebohm stated in evidence before the Committee on Banks of Issue, that "the large bank in Somersetshire (Stuckey's " Bank) would have to withdraw a considerable numberof branches " if they had not their issue."

5. The *periodic expansions* to which the English non-legal-tender note circulation is subject, *take place without affecting the reserve of the Bank of England*, and consequently without disturbing the rate of interest. Mr. Palgrave's tables show that on the average of the last ten years the English provincial circulation has expanded in obedience to the requirements of the public between August and October to the extent of 547,400*l.* per annum.

This normal expansion subsides only gradually, and if it had to be provided for from the reserve of the Bank of England, in addition to the November expansions of the Scotch and Irish circulations, the disturbance to the reserve of the Bank and to the rate of interest would necessarily be intensified at the very time when experience has shown the reserve is most liable to reduction and the London money market most keenly sensitive.

It can scarcely be seriously proposed to abolish the non-legal-tender circulation of Scotland. The banking system of that country has grown up with the aid of note issues. It would be utterly disorganised if these were withdrawn. The banks would suffer by the enforced suppression of a very large number of their smaller branches. The public would suffer by the withdrawal of many of their accustomed facilities, and by the increase of banking charges which must needs follow on the loss of the profit now derived by the banks from their circulation. The country is wedded to its system of note circulation, and would not listen for one moment to any proposal for its abolition.

Finally, the cost to the State for compensation would be very great. The direct value of their circulation to the Scotch banks may be estimated by calculating what the banks would lose if deprived of their issues.

	£
1. They would lose the profit on their notes in the hands of the public, amounting to	5,900,000
2. They would require to hold in legal tender as till money and reserves, say 6 per cent. of their liabilities, which, deducting circulation, are 86,500,000*l.*	5,190,000
They at present hold gold and silver	4,100,000
Additional legal tender to be held, at a loss of interest........	1,090,000
	6,990,000
Loss on that sum at 4 per cent.	279,600
Less present cost of circulation, at 1¼ per cent......................	73,750
Estimated net direct annual value of Scotch circulation to the Scotch banks	205,850

or exactly 3½ per cent. on the amount of notes in circulation.

The case of the Irish circulation is, I take it, pretty much the same as that of the Scotch, save that, though larger in amount, it is not quite so valuable to the issuers, in consequence of the larger proportion of coin held. But for their note circulation the Scotch banks would require to hold about a million more coin than they now do. The case seems to be reversed in Ireland. But for their note circulation, the Irish banks of issue would probably require to hold some 700,000*l.* less coin than they now do. The calculation stands as under:—

		£
Coin held by Irish banks of issue	....	2,800,000
Without issues their liabilities would be reduced to 35,700,000*l*., and if they held legal tender reserves and till money to extent of 6 per cent. of that amount, they would hold		2,142,000
Coin calculated as now held specially in respect of circulation		658,000
The Irish circulation amounts to	....	6,800,000
Deduct coin reckoned as held specially against it	....	658,000
		6,222,000
4 per cent. on this amount	....	248,880
Deduct present cost of circulation, at say 1¼	....	85,000
Estimated net direct value per annum of their circulation to the Irish banks of issue		163,880

or 2⅗ per cent. upon the average amount of notes in circulation.

Why the English non-legal-tender circulation should be suppressed if the Scotch and Irish issues are to be allowed to remain, it is very difficult to comprehend.

If the whole of the non-legal tender issues of England, Scotland, and Ireland, amounting to 17,700,000*l.*, were suppressed, the profit to the State would be at best, at 1⅜ per cent., 243,000*l.* per annum, which would be totally inadequate to compensate the issuing banks for a loss of direct annual profit amounting to, for

	£
England	150,000
Scotland	206,000
Ireland	164,000
Total	520,000

besides the loss of great indirect advantages, the money value of which cannot be appraised.

Retention and Proposed Reform of Non-Legal-Tender Issues.

The great practical advantages of the English non-legal-tender issues have been shown. It has also been proved that the important functions which they so well perform cannot by any possibility be fulfilled by the notes of a State bank.

The conclusion cannot then be resisted that the sound policy is to retain the English as well as the Scotch and Irish country issues. It is true that they all possess one defect. The security of the note depends solely on the solvency of the issuer. Banks may fail; banks do fail; and when they fail, their note holders may lose money; but this solitary defect admits of easy remedy.

Three courses suggest themselves:—

1st. To make the note a first charge on the issuer's estate in the event of failure.

2nd. To require Government securities to be lodged with the State to cover the amount of the maximum issue.

3rd. To combine the first two courses, *i.e.*, to make the note a first charge on the estate of the issuer, and to require security for the whole or part of the authorised maximum of circulation,

1. *To make the notes a first charge on the issuer's estate in the event of failure.* It has been objected to this suggestion, that in the event of a bank getting into difficulties depositors would run upon it in order to put themselves in the position of note holders. But it cannot be supposed that depositors who, under the present position of the issues, would not run upon the bank for legal tender, would, if the notes ranked preferentially to other liabilities, run upon the bank for payment in its notes. If a depositor doubted the solvency of the bank which held his money, he would demand payment of his deposit in legal tender, or if he took the bank's notes, it would be for the purpose not of holding them, but of paying them immediately to his credit with another banker, who would in due course present them for payment to the issuer.

To make the notes a first charge on the estate in the event of insolvency, would probably, in almost every case, protect note-holders from loss by the failure of the issuer, especially if every bank issuing notes were compelled to publish an audited and cer-tified balance sheet at least once a-year, and to make for publication in the "Gazette" and in a local paper a return of the monthly average of the weekly amount of the coin and Bank of England notes in its tills and reserves.

2. *To require each issuer to lodge with the State English Government securities to cover the amount of his maximum issue.* If it be objected that this might secure the ultimate payment of the note, but would afford no guarantee of its immediate convertibility, it may be replied that the State is by no means called upon to see to the immediate convertibility of a non-legal-tender note, though it may be politic to organise measures for the protection of the holder from loss; but in any case notes secured by the deposit of consols with the State would be practically convertible so far as the public were concerned, for as the discredit of the Government-Security note of one issuer might affect the notes of other issuers in the same district, it would be the policy of these issuers to give credit for the notes of the failed bank—knowing their ultimate sufficiency—rather than allow the system of note issues in which they were themselves interested to suffer discredit. This is precisely the course which the Scotch banks, after a couple of days' hesitation,

N

adopted with regard to the notes of the Western Bank when it failed, and they obtained a permanent accession of business by so doing, avoiding of course a loss of interest by having the notes marked as presented for payment.

But it may be argued further that the bank may have issued more notes than the amount authorised, or that its failure may take place during a panic, when consols are at 85, or during a war when they have fallen to 70, and those who held or took up the notes might ultimately lose a portion of their money. These points might be met by imposing a criminal penalty on issuing beyond the limit authorised, and by requiring that a margin of security should be established and maintained.

It is necessary to reckon whether the privilege of issue would be worth having if security had to be furnished for it in this manner.

The cost to the issuer of furnishing security for the maximum amount of his circulation may be estimated as follows :—

Let us assume the average amount of circulation to be represented by 100*l*. Let us allow 20 per cent. for fluctuations above the average, although Mr. Palgrave's tables show that during the five years 1870-74 the highest monthly excess over the year's average was 8 per cent. in England, 16 per cent. in Scotland, and and 12 per cent. in Ireland. The authorised limit of circulation, would then be represented by 120*l*. Security in consols would have to be provided for that sum, with a margin of 10 per cent., that is, for 132*l*. Assuming consols to yield 3¼ per cent., and the ordinary rate of interest obtainable by a bank on the average of its advances and investments to be 4 per cent., there would be a loss on the special investment of 132*l*. in consols of 0·99*l*. Then the State would have to make a charge for its trouble. From the paper put in by Mr. K. D. Hodgson, one of the directors of the Bank of England, in the course of his evidence before the Committee of 1875, it is calculated that the profit to the State on the Bank of England circulation, exclusive of stamp duty, is equal to 10*s*. 6*d*. per cent. on the average amount of the notes in the hands of the public. A Government duty of one-quarter per cent. on the amount of authorised non-legal-tender issues should amply suffice for the remuneration of the State, but let us assume a duty of one-half per cent., which would amount to 0·6*l*. in our calculation. It thus appears that the loss to the issuers by giving security may be estimated at 0·99 + 0·6 = 1·59, or in round numbers 1*l*. 12*s*. per cent.

For clearness the calculation is repeated:—

£

Average actual circulation 100
Authorised limit—20 per cent. for fluctuations 120
Security consols with margin of 10 per cent. 132

Loss of ¾ per cent. on investment in consols .... 0·99
Government duty ½ per cent. on authorised limit .... 0·60

Cost per cent. on average circulation of ⎫
providing security .... ⎬ 1·59
⎭

If the direct money value of the circulation in England, Scotland, and Ireland, has been correctly estimated, the result of giving security for it would be as follows in each division of the United Kingdom:—

Locality.	Present Direct Value.	Loss by giving Security.	Leaving net Direct Value.
	Per cnt. £ s.	Per cnt. £ s.	Per cnt. £ s.
England	3 –	1 12	1 8
Scotland	3 10	1 12	1 18
Ireland	2 8	1 12	− 16

Or 5s. per cent. more in each case if Government were satisfied with a duty of one-quarter instead of one-half per cent.

The effect which the possession of a perfectly secured issue would have on the amount of legal tender held by the issuers has not been taken into calculation. It would in most cases tend to diminish the amount of legal tender necessary to be held *in respect of issues*, and to that extent it would improve the net value of the circulation. Be that as it may, if the above calculation be approximately correct, it would certainly be worth while for the issuers to sacrifice even 1½ or 1¾ per cent. from the profit on their issues, in order to be enabled to retain them with all their concomitant advantages. The National Provincial Bank of England, before giving up their issues in consequence of opening a banking office in London, offered to deposit consols in security, and also to pay a tax of 1l. 5s. per cent. for the right of issue. Public policy does not require that the non-legal-tender issues should be abolished, but it does seem to require that they should be secured, and the cost of providing security must be borne by the issuers.

3. *To make the notes a first charge on the estate of the issuer, and to require security for the whole or part of the authorised maximum of circulation.* If the notes were made a first charge on the estate, it would probably be sufficient to require the provision of Government security for one-half of the maximum or authorised circulation.

The cost of this scheme to the issuer may be calculated as follows :—

	£
Actual circulation	100
Authorised maximum	120
Consols to be provided for	60
Loss on consols at ¾ per cent.	0·45
Government duty 10s. per cent. on 120l.	0·60
Cost per cent. to issuer	1·05

The result to the issuers would be to leave the net direct value as under :—

	£	s.	£	s.	£	s.
In England	3	—	— 1	1	= 1	19
„ Scotland	3	10	— 1	1	= 2	9
„ Ireland	2	8	— 1	1	= 1	7

or 5s. per cent. more in each case if Government were satisfied with a duty of one-quarter instead of one-half per cent. Probably if one half per cent. were charged, some relief might be got from the licence duty of 30l. per office at which notes or drafts under composition for stamp duty are issued ; an impost which now exercises rather a repressing effect on the extension of branches.

It seems to me that the third course is the one which legislation should take.

It would probably be quite unnecessary to bind the banks to hold coin or other legal tender. A bank failing to pay its notes on demand would forfeit the privilege of issue. This of itself ought to insure the maintenance of an adequate supply of legal tender ; but a monthly return should be required, for publication, of the average weekly amount of legal tender held, and every bank should be obliged to publish a balance-sheet annually in a prescribed form.

In providing for the maintenance and security of the English country issues, every facility should be given for their consolidation by the withdrawal of all restrictions upon the number of partners in private banks, and of all provisions directed against the amalgamation of issues. The exclusion of English joint stock banks of issue from banking in London should also be abolished.

Proposed Extension of Non-Legal-Tender Issues.

If the non-legal-tender issues were thus secured and reformed, justice as well as the interest of the public requires that they should no longer remain the exclusive privilege of the existing banks of issue, but that alike in England, Scotland, and Ireland, any well established bank should be allowed to participate in the privilege.

The forty-three purely provincial English joint stock banks of non-issue have a paid-up capital of 10,545,000*l.*, and the London and provincial banks have a paid-up capital of 4,425,000*l.*, making a total paid-up capital of 15,000,000*l.*

There are eighty-three purely provincial private banks of non-issue in England and Wales, and the privilege of issue could not be withheld from these if they came under the prescribed conditions.

It would, however, be most expedient to avoid a multiplicity of small issuers, and this might be effected by providing, 1, that no new right of issue should be granted for a less sum than 50,000*l.*, and 2, that all issues actually under 10,000*l.* on the average of, say the year 1885, and all under 25,000*l.* on the average of, say the year 1890, should be forfeited. The latter provision, coupled with the removal of all restrictions on amalgamation, would speedily lead to a very desirable consolidation of the smaller ·issuers without inflicting on them any loss or injustice.

Should it be urged as an objection to the extension of the country issues, that the pressure on the Bank of England during a time of crisis or threatened crisis, already too great, would be intensified, as the provincial banks would have not only their deposits but likewise their circulation to protect, and would require to hold for that purpose an increased amount of legal tender, it may be replied that the notes would command confidence by bearing on the face of them the conditions as to security under which they were issued. Moreover, it is to be hoped that the days of the reliance of our banking system on the single attenuated reserve of the Bank of England are already numbered, and that the regular publication of the amount of legal tender held by each bank will be enforced to secure the permanent maintenance by every considerable bank of a tangible reserve in coin or legal tender notes. The extension of the country issues would facilitate the formation of such reserves by throwing free a considerable amount of the legal tender now in circulation.

The fact is that we have in the country a very ample amount of coin and legal tender notes. Mr. Palgrave, in the course of his very interesting and instructive evidence before the Committee of 1875, gave the following statement of the estimated actual gold circulation in England :—

[000,000's omitted.] £

Amount of gold coin in Great Britain and Ireland, as per
   estimate of Mr. Hendriks...} 100,

Add gold bullion in Bank of England 15,

„ Bank of England active circulation 26,

„ country note circulation 5,

                    146,

Deduct— £

   In Bank of England, gold coin and bullion 24,

   „ other English banks, gold coin 16,

   „ Scotland, gold coin in banks and circulation 5,

   „ Ireland,   „   7,

                    52,

Total circulating medium in hands of public in England,
   including Bank of England notes held by other banks } 94,

Deduct Bank of England notes.. 26,

Less   „   abroad............................... 3,

                    23,

Country notes ....,.............. 5,

                    28,

Estimated gold coin in hands of public in England 66,

Assuming roughly that of the 23,000,000*l.* of Bank of England active circulation estimated to be in this country, 13,000,000*l.* are in the hands of the banks and 10,000,000*l.* in the hands of the public, we should have a total legal tender circulation in the hands of the public of 76,000,000*l.*

Now if this estimate be at all an approximation to the facts, we would appear to be unduly lavish in our currency arrangements in one direction, and unduly economical in another. We have some 76,000,000*l.* of gold and legal tender notes sunk in the hands of the public in England, and only 10,000,000*l.* or 12,000,000*l.* free as a reserve against the gigantic banking liabilities of the entire United Kingdom.

The legal tender in the hands of the banks cannot be reckoned as a reserve. It is simply till money—an implement necessary to the daily operations at the counter; and instead of being available as a reserve to fall back upon in a time of crisis, the stock of it then requires augmentation.

Neither can the gold and legal tender notes in the hands of the public, as distinguished from the banks, be regarded in the light of a reserve. It is true that they have been so regarded by authorities whose opinion is entitled to the greatest respect. It seems to be clear, however, that legal tender notes and gold in the hands of the public are merely instruments for effecting some of the cash payments of the country. The public will not keep in its hands systematically a larger quantity of these instruments than it requires, and it is very questionable if the quantity can be rapidly or appreciably diminished even by the advance of the rate of interest to a high point. Mr. Sampson Lloyd, in questioning Mr. Jervoise Smith in the Committee of 1875, brought out this point very distinctly— *Question :* " I presume the primary mode in which the Bank of " England would meet a foreign drain of gold would probably be by " attracting it from abroad ?" *Answer :* " Yes, by raising the rate." *Question :* " And the only way in which it would diminish the " circulation of sovereigns would be by the exercise of pressure to " cause such a cessation of the transactions, or such a lowering of " prices as that gold ceases to be employed in the country, and so " filters gradually into the Bank ? " *Answer :* " Yes." The operation of this process must needs be very slow—so slow in fact that the gold which it brings in will reach the central reserve only after the emergency is over, and when it is no longer wanted. The mass of legal tender circulation cannot thus be looked upon as a fund to be drawn upon in order to mitigate a crisis, or to replenish bullion reserves depleted by a foreign drain. It is quite true that in the event of war much of the gold in the country could be made available for export by the substitution of notes, and especially 1*l.* notes, but until liberated by such an expedient, gold in circulation cannot be held to answer the purposes of a reserve.

Therefore it would appear that in a great measure we have our legal tender in the wrong place. If we could take even 20,000,000*l.* of it out of circulation and place it in reserve, we should be in a much stronger position. The banking liabilities resting ultimately on the Bank of England reserve have been estimated in the foregoing pages to amount to 635,000,000*l.*, and assuming the Bank of England reserve to be 11,000,000*l.*, the ultimate bullion reserve is only 1¾ of the liabilities. If, however, we could, by the issue of well secured country notes, add 20,000,000*l.* to the reserve, we should attain much greater strength. We should have banking liabilities of 655,000,000*l.*, and legal tender reserves of 31,000,000*l.*, or nearly 4¾ per cent. of our banking liabilities, irrespective of the till money now held by the banks.

It would, however, be impossible to transfer even 20,000,000*l.* of legal tender from circulation to reserve without the issue of 1*l.* notes ; and the feeling in England seems to run very strongly against the reintroduction of small notes; but an addition of 10,000,000*l.* or 11,000,000*l.* to the legal tender reserves by means of well secured country notes of 5*l.* and upwards might be quite practicable, and the coin in the Scotch and Irish banks, 7,000,000*l.*, being no longer tied up against circulation, would, to extent of at least 5,000,000*l.*, become available as a bullion reserve.

Supposing, however, a transference of legal tender from circulation to reserve effected to a certain extent, what guarantee should we have that the legal tender would be retained in reserve ? Would not the Bank of England notes find their way to the Bank, and would not the gold tend to disappear by export? The publication of the stock of legal tender held by each bank would, I think, effectually prevent this. Public attention and public criticism would be directed to the amount held, and a wholesome regard for public opinion would constrain each bank to maintain a legal tender reserve adequate to its liabilities.

It will thus be seen that the suggestion which has been made for securing and extending the non-legal-tender issues would not diminish the circulation of the Bank of England. It would displace some of their notes in the hands of the public and transfer them to the hands of the banks, there to remain as a legal tender reserve against general liabilities; but so far as the Bank of England was concerned the notes would still be in the circle.

One important effect of the proposed arrangement would be to enable the circulation in Scotland and Ireland to pass through its normal periodic expansions without any strain on the Bank of England reserve, which as matters now stand is generally drawn upon in May by the Scotch banks to extent of three-quarters of a million, and in October and November by the Irish and Scotch banks together to extent of not less than a million and a half.

Another effect would be to remove inequalities of privilege as between bank and bank, by giving to each the amount of circulation which it could use.

At present, in England, many of the issuing banks could readily double or treble their circulation if they were not prevented by law from exceeding their fixed limits. Others, again, have not now an outlet for more than a fractional part of their authorised issues.

In Scotland, where all exceed their fixed or credit issues, there are wide and unjust differences of privilege. The British Linen Company and the City of Glasgow Bank are banks of about the same magnitude. The one has a credit circulation of £438,024l., the other has only 72,921l., and the bank which has the smaller credit circulation has by 143,000l. the larger actual circulation. The figures of the two banks are as under:—

[Cols. 6, 7, and 8 are taken from Mr. Palgrave's Tables.]
[000's omitted in Cols. 2, 3, 4, and 6.]

1	2	3	4	5	6	7	8
When Established.	Paid-up Capital.	Reserve Fund.	Money Lodged.	Number of Branches.	Average Actual Circulation, 1874.	Authorised Issue.	Proportion of Actual to Authorised Issue. Authorised Issue = 100.
	£	£	£		£	£	
British Linen Company.... 1746	1,000,	390,	7,957,	67	530,	438,024	121
City of Glasgow Bank... 1839	1,000,	451,	8,489,	122	673,	72,921	925

Thus the law compels the City of Glasgow Bank to hold upwards of 600,000*l.* of coin, whilst the British Linen can fulfil the conditions of the Act with less than 100,000*l.* The sole reason for this discrepancy is, that the City of Glasgow Bank was a young and a small bank, whilst the British Linen Company was a century old when Sir Robert Peel applied his rigid rule to the Scotch banks.

In Ireland, the Bank of Ireland's actual circulation in 1874 was 77 per cent. of its authorised circulation, whilst the actual circulation of the Ulster Banking Company was 221 per cent. of its authorised circulation.

All this inelasticity would be put an end to by the scheme proposed.

That scheme would also put a stop to the monopoly of issue and banking in Scotland, by enabling new banks to acquire the same privileges as the old banks.

The non-legal-tender note circulation should not be international. · It should retain its local character. The issues in England should be confined to English banks, in Scotland to Scotch banks, and in Ireland to Irish banks.

An entirely different scheme from those which have been already adverted to has been suggested, viz., that the coin now held by the Scotch and Irish banks in respect of their excess of credit' issues, should be specially "earmarked" against the circulation; and that the English provincial issues should be put upon a similar footing.

This would, in effect, create in each bank of issue an issue department separate from the banking department. It would be somewhat difficult of adjustment. We have seen that the Irish authorised credit issues are very large compared with the Scotch. The Irish banks hold 576 per cent. more coin than covers their excess of issue, whilst the Scotch banks hold only 30 per cent. of coin beyond the amount of their excess of issue. Yet the coin in the Scotch banks is 70 per cent. of their average circulation, whilst the coin in the Irish banks is only 41 per cent. of their average circulation. Moreover, similar inequalities exist between bank and bank, both in Scotland and Ireland. In England too, though no excess of the fixed limit of issue is permitted, and though there is no statutory provision for coin being held, the inequalities are extreme, some banks, as has been stated, having habitually in circulation nearly the whole of their authorised issue, and others finding an outlet for only a small fraction of their authorised amount.

In order, therefore, to apply the scheme equitably, it would be requisite to cancel the present credit limits, and to provide that, say 50 per cent. of the actual circulation should be secured by coin specially hypothecated against it. If, in addition to such a provision, the circulation were made a first charge on the estate of the issuer, there is no doubt that the notes would be abundantly secured. But two grave objections present themselves.—1. It would be impossible, with a multiplicity of issuers, to keep any check over the amount of coin held. 2. A very large aggregate amount of coin would be specially locked up against circulation, which would be much more advantageously employed as a reserve against general banking liabilities. These two objections, but especially the latter, seem to me to render the scheme inadmissible.

The Intrusion of the Scotch Banks into England.

The question of the intrusion of the Scotch banks into England stands some chance of being thrown into the shade by the more momentous controversy which it has raised, as to what is to be done with the country issues.

It may at once be conceded that there might possibly be some gain to the English public from the admission of Scotch and Irish banks to English soil. There would be increased competition, followed possibly in some provincial districts by a slight reduction of the terms of business. Banking, it is true, is already free in England. Any man or body of men may establish a bank in England, and new banks are opened year by year; but if increased competition in banking be a public desideratum, it is possible that the competition of these new, small, and untried banks may not be so advantageous to the English public as the competition of the large, well-established banks of Scotland, with their ample resources, and sound traditions of management. On the other hand, in establishing a footing in England, the Scotch banks would be at the disadvantage of not possessing local influence and local prestige in anything like the same degree as the established banks with which they ventured to compete.

Except on the borders and in cities like London, Liverpool, and Manchester, where the population includes a large and influential Scotch element, their progress would probably be discouragingly slow, notwithstanding their character for solidity and prudence; but if it be legal for them to come, as to which some doubt exists, and if they elect to take their chance, the question to be faced is, why should the English public be deprived of the benefit of such competition as they would create?

Under existing circumstances the answer is two-fold: 1, because their competition would be unjust to the English banks; and 2, because their extension beyond Scotland would be prejudicial to the interests of the Scottish public, and especially of the Scottish note holders.

1. The condition of Scotch and English banking is widely different, and that difference results from the utterly diverse manner

in which the two systems have, *ab initio*, been dealt with by legislation. In Scotland, freedom from legislative restrictions has favoured the development of large and strong banks, with numerous branches. In England, a long course of legislative restrictions has kept banking, with some exceptions, in the hands of comparatively small banks, with a distinctly local character. Legislation has given the Scotch banks the lucrative privilege of unlimited issues. It has denied that privilege to the English banks. Legislation prevents English banks from competing on equal terms with Scotch banks on Scottish soil. It is therefore unjust that Scotch banks, with all these legislative advantages at their back, should be allowed to compete on English soil on equal terms with English banks which have no such advantages.

The monopoly of issue and banking which the Scotch banks now enjoy in their own country is in reality the most remarkable instance of protection which retains at this day the sanction of the British Legislature. The English non-issuing banks, including all the banks in London except the Bank of England, are not protected at all, and the English banks of issue enjoy a measure of protection which is trivial compared with that allotted to the Scotch banks. Is it, then, consistent with free trade principles to admit these highly protected institutions to competition with institutions which are totally unprotected? It cannot be supposed that the Legislature would sanction such a flagrant and unjust violation of the sacred principle of free trade, even if the prospective advantage of such a course to the English public were ten times as great as it can possibly be proved to be.

2. Justice to Scotland forbids the ramification of the Scotch banks beyond the confines of their privileges. The author of a pamphlet printed in Glasgow in 1875 for private circulation, points out with great force that Parliament having tied the people of Scotland to her banks, it is only fair that the banks should be tied to Scotland. "In other words," he says, "the ramification of " our banks beyond Scotland into fresh fields of business is not " fairly allowable, their depositors and note holders being not " equally free to find themselves new banks and new note issuers."

The Act of 1845 confided to the Scotch banks the solemn and important trust of providing a sound bank note currency for their own country. This great trust was confided to them as purely Scotch banks, and it may justly be held that they betray that trust, and forfeit their right to their exclusive privileges, when by entering on the field of English banking they cease to be purely Scotch banks. There is no doubt the features of Scotch banking have already undergone a very marked alteration since 1845. Table LXXVII gives the progress since that date :—

TABLE LXXVII.—*Progress of Scotch Banking*, 1845 to 1875.

[Compiled chiefly from the evidence of Mr. Davidson, of the Bank of Scotland, before the Committee of 1875.]

	Num- ber of Banks.	Paid-up Capital.	Bank Offices.			Mouey Lodged.			Note Circulation.		
			Num- ber.	Propor- tion to Number in 1845.	Number of Inha- bitants to each Office.	Amount.	Propor- tions to Amount in 1845.	Amount per Head of Population.	Amount.	Propor- tions to Amount in 1845.	Amount per Head of Popn- lation.
		£				£		£ s. d.	£		£ s. d.
1845	19	10,793,415	382	100	7,178	33,192,105	100	12 2 1	3,087,209	100	1 2 7
'55	17	11,456,055	480	126	6,204	43,270,612	130	14 10 7	4,104,582	133	1 7 7
'65	13	9,431,000	654	171	4,870	56,185,061	169	17 12 10	4,382,600	142	1 7 7
'75	11	9,785,888	884	231	3,954	78,405,261	239	22 8 8	5,904,586	191	1 13 10

From this table it is apparent that with an actual diminution of paid-up capital, the Scottish note circulation has been nearly doubled, and the deposits have been considerably more than doubled. Moreover, many of the Scotch banks, and especially those which are in London, have entered largely on the system of accepting bills, an entirely new feature in Scotch banking since 1845. The acceptances of the eight leading Scotch banks amounted in 1873 to 6,100,000l., and in 1874 to 5,120,000l. Four of them have entered on the comparatively unlimited field of business south of the Tweed. Without impugning the soundness of any Scotch bank, Parliament is bound, as guardian of the interests of the note-holders of Scotland, to consider whether the conditions under which so grave and responsible a trust was confided to these banks, are not now so seriously affected by the altered policy of several of them, as to endanger the soundness of the time-honoured note circu- lation of Scotland, and to render legislative interference not only desirable but necessary.

On these distinct and weighty grounds of justice to English bankers, justice to the public of Scotland, and consistency with the principles of free trade, it is contended that if under existing legisla- tion the Scotch banks are to retain their exclusive privileges in Scot- land, they should be required to confine their banking operations to Scotland. This is the sound and intelligible principle of Mr. Göschen's Bill, which was held in abeyance, pending the report of the Committee of 1875.

The National Bank of Scotland and the Bank of Scotland have since 1864 and 1867 respectively had banking offices in London, and the Royal Bank in 1873 obtained an Act altering its constitution so as to enable it to open a banking office in London, which it did in 1875. Whether the National Bank of Scotland and the Bank of Scotland have been in London all these years contrary to law is open to discussion, but if not it would be a hardship on them to drive them away now without compensation.

If the English, Scotch, and Irish issues were suppressed in favour of the issues of the State or a State bank, which I have endeavoured to show would be a most impolitic step, all the banks would be placed upon an equality, and those of one division of the United Kingdom need no longer be debarred from extending into the other divisions.

Similarly if Parliament agreed to reform and extend the system of ·non-legal-tender issue in England, Scotland, and Ireland by admitting all banks on certain conditions to the privilege of issue, which I have ventured to advocate as the most politic step in the circumstances, banking in each division of the United Kingdom might fairly be thrown open to the banks of the other divisions. It is true that if $1l.$ notes continued to be prohibited in England the privileges of the English banks would not be on a par with those of Scotland and Ireland, but the Scotch privileges would have been docked of some of their profit, the Scotch monopoly would have ceased to exist, and the just objections now existing to the intrusion of Scotch banks on English soil would be in a great degree removed.

HARRISON AND SONS, PRINTERS IN ORDINARY TO HER MAJESTY, ST. MARTIN'S LANE.

www.ingramcontent.com/pod-product-compliance
Lightning Source LLC
Chambersburg PA
CBHW031104020726
47495CB00007B/2042

*9 7 8 3 3 3 7 1 4 6 8 4 9 *